MODERN THEORIES
OF CRIMINALITY

THE MODERN CRIMINAL SCIENCE SERIES
Published under the Auspices of
THE AMERICAN INSTITUTE OF CRIMINAL LAW AND CRIMINOLOGY

Modern Theories of Criminality

By C. BERNALDO DE QUIRÓS

Translated from the Spanish
By ALFONSO DE SALVIO, Ph. D.
Assistant Professor in Romance Languages
Northwestern University

WITH AN INTRODUCTION BY Wm. W. SMITHERS, Esq.

AGATHON PRESS, INC.
New York, N.Y.
1967

Reprinted 1967, with permission, by
AGATHON PRESS, INC.
150 Fifth Avenue
New York, N.Y. 10011

Library of Congress Catalog Card Number: 67-20716

Printed in U.S.A. by
NOBLE OFFSET PRINTERS, INC.
NEW YORK 3, N. Y.

TO MY SONS

JUAN AND CONSTANCIO

IN MEMORY OF MY PARENTS

GENERAL INTRODUCTION TO THE MODERN CRIMINAL SCIENCE SERIES.

AT the National Conference of Criminal Law and Criminology, held in Chicago, at Northwestern University, in June, 1909, the American Institute of Criminal Law and Criminology was organized; and, as a part of its work, the following resolution was passed:

"*Whereas*, it is exceedingly desirable that important treatises on criminology in foreign languages be made readily accessible in the English language, *Resolved*, that the president appoint a committee of five with power to select such treatises as in their judgment should be translated, and to arrange for their publication."

The Committee appointed under this Resolution has made careful investigation of the literature of the subject, and has consulted by frequent correspondence. It has selected several works from among the mass of material. It has arranged with publisher, with authors, and with translators, for the immediate undertaking and rapid progress of the task. It realizes the necessity of educating the professions and the public by the wide diffusion of information on this subject. It desires here to explain the considerations which have moved it in seeking to select the treatises best adapted to the purpose.

For the community at large, it is important to recognize that criminal science is a larger thing than criminal law. The legal profession in particular has a duty to familiarize itself with the principles of that science, as the sole means for intelligent and systematic improvement of the criminal law.

Two centuries ago, while modern medical science was still young, medical practitioners proceeded upon two general assumptions: one as to the cause of disease, the other as to its treatment. As to the cause of disease, — disease was sent by the inscrutable will of God. No man could fathom that will, nor its arbitrary operation. As to the treatment of disease, there were believed to be a few remedial agents of universal efficacy. Calomel and blood-letting, for example, were two of the principal ones. A larger or smaller dose of calomel, a greater or less quantity of bloodletting, — this blindly indiscriminate mode of treatment was regarded as orthodox for all common varieties of ailment. And so his calomel pill and his bloodletting lancet were carried everywhere with him by the doctor.

Nowadays, all this is past, in medical science. As to the causes of disease, we know that they are facts of nature, — various, but distinguishable by diagnosis and research, and more or less capable of prevention or control or counteraction. As to the treatment, we now know that there are various specific modes of treatment for specific causes or symptoms, and that the treatment must be adapted to the cause. In short, the individualization of disease, in cause and in treatment, is the dominant truth of modern medical science.

The same truth is now known about crime; but the understanding and the application of it are just opening upon us. The old and still dominant thought is, as to cause, that a crime is caused by the inscrutable moral free will of the human being, doing or not doing the crime, just as it pleases; absolutely free in advance, at any moment of time, to choose or not to choose the criminal act, and therefore in itself the sole and ultimate cause of crime. As to treatment, there still are just two traditional measures, used in varying doses for all kinds of crime and all kinds of persons, — jail, or a fine (for death is now employed in rare cases only). But modern science, here as in medicine, recognizes that crime also (like disease) has natural causes. It need not be asserted for one moment that crime is a disease. But it does have natural causes, — that is, circumstances which work to produce it in a given case. And as to treatment, modern science recognizes that penal or remedial treatment cannot possibly be indiscriminate and machine-like, but must be adapted to the causes, and to the man as affected by those causes. Common sense and logic alike require, inevitably, that the moment we predicate a specific cause for an undesirable effect, the remedial treatment must be specifically adapted to that cause.

Thus the great truth of the present and the future, for criminal science, is the individualization of penal treatment, — for that man, and for the cause of that man's crime.

Now this truth opens up a vast field for re-examination. It means that we must study all the possible data that can be causes of crime, — the man's heredity, the man's physical and moral make-up, his emotional temperament, the surroundings of his youth, his present home, and other conditions, — all the influencing circumstances. And it means that the effect of different methods of treatment, old or new, for different kinds of men and of causes, must be studied, experimented, and compared. Only in this way can accurate knowledge be reached, and new efficient measures be adopted.

All this has been going on in Europe for forty years past, and in limited fields in this country. All the branches of science that can help have been working, — anthropology, medicine, psychology, economics, sociology, philanthropy, penology. The law alone has abstained. The science of law is the one to be served by all this. But the public in general and the legal profession in particular have remained either ignorant of the entire subject or indifferent to the entire scientific movement. And this ignorance or indifference has blocked the way to progress in administration.

The Institute therefore takes upon itself, as one of its aims, to inculcate the study of modern criminal science, as a pressing duty for the legal profession and for the thoughtful community at large. One of its principal modes of stimulating and aiding this study is to make available in the English language the most useful treatises now extant in the Continental languages. Our country has started late. There is much to catch up with, in the results reached elsewhere. We shall, to be sure, profit by the long period of argument and theorizing and experimentation which European thinkers and workers have passed through. But to reap that profit, the results of their experience must be made accessible in the English language.

The effort, in selecting this series of translations, has been to choose those works which best represent the various schools of thought in criminal science, the general results reached, the points of contact or of controversy, and the contrasts of method — having always in view that class of works which have a more than local value and could best be serviceable to criminal science in our country. As the science has various aspects and emphases — the anthropological, psychological, sociological, legal, statistical, economic, pathological — due regard was paid, in the selection, to a representation of all these aspects. And as the several Continental countries have contributed in different ways to these various aspects, — France, Germany, Italy, most abundantly, but the others each its share, — the effort was made also to recognize the different contributions as far as feasible.

The selection made by the Committee, then, represents its judgment of the works that are most useful and most instructive for the purpose of translation. It is its conviction that this Series, when completed, will furnish the American student of criminal science a systematic and sufficient acquaintance with the controlling doctrines and methods that now hold the stage of thought in Continental Europe.

Which of the various principles and methods will prove best adapted to help our problems can only be told after our students and workers have tested them in our own experience. But it is certain that we must first acquaint ourselves with these results of a generation of European thought.

In closing, the Committee thinks it desirable to refer the members of the Institute, for purposes of further investigation of the literature, to the " Preliminary Bibliography of Modern Criminal Law and Criminology " (Bulletin No. 1 of the Gary Library of Law of Northwestern University), already issued to members of the Conference. The Committee believes that some of the Anglo-American works listed therein will be found useful.

COMMITTEE ON TRANSLATIONS.

Chairman, WM. W. SMITHERS,
> Secretary of the Comparative Law Bureau of the American Bar Association, Philadelphia, Pa.

ERNST FREUND,
> Professor of Law in the University of Chicago.

MAURICE PARMELEE,
> Professor of Sociology in the State University of Kansas.

ROSCOE POUND,
> Professor of Law in the University of Chicago.

ROBERT B. SCOTT,
> Professor of Political Science in the State University of Wisconsin.

JOHN H. WIGMORE,
> Professor of Law in Northwestern University, Chicago.

INTRODUCTION TO THE ENGLISH
VERSION.

THE science of criminology is a secondary evolutional consequence of the study of penology. The early writers who
from humanitarian impulses condemned the severities
attending the administration of criminal law in both its
evidential and punitive features had no thought of creating
a new science. While they secured great penological
reforms they never departed from the traditional theory
that a law broken meant that there was a wilful trans-
gressor, who deserved to suffer retributively. The conception of imposing punishment was as impersonal as it
was instinctive. Only in degree was there any amelioration of the ancient savagery. From the time when Mon-
taigne wrote " How many sentences I have seen more
criminal than the crimes themselves! " until Servan, the
great French jurist, declared " Humanity is a sixth sense,"
although in the interim D'Aguesseau, Montesquieu,
Beccaria and Blackstone had written, the offense, — the
manifestation of contempt for the majesty of the law —
continued to be the pole-star of all criminal law. Even after
Howard, Bentham, and Romilly had secured substantial
prison reforms in England, evidential torture had ceased
on the Continent, and through the efforts of Rush, Vaux,
and Livingston the Pennsylvania system of penitential
incarceration had become generally recognized in this
country as the most rational and humane the world had
until then known, still criminology was so inextricably
entwined with penology that its true principles were over-

shadowed and undefined. The field of the causes and nature of crimes and the treatment of criminals from their psychological, physiological and social relations to the offense lay practically unexplored. The offender was observed but not studied. He was pitied and his sufferings humanely ameliorated but he steadily remained a logical object of vengeance because he had done that which a law had forbidden him to do.

This deeply imbedded tradition was not easily cast aside and even when by force of treating the results of crime men fell to questioning the causes the new thought had to occur again and again, be expressed with misgivings, dallied with as a novelty and derided as a sophistry until familiarity of suggestion lodged the thought of its possibly being a matter worthy of real attention and reflection. However, every attempt to adopt a theory was trammeled by the phantom tradition of the centuries, — the cry for vengeance by the outraged law. It took more than a hundred years for shaded and vague expressions to emerge into positive assertion by any considerable number of savants that the criminal and not the crime should be the object of investigation and study.

Supported finally during the past fifty years by the greatest legal, medical and social philosophers, the true lines of criminology have gradually become clearly defined and the materials for its true application are constantly increasing. By its principles the problems which were perplexing, because beclouded by ancient errors, are being solved in consonance with the progress which has marked other phases of life. The bases of action are appreciated and the proper remedies being provided by close study and statistical records. A rational theory has been perceived and adopted.

Obedience to the law is recognized as a normal condition. It is now admitted that moral character depends upon a condition of equilibrium amid the emotional, volitional, and intellectual forces. When that equilibrium is disturbed to the point of law-breaking then the criminal becomes a special object of consideration and the causes of his abnormal state a matter for study. Those causes have already been ascertained to a large extent. The criminal being the product of cosmic, biological, or social influences which put him out of harmony with conventional morality and cause him to disturb the recognized aims of community existence, must be treated as a ward of the State for the purpose of curing his impairment and meanwhile keeping him so sufficiently restrained as to prevent injury to others. These are the practical guiding principles which the true science of criminology is rapidly making more accurate and more capable of application.

It is not enough, however, for a student to know the definition of a science which is a product of evolution and therefore progressive. It is indispensable that he be familiar with every phase of its development and be able to distinguish the real and durable amid the exaggerated, the false and the ephemeral. Since the impetus to the study given by Dr. Paul Broca in founding the Anthropological Society of Paris in 1859 many distinguished scholars have written upon different phases of criminology and advocated a variety of theories as to which they have differed not a little. Several schools have arisen, none of which is without followers, and many have abundant adherents and earnest teachers.

The great work of Señor de Quirós, — *Las nuevas teorias de la criminalidad* (Modern Theories of Criminality), — now presented for the first time in the English language,

reveals all the shades of thought which have marked the
development of the science and constitutes a compendium
that no student of the subject can ignore without disad-
vantage. It is a concise survey of all the European
writers on Criminal Science during the last century, by
one whose untiring attention to details, earnest effort for
accuracy, and pre-eminent faculty of comparison and
analysis, have given him a deservedly high place among
the scholars of Europe.

Señor C. Bernaldo de Quirós was born in Madrid
December 12, 1873, and was licensed to practise law in
1894. While pursuing the ordinary lines of his profession
he became an interested, searching and zealous student of
criminology, and devoted several years of study of the
great mass of European literature on the subject. After
diligently and discriminately gathering his materials as a
a basis for sound deduction and means of weighing the
theories of the rapidly developing schools, he spent some
years in writing this work, and finally published it in 1898.
Its immediate and lasting success removed any doubt
that he might have entertained concerning his life work.
He shortly after began preparing the data for his next
offering on the subject, which was published in 1901 under
the title *La mala vida en Madrid* (Low Life of Madrid)
written in collaboration with J. M. Llanas Aguilaniedo.
This work is a highly meritorious and valuable psycho-
sociological treatment of criminals, prostitutes, beggars,
and that multitude of degenerate human flotsam and
jetsam known in modern Spanish as *golfos*, a term which
embraces all and more than our word " vagabonds."

This book marked the line of efficiency for Señor de
Quirós, and he earnestly accepted the burden of joining
his manifestly special abilities to those of the other great

Continental writers in promoting the science of criminology. In 1903 he published *El Alcoholismo*; and the next year his article on *Literatura española del alcoholismo* appeared in the *Bibliographie der gesamten wissenschaftlichen Literatur über den Alkohol und den Alkoholismus* (Bibliographical Collection of the Scientific Literature on Alcohol and Alcoholism) of Dr. Abherhalden, which was a recognition given only to those standing high among Continental scholars. In the same year he wrote *Biblioteca de ciencias penales* (Library of Penal Science), and also *Alrededor del delito y de la pena* (Concerning the Offense and the Penalty). In 1906 the *Instituto de Reformas Sociales* was founded and he was chosen one of its staff of governing officials, a position which he still occupies. He signalized this definite acceptance of his mission by publishing in the same year *Vocabulario de Anthropología criminal* and *Criminología de los delitos de sangre en España* (Sanguinary Crimes in Spain). Both works bear his characteristic marks of careful preparation and scientific treatment. The latter deservedly ranks high among the foremost collection of works on crime in particular countries. In 1907 he published *La Picota* (The Head-Exposure Post) comprising a most interesting account of crimes and punishments in the Castilian country during the middle ages. The effort to be accurate historically is so apparent that trust in his honesty of purpose and thoroughness of research cannot be withheld.

In 1908 the general acceptance of Señor de Quirós as the leading Spanish writer on criminology was such that a second edition of his earliest work became imperative; but he permitted it only after a most careful review of the whole text and revision of certain parts which he deemed would contribute to its completeness as a practical guide to those bent on basic research. It is from this second edition that the present translation has been made. He has personally revised a copy for our translator. During its progress he has also published (1909) *Figuras delincuentes* (Some Types of Offenders), containing several antique judicial records.

Appreciation of his researches and views has recently (1910) been expressed by a translation into German of *La mala vida en Madrid* by Dr. Bloch of Berlin, with an introduction by the late Dr. Caesar Lombroso, penned by that distinguished criminologist and statistician not long before his death.

Such a work from such an author becomes invaluable to every student of criminology.

W. W. SMITHERS,

Chairman of the Committee on Translations of the American Institute of Criminal Law and Criminology, and Secretary of the Comparative Law Bureau of the American Bar Association.

PHILADELPHIA, PA., December 1, 1910.

PREFACE TO THE FIRST SPANISH EDITION.

THE interest that penal questions awoke in me, as soon as I came to know them, found its most favorable opportunity for application while following the courses in the Philosophy of Law given at the Central University by Don Francisco Giner de los Ríos.

Among the various subjects, which, according to their tastes and likings, the students of this department — a true laboratory of social and legal sciences — brought up for discussion, I presented for three years the question of modern theories of criminality. At the end of that time, the books and publications consulted, the conversations held among all present, and the constant stimulus exercised upon the mind from various directions formed a material of no mean importance and consideration, which, if put together and revised once more, I thought could be presented to the public in the hope that it might prove useful for the knowledge and diffusion of such an interesting subject.

Thus grew this work; and in publishing it, not only I fulfill a duty, but I also experience the long-awaited pleasure, marred only by the knowledge of the scant value of the work, of paying the most sincere and respectful homage of lasting gratitude to the instruction of that beloved teacher, whose delicate modesty prevents my saying more at the very start. Nevertheless, I am extremely anxious that he be not held responsible for the ideas my book may contain: useless precaution, after all, when the essence and method of his teaching are so well known to all.

While I take pleasure in writing these pages, I do not wish

to forget any one of those who have brought within my reach books, reviews, pamphlets, and information, thus making possible the production of such a work, which necessitates the largest possible number of data. I take occasion, therefore, to openly express to them my heart-felt thanks. Finally, my fellow students will surely permit me to remember them in a book full of quotations from authors and works which have not given me the assiduous collaboration and kind advice that these friends have; we all know that the real upbuilding of knowledge is due more to a bee-hive process than to single-handed labor.

And now a few words concerning the book itself.

There are in Spain two other works of the same character. Their worth is such that I shall have to refer to them throughout. They are Dorado Montero's " Criminal Anthropology in Italy," and Aramburu's " Modern Penal Science." [1] However, of the modern theories of criminality both treat only the anthropological, to be sure the most novel on account of its extraordinary apparatus unknown to jurists. Moreover, they limit themselves to expounding its operation in only one country, Italy.

Again, they were published ten years ago. Therefore, my work comes to complete and continue them to the best of my ability. The movement of penal science and its auxiliary disciplines, set forth by those writers in its beginnings, has grown to such an extent and has become so intricate and all-inclusive, that many times in looking through my pages for a picture of the movement, I have been haunted by the suspicion lest some one, in reading them, should say: " Was it necessary in this book to re-write twenty years of general history? "

[1] Dorado Montero's *Antropología Criminal en Italia* ; and Aramburu's *Nueva Ciencia Penal.*

I hasten to acknowledge beforehand that, although one may see only the phases of the subject presented by me, much more has been done and discovered in reference to modern theories than is here set forth even if it be only the first form of discovery, namely, the recognition of problems. But a work such as this with the limitations imposed by various reasons can only look at the subject from a point of view so distant that only the most salient outlines become visible.

I will add no more concerning the work, since it is already before the reader. I must only repeat that it is a work essentially of information, seldom altered by the personal reflection of the author. Incomplete or badly interwoven as the latter may be, the author believes that the work will not be altogether fruitless in our western and remote Spain. May God give it power to suggest and stimulate the serious and thoughtful study of crime and punishment, a study which, to-day more than ever before, calls for men willing to devote to it their whole life.

CONSTANCIO BERNALDO DE QUIRÓS.

AUTHOR'S PREFACE TO THE AMERICAN EDITION.

In presenting to the American reader a new edition of this work, I am glad to be able to correct not a few structural, historical, and typographical errors of the first edition, and, at the same time, to trace the history of the movement up to the present day.

I will add that these two are not the only innovations made in this edition. The entire contents of the book have been recast in a new mold, which the author considers preferable. The last chapter on " The Scientific Investigation of Crime " is altogether new.

It only remains to be said that the author, after a careful selection, mentions and expounds only what, in his opinion, is fundamental or characteristic. It would be in vain for him to suppose that nothing remains beyond this limit. Perhaps this final remark was not needed.

The author is much pleased to see this book, originally written in Spanish, translated into English: a language so different in idiomatic expression.

C. B. DE Q.

MADRID, December 1, 1910.

CONTENTS

CONTENTS

MODERN THEORIES OF CRIMINALITY.

CHAPTER I

CRIMINOLOGY.

I.

ORIGINS.

Section 1.

BEGINNING with the middle of the nineteenth century, people have been speaking more and more of the criminal in the same naturalistic sense which, in our days, found its culminating expression in Professor Cesare Lombroso.

Original and strange as this sense may appear, it is certain that history was preparing its way and that in it we find its laborious genealogy and gestation. History, like nature, does not advance by leaps. Its ages preserve the footprints of forerunners and founders just as the geologic strata preserve the fossilized species from which are derived those that people the earth to-day.

Among the great complexity of forces that have determined the new direction of modern penal thought, observation discovers immediately a number that are nearer, more manifest, purer, and of such a decisive influence on the origin and tendencies of modern criminology, that, as a writer says, once granted their existence, what Lombroso has done would have been realized, even if he and his collaborators had not existed. These forces are:

a. The old preoccupation and longing to discover in man the relations between body and soul, the correspondence between spirit and matter;

b. The development of psychiatry; and

c. The rise of statistic science.

Section 2. (1) OCCULT SCIENCES. — PHYSIOGNOMY, PHRENOLOGY.

Lauvergne, Carus, Casper.

The first factor is the same as that which has changed astrology into astronomy, alchemy into chemistry, and demonology into psychiatry. In fact, criminology, through the doctrine of the criminal man, and especially through its derived doctrine of the type, is connected with all those occult sciences, like chiromancy, metoscopy, podology, ophthalmoscopy, etc., which sought the sensible expression of the spirit in every part of the human body. Antonini has been able to write an interesting book on this subject, entitled "The Precursors of Lombroso." [1] Nevertheless, in his account, many names have been necessarily omitted. As for the Spanish precursors, Antonini's book can be complemented by Montes' "Studies of Old Spanish Writers (Romano, La Fuente, Estella, Vives, Huarte, Guevara, Zabaleta, Ponce de León, etc.) on the Perpetrators of Crime." [2]

Among those sciences, which were as numerous as the various organs and functions of the body, natural selection supported *physiognomy*, on account of the vague prejudice

---

[1] Antonini, *I precursori di Lombroso*, Turin, 1900.

[2] Montes, *Estudios de antiguos escritores españoles sobre los agentes del delito;* en la Ciudad de Dios, 1902 and ff.

which considers the face as the most noble part of the body
and as the most worthy of manifesting the soul. The same
cause gave rise to *phrenology;* and both sciences, or pseudo-
sciences if you prefer, with more and more scientific apparatus,
spread everywhere with no less debate than criminal anthropology has done in our days. Lavater (1741–1801) and Gall
(1758–1828), to mention only the most famous, are the direct
ancestors in ascending line of modern penal science. To be
sure they are separated by a considerable distance, but not by
a leap. A fervent disciple of Gall's, Lauvergne, studies the
convicts of Toulon, and, after attributing their criminal
instincts to the abnormal development of a part of the brain,
he describes the criminal type in strokes reproduced later by
Lombroso.

Speaking of cold-blooded assassins, whom he classifies as
" a rare species coming from the mountains and from out-
of-the-way regions," he says: " They possess marked protuberances and a peculiar face stamped by the seal of a
brutal and impassible instinct. Their heads are large and
receding with notable lateral protuberances, enormous jaws
and masticatory muscles always in motion." [1]   Yet, a year
before, the physiologist Carus (1789–1869), in his " Principles of a New and Scientific Craniology," [2] insisted upon the
anomaly in the cranial formation of delinquents. He stated
that they are distinguished by a narrow forehead, the insufficient development of the occiput, and the length of the
cranium. In his opinion, they are beings who tend exclusively
to a vegetative life and to the satisfaction of their material
life, lacking in reason and will-power and prone to offend

---

[1] *Les forçats considerés sous le rapport physique, morale et intellectuel
observés au bagne de Toulon*, Paris, 1844.

[2] *Grundzüge einer neuen und wissenschaftlichen Kranioscopie*, Stuttgart, 1840.

at the first occasion. Similar references could be multiplied
till reaching Casper, who published a minute study of criminal
physiognomy in the "Quarterly Review for Medical Jurisprudence, 1854." [1]

Disgusted at times by this kinship to occultism and super-
stitions, and compelled at other times, as if by necessity like
all other reformers, Lombroso tells us how "the novelty of
my most discussed conclusions goes back to prehistoric times.
Homer speaks of Thersites, Salomon writes that the heart
alters the face of the evil man, and, above all, Aristotle, Avi-
cenna, and J. B. Dalla Porta discussed extensively criminal
physiognomy, the last two going perhaps further than we
ourselves. What else shall be added, when Polemon, after
having insisted upon the narrow forehead of criminals, speaks
even of their *mancinismo* (left-handedness), an observation
which I thought to have been the first to make?"

The people also preserve in their proverbs, sayings, and
phrases an entire folk-lore of criminal anthropology, in which
one perceives traces of the same problem, constantly stated,
concerning the relations of body and soul. We find it also
in literature and art, fields already investigated by the modern
penal school. Worthy of mention are Lefort's monograph
"Criminal Type according to Scholars and Artists," [2] and
Ferri's "The Delinquent in Art." [3] Other works of a more
specialized nature are Niceforo's "Criminals and Degenerates
in Dante's Inferno"; [4] Roux's "Balzac, Jurisconsult and
Criminalist"; [5] and Koni's "Dostoyewsky as a Criminalist." [6]

Nor does the past lack judicial applications in reference to

[1] *Morder Physiognomien*, in *Viert. f. gerich. Mediz.*, 1854.
[2] *Type criminel d'après les savants et les artistes*, Lyon, 1892.
[3] *I delinquenti nell'arte*, Genoa, 1896.
[4] *Criminali e degenerati dell' Inferno Dantesco*, Turin, 1898.
[5] *Balzac jurisconsulte et criminaliste*, Lyon, 1906.
[6] *Dostoyewsky criminaliste*, Paris, 1898.

the criminal type. Valerio, for instance, records a mediæval edict ordering that in case of doubt between two suspects, the one showing more deformity was to undergo torture. The chronicles speak of a Medici who reserved final judgment till the criminal had been examined physically: "Having seen your face and examined your head, we do not send you to prison but to the gallows." Under the old régime, as Loiseleur affirms in his "Crimes and Punishments," [1] the commentators Jousse and Muyart de Vouglans enumerated, among the reasons for suspicion, the unfavorable physiognomy of the accused. "And, in reality," adds Tarde, who quotes from Loiseleur, "what more do we need to-day to decide a judge who wavers among many suspects?"

Section 3. (2) PSYCHIATRY. — FIRST THEORIES OF CRIMINALITY. — DEGENERATION AND MORAL INSANITY.

Morel, Despine, Maudsley.

Psychiatry, more than any other science, can be called a product of our century. In fact, in 1801, there appeared a "Medical and Philosophical Treatise on Mental Alienation," [2] by Pinel (1745–1826), a work which inaugurated the age of science and put an end to the age of corrective and penal methods, properly speaking, against the insane; an age, which the people record in one of their proverbs: "The insane is sane for punishment." Although late in coming, psychiatry met with a rapid development. After Pinel came Esquirol, who was in turn followed for the space of a century and a half by a great generation of alienists, who have contributed in a decisive manner to the creation of criminology.

The ideas and even the words met in this science are found,

[1] *Les crimes et les peines*, Paris, 1865. Quoted by Tarde in his *La criminalité comparée*, p. 21.

[2] *Tratado médico filosófico sobre la enajenación mental.*

at least potentially, in the works of these predecessors. The ideal portrait of the insane created by law begins from that time on to disappear, and in its place there appear the outlines of the criminal. The long list of the manias and alterations of a single chord of the psychic key-board, its forms less and less objective and more delicate and hidden to the mere eye and good sense, the only criteria employed in former times; the lack of crisis, spasms, and deliriums; its relative character, in the double sense of manifesting itself in a single idea or sentiment, and in mingling at the same time with the conditions of health instead of successions as claimed by the old theory of lucid intervals; the reproduction of juridical portraits of crimes on account of the inexhaustible and innumerable psycopathies, and many other items of analogous significance, have all extended the boundaries of mental infirmity, reduced the field of delinquency, and prepared the explanation of the morbid nature of crime. It is to be noted that in those days the practical aspect of penal reform was not lacking; this is shown by a complete set of works which fall under the general title of " Conflicts between Psychiatry and the Code."

It is in the midst of frequent experiments that the first two theories of criminality, *degeneration* and *moral insanity*, begin to form themselves.

Three generations after the beginnings of psychiatry, the theory of *degeneration* is set forth in France by Morel.[1] Nevertheless, according to Dallemagne,[2] he rather owes his ideas on degeneration to natural sciences. Morel, in his classical treatise " Physical, Intellectual, and Moral Degeneration of the Human Species," [3] looks upon degeneration as a kind of

---

[1] Pinel, predecessor of Esquirol; Esquirol, teacher of Falret senior; Falret, teacher of Morel.

[2] *Dégénérés et déséquilibrés*, Brussels, 1894, p. 99.

[3] *Degeneraciones fisicas, intelectuales y morales de la especie humana*, Paris, 1857.

retrogressive natural selection, a degradation, using the word
not in its ethical sense and without any meaning of contempt.
His starting point is " the existence of a primitive type which
the human mind reproduces in its own thought as the master-
piece and culmination of creation — a view which agrees
so well with our own ideas, — and that the degeneration of
our nature is due to the going astray of the primitive type,
which contains in itself all the necessary elements for the
preservation of the species." Intent upon making the latest
scientific discoveries come within the scope of the purest
orthodoxy, Morel establishes as the starting point of degeneration " the combination of the new conditions brought about
by the original fall." Then he studies the rôle heredity plays
— a theory already confirmed in relation to the transmission
of crime by Lucas, in his " Treatise on Natural Heredity " [1]
— in the genesis and development of the deviation of the
primitive type; and, tracing through the generations the
evolution of the psychopathic process, succeeds in establishing for the first time the relation between criminality
and degeneration. " The strange and unknown types which
people our prisons," said he, " are not so strange and
unknown to those who study the morbid varieties of the
human species from the double point of view of the psychic
and moral condition of the individuals that compose them.
They personify the various degenerations of the species,
and the evil which produces them constitutes for modern
society a greater danger than the barbaric invasion did for
the old."

Not less noteworthy among the precursors of criminal
anthropology is Despine, the author of " Natural Psychology,
an Essay on the Intellectual and Moral Faculties in their
Normal State and Abnormal Manifestations in the Insane

[1] *Traité de l'hérédit naturelle*, Paris, 1847.

and the Criminals." [1] " His name," says Francotte,[2] " ought to occupy a prominent place. The object of his investigations was, above all, the psychological side of the criminal; for, according to him, the habitual criminal suffers a moral anomaly characterized by the absence of remorse."

In the meantime, psychological studies of the criminal were progressing in England, and we have Clapham and Clarke's " The Criminal Outline of the Insane and Criminal," London, 1846; Winslow's " Lettsonian Lectures on Insanity," London, 1854; and Thompson's " Psychology of Criminals," London, 1870; and " The Hereditary Nature of Crime," in the " Journal of Mental Science," October, 1870. After them we come to Maudsley, one of the most remarkable names in contemporary mental science.

The most characteristic features of Maudsley's theory [3] are the diagnosis of the criminal as morally insane, and the existence of a vast middle zone between mental disease and delinquency.

Pritchard was the first to employ the phrase *moral insanity* [4] to designate a psychic overthrow falling upon the emotional sphere, and consisting in the benumbing or the deprivation of the moral sense. It is the *rational* or *emotional monomania* of Esquirol, the *instinctive* or the *impulsive* of Morel, the *insanity of action* of Briérre de Boismont, the *mania of character* of Pinel, the *lucid insanity* of Trélat, and the *insanity with conscience* of Baillarger. In short, it is a peculiar condition in which the intellectual faculties are not affected, but remain intact; hence, the appellations *lucid, with con-*

---

[1] *Psychologie naturelle, essai sur les facultés intellectuelles et morales dans leur état normal et dans leurs manifestations anormales chez les aliénés et chez les criminels*, Paris, 1868.

[2] *L'Anthropologie criminelle*, Paris, 1891, Introduction.

[3] Cf. *Mental Responsibility*, London, 1873.

[4] *A Treatise on Insanity*, London, 1835.

science, without delirium, rational. The alteration or the deprivation falls upon the emotional or the affective faculties. The idea seems altogether of English origin. Franzolini tells us that, in the 16th century, the Scotchman Thomas Abercromby, physician of James II, spoke in his "Treatise on the Mind" (1656) of *moral insanity,* "in which all the upright sentiments are eliminated, while the intelligence presents no disorders." He showed by long psychologic analyses how the influence of the moral sense upon conscience can be altered or lost without disturbing the intelligence.[1]

With Maudsley, moral insanity assumes a special character through the addition of another theory: the *borderland* or the *middle zone* theory. Between crime and insanity, says this writer, there exists an intermediate zone, in one of whose borders one observes a little insanity and much perversity, while in the other the contrary takes place, namely, less perversity and more insanity.

Section 4. (3) STATISTICS.
Quételet.

Meanwhile, the science of statistics was being formed.

Social Physics, as Quételet calls it, anticipating Comte who reserved it for his sociology, ascertained, from its very beginnings and with all its graphic procedure, a general European fact, namely, the increase of crime in the form of relapse, which was able to suggest the idea of an incorrigible criminal; and, at the same time, the phenomena of regularity in crime with their relation to social facts, which suggested the possibility of probable laws for crime and vice analogous to those which for the first time had been enacted for economical relations.

[1] *I giudizii sullo stato mentale alla Corte d'Assise e la Giuria supletoria,* Venice, 1877.

Quételet himself (1796–1874), whom we can consider the first social criminologist, pointed out some of these laws, especially that called *thermic law of delinquency*, according to which crimes of blood are prevalent in the south and those against property in the north. It was the first expression of the theory of physical factors developed later by criminal anthropology. He went so far as to say: "Society prepares crime; the criminal becomes its executive." [1]

II.

THE THREE INNOVATORS.

Section 5. (1) CESARE LOMBROSO.

1836-1909.

Between 1871 and 1876 there began to appear in Italy the studies on the male offender by an original physician, Darwinist from the very start, Cesare Lombroso.   Travelling through Italy in 1869, Emile Laveleye noted this in his diary: " There has been introduced to me in Milan an unknown young scholar, Dr. Lombroso. He spoke of certain anatomical signs by which he can recognize criminals. What a useful and convenient discovery for committing magistrates!" "Mr. Laveleye," says Tarde, in recording the first allusion to a name that was destined to become famous, " writes four or five lines more about him and then stops." [2]

In fact, who was there at the time that expected more ideas on the subject?

Nevertheless, these ideas were to be found in the environment. The causes that led Lombroso to their discovery are the same as those which his school finds in every human

[1] *Physique Sociale*, 1869.

[2] *A propos du Congrès de Génève;* a discourse delivered before the General Prisons Congress, November 18, 1896; *Archives d'Anthropologie criminelle*, May, 1897.

action. Individual, physical, and social factors, heaven and earth, as Goëthe would say, have determined the birth of the male offender and of the modern school of criminal law.

The birthplace of this science is Italy; perhaps, as it has already been remarked, for the same reason that, in the same country, Beccaria wrote on crimes and punishments; and, before him, Farinacio, Claro, Marsilio, etc., had treated the same problem with some degree of continuity as far back as the great classical jurisconsults.

Moreover, what shall we say of the influence of the social medium already saturated with the ideas which to-day are crystallized? To speak of it would be to repeat words already uttered; but it is important to note the fact, because when it is a question of science and scientists, there still persist, even in modern science, the legend of Minerva's birth and a class prejudice which reduce the rôle played by the medium of environment and of the public which compose it to that played by the Greek chorus around the hero or the genius.

"The Criminal, in Relation to Anthropology, Jurisprudence, and Psychiatry,"[1] originally a small pamphlet, grew into a work of three volumes: the fifth and last edition containing also an atlas. In spite of this and other observations, applicable to all historical events and to be kept in mind in dealing with them, the above work is the starting point from which criminal anthropology plunges forth and finds, at the same time, its most characteristic expression.

His later works "The Female Offender," "Political Crime and Revolutions," "The Anarchists,"[2] and others, show amplified details of the whole.

[1] First edition, 1876; last edition, 1897–1900.

[2] *La donna delinquente, prostituta e normale*, in collaboration with G. Ferrero, Turin, 1893; *Il delitto politico e le rivoluzioni*, in collaboration with R. Laschi, Turin, 1890; *Gli Anarchici*, Turin, 1894.

The complete account of Lombroso's works may be found in the book prepared by his daughters Paola and Gina: *Cesare Lombroso,*

Lombroso begins by discussing what has been called *the embryology of crime*, which constitutes an indispensable first chapter in the monographs of the school.

The author studies crime among the lower organisms, detecting it even in the vegetable world.[1] Then he studies it among the animals, and finally in the human realm; in the infancy of the individual and of the species, in the child and the savage. Later, as the book develops, there appears an ethical variety of the *genus homo*, the male offender, distinguished by numerous characteristics which constitute the type.

The conclusion that can be drawn from the data accumulated by the author is the indissoluble relation between certain deeds which man calls crimes and all living organisms in an indifferent and normal condition. The activity displayed in the form of crime bears these marks in both the vegetable and the animal worlds, and would bear them even among men if one did not see in the latter another element of the historical development of their nature, namely, the genesis and development of the moral sense; after which, what could be called physiologic criminology — being a stage of the normal process of the organisms characterized by the absence, also normal, of the fundamental altruistic sentiments — becomes pathologic and abnormal. But this growth and correlative elimination do not always take place,

Turin, 1906. As for his personality, consult the various writings contained in a volume published on the occasion of his scientific jubilee, entitled: *L'opera di Cesare Lombroso nella Scienza e nelle sue applicazioni*, Turin, 1906.

[1] Enrico Ferri, in his "*Omicidio nell Antropologia Criminale*," Turin, 1895, has rectified the illustrations proposed by Lombroso as manifestations of crime among vegetables (insectivorous plants, etc.). He attributes them not to delinquency which supposes an analogy of species between the victim and the author of the assault, but to the law of the struggle for existence.

either through causes connected with the organism itself which is paralyzed in its evolutionary process or stricken and torn by atavistic and pathologic heredity, or through the influence of the social medium that surrounds the individual; a medium, which weighing unconsciously upon him like the atmosphere, hinders him without his own co-operation. The abnormal continuance of the criminal physiological condition by means of many physical and social causes forms, in short, the criminal with his manifold epileptic, alcoholic, hysteric, and other varieties. Our author has studied almost exclusively the varieties that, in his opinion, are due to individual factors.

The first explanation for the phenomenon of congenital criminality was found by Lombroso in *atavism*.

Literally speaking, atavism means hereditary transmission from forefathers or remote ancestors. Not from Adam and Eve to be sure; the general conception of man and his origins has radically changed, thanks to the theory of transformation which replaces the first couple stained by one original sin by the primitive man scarcely freed from the animality of the anthropoid.

Atavism, then, is the tendency of living beings to return to a distant type from which intermediate generations have made them deviate. Unlike direct heredity, with which, however, it preserves the stability of the species, atavism is characterized by the reappearance of unusual traits in most recent ancestors, which were characteristic of that distant race.

The criminal goes back to the savage type. In order to reach the hypothesis for his regression, the following process seems to have been followed:

a. Organic and psychic comparison of the present criminal with the savage and the primitive man;

b. Accumulation of documents showing that with them "crime is not the exception, but the general rule."

a. When the comparison is undertaken, we find that in the criminal there are numerous *anatomic* traits, especially craneologic, that suggest the structure of primitive men and even of the leading mammals. These *anatomic* traits are: the narrowness of the forehead; an exaggerated development of frontal sinuses; a great frequency of median frontal sutures, of the median fossa of the occipital crest, and of the Wormian ossicles; abnormal development of the cranial vault; disproportionate development of the mandibles and cheekbones; prognathism; obliquity and great capacity of the occipital orbits and foramen, etc. Among the *physiologic* traits we may mention: obtuse sensibility, invulnerability and in consequence longevity, absence of vascular reactions, left-handedness, etc. The *psychologic* traits are: moral and affective insensibility, idleness, absence of remorse, want of foresight, etc. And, finally, among the *social* traits, we find tattooing, language, etc.

b. On the other hand, the delinquency of the savage and of primitive man is demonstrated: (a') by *physiologic* arguments that prove the absence in the beginning of any distinction between the idea of action and that of crime,[1] the frequency of actions which, on account of numerous synonyms, we call crimes,[2] and the impure origins of some institutions;[3] (b') by *mythologic* arguments, like the existence of gods and goddesses for every offense and for all crimes; (c') by *historic*

---

[1] *Crime* from the Sanskrit *karman* is equivalent to action, according to Pictet; *guilt* (culpa) from the Sanskrit *halp, hlrp*, meaning to do, to execute, acording to Pictet and Pott; *faccinus* from *facere*, etc.

[2] Pictet says that in Sanskrit there are about a hundred roots expressing the idea of killing and wounding, without counting the secondary divergencies.

[3] According to Lombroso, all languages agree in pointing to robbery and murder as the first methods for acquiring property.

arguments found in the copious material of description of savage tribes and races, collected by travellers and scientists who show them to us living a life of crime with indifference when not as a display of heroism.

In short, according to all these arguments, crime resembles a remote anachronism; the criminal, that is, the man in whom heredity goes back to his first ancestors, leaves a gap which in other beings is filled by the historical product of moral selections transmitted by later generations.

The type of the born criminal was a reproduction of the rude morphology of the savage. From the deformed cranium down to his tattooed skin, all pointed to that. There remained, however, a few stigmata, crept into the type, which could not be called atavistic. According to Lombroso, it was only later that he saw that these characteristics coincided with those attributed to the morally insane and were connected with other pathologic and not atavistic peculiarities. It was only when preparing his study on the epileptic criminal, and at the third edition of his book, that he saw that this family group could perfectly include the born criminal, a discovery that enabled him to solve all difficulties. Nevertheless, in his opinion, atavism did not fail; for there does not exist in pathology any other infirmity more calculated to fuse and combine morbid and atavistic phenomena than epilepsy. The epileptic, for instance, barks, eats human flesh, etc.; two marks of prehistoric and savage cannibal atavism.

The frequency of crime among epileptics was well known and had been remarked by all writers. Thus, according to Maudsley, the most diverse cases of homicidal impulses are connected with epilepsy. Burlureaux writes: " When an inexplicable crime, completely out of harmony with the culprit's antecedents who is not insane, is committed with unusual rapidity, ferocity or multiplicity of extraordinary aggressions, foreign to the usual mechanism of crime and without complicity; when the culprit has lost all remembrance and seems a stranger to the act, or when he has only a vague consciousness of the deed and speaks of it with indifference as if another had committed it; then it is necessary to look for epilepsy." [1]

It would not be difficult to look for epilepsy in these symptoms so characteristic of the *grand mal;* but, side by side with them, there exist other marked forms discovered by modern science, which embrace even the state of temporary insensibility, want of foresight, or the short choleric and wrathful attack, which are the psychic equivalent of muscular epilepsy. If the reader wished to know, definitely, what this morbid state is, we would answer that only a few years ago it would have been possible to define it, but that, to-day, like degeneration and neurasthenia, it represents a protean body personifying for some the entire mental pathology. Being the effect of the irritation of the cerebellar or of the medullar cortex, its reaction is characterized by a rapid and excessive discharge of latent forces in intermittent and unstable impulsions.

It is exactly in this very wide sense that Lombroso considers epilepsy as forming with atavism the *substratum* upon which is based the criminal world.

I sum up my ideas, says he, for greater clearness, in the following graphic lines:

EPILEPTOIDS
1. Occasional criminal _____
2. Emotional criminal _____
3. Born criminal   _____
4. Moral insane   _____
5. Masked epileptic   _____

His latest theory is composed of three chief factors: *atavism,*

[1] Cf. the article *Epilepsie* in the *Dictionnaire des Sciences médicales,* 1886.

moral insanity, and *epilepsy;* hence its name of *triple* theory. A German criminalist, Näcke, has summed up Lombroso's latest position with sufficient exactness. His point of view, says Näcke, is summarized in the following conclusions:

(a) the criminal, properly speaking, is *born* so;

(b) the same as the *moral insane;*

(c) on *epileptic* basis;

(d) explicable chiefly by *atavism;* and

(e) forms a special *biologic* and *anatomic* type.[1]

And now we come to the theory of the type of *the born criminal,* which for many embraces all criminal anthropology. The reason for this is found in the fact that, in its gradual process not unlike other subjects, this science, from the book and the review down to the daily paper and anonymous oral literature, as it reached the different social strata represented by these mediums, has lost so much of its contents as each of them has been able to assimilate, until at last it is reduced to the romantic and extraordinary form of the type of the born criminal. Criminal anthropology has, in a short time, reached people and regions that science could not have reached if we consider the latter in all its classical apparatus, and has given rise to so many discussions that if, for instance, Flaubert had written *Madame Bovary* in 1887 instead of 1857, Mr. Homais and the curate of his town could not have discussed any other subject but Lombroso and his theories.

Considering the nature of this work, it would be indeed impossible to give a full account of the traits, marks, and stigmata of the type of the born criminal. Impossible, because it would presuppose the most complete and minute autopsy in which bones, viscera, and tissues should be examined one by one in their respective relation, and the keenest

[1] *Lombroso and Modern Criminal Anthropology,* in the *Zeitschrift für Kriminalanthropologie,* Berlin, 1897.

observation of the whole physiology and mechanism of life and of psychology, sounded and estimated by means of all modern procedures. The criminal type, as the scholastics said of the soul, is in its entirety in the whole body and in each of its parts.

The history of its elaboration, then, can be considered from the standpoint of the method adopted for its construction, and from that which refers to the nature of its characteristics.

As for the method, we can easily perceive that in the beginning it consisted in the mere accumulation of all that appeared abnormal and teratologic, namely, the *criminalization* of every unusual trait, which, as a result, gives us a type of the most abstract nature. The period of selection follows with great delay. With the adoption of better methods which made possible the grouping of the more evident and frequent characteristics and the elimination of not a few incompatibilities, the type dissolves itself into different types, especially physiognomical, of assassins, swindlers, thieves, etc. Thus the Galtonian photograph of some criminal skulls shows, according to Lombroso, in the case of assassins, developed frontal sinuses, very large cheek and jaw-bones, large and far apart orbits, facial asymmetry, the ptelea-shaped type of nasal cavity, and the lemuridous appendix of the jaw-bone. The skull of swindlers and thieves offers less visible results; but the living head, studied by Garofalo and Ferri more than by Lombroso, presents a contrast between the extreme mobility of the thief's whole face and the impassible and cold fixity of the assassin's.

If from the method we pass to the nature of the characteristics classified by Lombroso, we find that all writers continue to point out the progress made not long ago in the fields of anatomy, physiology, and psychology.

In the field of anatomy, the type presents a plastic picture in such relief and so sensible to the five senses as mother nature made them, that, without instruments to render it more keen and sensitive, the eye alone could discover the picture; and not alone the clinical eye of the scholarly anthropologist and of the old magistrate, but also that of a child and of the most ignorant in science.

Later, when gross anatomy is completed by histology, the type shrinks, evaporates, is entirely lost under the action of well-defined factors, and we have what the discoverer himself has called " delinquents of genius," without hindering a certain tendency in the type to reëstablish itself enveloped in characters of opposite biological significance (prophetic, for instance, and not atavistic).

In spite of all, we can affirm that the anatomic features continue to characterize the Lombrosian theory, although not as in the past by exclusion or greater significance, but by their mere presence, due perchance to the integral study of the criminal which the author has been obliged to make.

Section 6. (2) ENRICO FERRI.

Lombroso's discovery gave Enrico Ferri the point of view for his " New Horizons of Criminal Law and Penal Procedure." [1] His work in the modern science began, however, a few years before by a denial of free will and the formulation of the theory of responsibility.[2] After that his works multiply. We will mention only " The Homicide in Criminal Anthropology," " The Criminals in Art," and " Socialism and Criminality." [3] Most of the theories that to-day are complete

---

[1] *Nuovi orizzonti del diritto e procedura penale*, Bologna, 1884; fourth edition under the title of *Sociologia criminale*, Turin, 1900.

[2] *Teorica dell' imputabilitá e la negazione del libro arbitrio*, Florence, 1878.

[3] *L'omicidio nell' Antropologia criminale*, Turin, 1895; *I delinquenti nell' arte*, Genoa, 1896; *Socialismo e criminalità*, Turin, 1883.

and crystallized take their rise from these books which represent the application of positivistic philosophy to crime and punishment. In them we find the theory of criminal factors, which is the key to the modern theories of criminality; also the most largely adopted classification of criminals, the penal function conceived in the social body defending itself, the penal substitutes, the transformation of criminal jurisprudence into *sociologic* science, forming thus a complete organism so readily adaptable to the medium, that it appears to be the winner and favorite in the vital competition of modern theories.

We shall begin with the *theory of the factors.*

In " Studies on Criminality in France from 1826 to 1878," [1] Ferri states for the first time the theory as follows: " Crime is the result of manifold causes, which, although found always linked into an intricate net-work, can be detected, however, by means of careful study. The factors of crime can be divided into *individual* or *anthropological, physical* or *natural,* and *social.* The anthropologic factors comprise age, sex, civil status, profession, domicile, social rank, instruction, education, and the organic and psychic constitution. The physical factors are: race, climate, the fertility and disposition of the soil, the relative length of day and night, the seasons, meteoric conditions, temperature. The social factors comprise the density of population, emigration, public opinion, customs and religion, public order, economic and industrial conditions, agriculture and industrial production, public administration of public safety, public instruction and education, public beneficence, and, in general, civil and penal legislation.

To these factors we could add many others without ever exhausting them, since they include all that the Universe

[1] *Studi sulla criminalità in Francia dal* 1826 *al* 1878, Rome, 1881.

contains, not omitting a word or a gesture. What we must add, however, is the fact that as a whole they determine the *law of criminal saturation:* " Just as in a given volume of water, at a given temperature, we find the solution of a fixed quantity of any chemical substance, not an atom more or less, so in a given social environment, in certain defined physical conditions of the individual, we find the commission of a fixed number of crimes."

Ferri's theory is the most scientific production of modern studies. " Crime," says he, " is a phenomenon of complex origin and the result of biological, physical, and social conditions. Certainly, the dominant influence of this or that factor determines the bio-sociologic variety of the criminal, but there is no doubt that every crime and every criminal is always the product of the simultaneous action of biological, physical, and social conditions." In order to reach this position he has passed through two phases, representing as many oscillations: first, through that of the individual factors, as when in his " New Horizons " he wrote, to quote only one of many analogous sentences, that " without special individual inclinations, the external impulses would not be sufficient; " and then through that of the social factors, at the time of his conversion to socialism, of which conversion and influence on criminology we shall speak when we treat that subject.

Mention has been made of the bio-sociological varieties of criminals. What are they?

As a starting point for the classification, Ferri makes use of the *a priori* existence of two great classes sufficiently known by all and which can serve as a starting point for further distinctions. These are the classes of *habitual* and *occasional* criminals.

"Above all," says Ferri, "from the group of habitual criminals there stand out the victims of a clear, evident, and

common   mental   alienation   which   causes   their   criminal
activity. In the second place, even among habitual criminals
not insane, we find a class of individuals, physical and moral
wretches from infancy, who live in crime from a congenital
necessity of organic and psychic adaptation and who are
nearer to the lunatics than to the sane; a class which is distinguished from another class of individuals living in crime
and for crime by a dominant complicity of the social environment in which they were born and raised, and also by an
unfortunate organic and psychic constitution; individuals
who, undoubtedly, once having reached the chronic state of
crime, are incorrigible and unfortunate as the other class of
habitual criminals, but who, before falling from the first crime
to the final abject condition, could have been rescued by
preventive institutions and by a less vitiated environment.

" On the other hand, in the group of occasional criminals
we have a special category distinguishable less by a variety of
characteristics than by the typical exaggeration of their more
or less varying organic and psychic traits. In all these it is
the impulse of opportunities more than the innate tendency
that determines the crime. But, while in most of them the
determining opportunity is a sufficient and almost common
stimulus, in others it is the extraordinary impulse of a passion,
a psychologic storm, that alone could attract them to crime;
persons, who, as if completing the circle, as it has already
been remarked by Delbruck and Baer, approach very closely
the group of the criminal lunatics, if not through a permanent
form of insanity at least through a psychic disturbance which,
more or less latent before, breaks out at last into criminal
transgression.

" Therefore, all criminals can be classified under five
groups which I have called: a. Criminal *lunatics;* b. Criminals
born incorrigibles; c. *Habitual* criminals, or criminals from

acquired habit; d. *Occasional* criminals; and, e. *Emotional* criminals."

With classical illustrations from universal literature, as, for instance, the Shakspearean criminals Macbeth, Hamlet, and Othello, perfect types of the born criminal, the criminal lunatic, and the emotional criminal, the author has again made use of the above classification in his " Criminals in Art," a valuable monograph purporting to show the empirical and unconscious origins of criminal anthropology in art. We find it also in his voluminous and remarkable work " Homicide in Criminal Anthropology," stated more extensively and supported by numerous observations, although limited to a single form of delinquency.

The first and the most salient and discussed class is that of the *born criminals*. According to Ferri, *race* and *temperament* combined with *degeneration* are the chief factors of this inborn tendency; the type, especially the physiognomic and imitative one, constitutes its visible mark. An unfortunate hereditary state suppresses or atrophies in the born criminal his moral sense without altering in many cases the intellectual faculties, which can be better than the average. Under the pressure of the social environment, there develops in him an enormous aggressive power, which is not always ferocious, brutal, and violent; for, as according to Spencer the different classes of society from the warrior to the merchant find themselves in the course of transformation, so delinquency is losing those traits and appears shrewd and voluptuous with all the characteristics of the modern phases of culture.

The difference between the born criminal and the criminal *lunatic*, which forms the second class, is found in the insanity of the latter. It is better to adopt the term *lunatic* for this class, so as to distinguish it from the congenital moral insane, as he is called. A kind of dual personality constitutes the chief characteristic of this class of criminals. In fact, " the chief trait of insanity," says Taylor,[1] " is a great change of character; a man affected with mental alienation is different than he was before." " He is not the same," adds Griesinger,[2] " his former *ego* has changed and becomes estranged from itself." Legrand du Saulle writes:[3] " Man begins to be ill when he begins to differentiate himself from himself." Maudsley has well described this process, of which even every day speech gives a clear idea when it uses the word *alienation*.

The crime of the lunatic is characterized by its marked and startling forms: violent delirium, ferocity, multiplicity of aggressions, unusual suddenness. It has been maintained for a long time that for him crime is not a means as in the other criminals but an end; but the range of this observation diminishes from day to day through the psychologic study of the madman's strange conceptions, his latent impulses, hallucinations, etc. In most cases there exists no premeditation, although in others he goes so far as to plan an alibi. Only in a limited number of cases we find accomplices; but, on the other hand, these cases often belong to the collective form of delinquency, called the criminal *mob*, which surpasses the first in frequency and extension. The victim belongs either to the social environment close to the lunatic, like family, friends, companions; or to the most foreign to him, like the first person he happens to meet. The space intervening between the two extremes is hardly touched upon by statistics. Finally, his attitude after the deed is one of stupor or imbecility, indifference, and forgetfulness.

We find a marked analogy between the lunatic and the *emotional criminal*. Like the lunatic the emotional criminal

---

[1] Quoted by Joly, *Le crime*, p. 337.

[2] *Traité des maladies mentales*, Paris, 1865, p. 136.

[3] *Traité de Médicine, légale*, Paris, 1886.

has no accomplices, does not premeditate his crime, and his victim is generally on intimate terms with him. In him also personality suffers a sudden paroxysm. If to-day we speak of the madman's lucid intervals, why not say, then, in comparing the two classes, that the emotional criminal is a sane and normal man subject to momentary paroxysms and intervals of insanity? Paroxysm characterizes him more and better than emotion. It is only when the latter manifests itself in an *acute* manner that we have the real emotional criminal. *Chronic* emotion constantly renewed and repeated forms the basis of an altogether different delinquency. We must also remark that most crimes committed by emotional criminals are numerically few in comparison with those of other classes, and that they are due to the group of the so-called *noble* emotions.

Anatomy discovers nothing abnormal in this class of criminals, sung and glorified at times as a source of poetry. Their physiological characteristics seem to be only a certain nervous debility and excessive sensibility. Their face and their body are not different from those of the anti-criminal type. Especially in the political criminal, the nobler the motive for the crime the more noticeable are these characteristics.

In order to detect the emotional crime one must study the motive. Between the two there exists a real proportion. Moreover, the motive is generally of very recent date. When it is not, the time that separates it from the deed is filled by an extraordinary agitation. Yet, during this interval, nothing is premeditated, no weapon is chosen, and no accomplice is sought. The crime takes place during a real psychologic storm, says Ferri, in full daylight, before witnesses, and in public places. Usually, only one blow is struck, since emotional crimes are almost always against the person; but, at times, its fury and multiplicity remind one of the great epileptic crimes. The analogy, however, soon disappears; for there comes a sudden reaction, and the culprit passes through a variety of sensations, ranging from instant suicide to an immediate acknowledgment of the crime. Finally, the desire for punishment, repentance, and reform complete the history of the crime.

The two classes of *occasional* and *habitual* criminals are difficult to define. They are distinguished from each other so far as two things, whose difference is found in the greater or less extension of a third, can be distinguished. According to Ferri, the former class has no other distinct characteristic than less relapse and less precocity. The general impression which I am able to gather is not less volatile and unstable. I would say that, while with habitual criminals it is the criminal himself who acts upon the environment in order to produce and repeat the opportunity, with the occasional criminal it is the opportunity which acts intermittingly and extraordinarily upon the criminal in order to cause the crime.[1] Here, then, we confront the serious psychological problem of the rôle that opportunity plays in the genesis of crime. According to the old saying, it is the opportunity that makes the thief, or must the thief possess a natural latent tendency for theft in order to take advantage of the opportunity?

And now, after having by these studies revealed a universal coercion in the cause of human deeds, we may ask: why should the penal function be maintained? *E pur si muove;* perhaps it will be even more necessary and more energetic, not as a means of retribution and reward, but as a necessity and defense.

It is not a question of defense, as Beccaria and the philanthropists imagined, upon the basis of the social contract

[1] I am pleased to see this observation repeated almost literally by Vargha in *Die Abschaffung der Strafknechtschaft,* Graz, 1895–1896.

theory. The ruling conception, that makes of the human race a living organism, above man, and the last in complexity in the zoölogic scale, makes the social defense appear as a natural movement corresponding to the irritability of the lower animals and to the reflex action of those which have a differentiated nervous system so perfected as to correspond to the high nature of man.

Of this we shall speak more at length in the chapter devoted to Penology. But it is necessary to mention at this point a new idea.

To the elementary defensive methods against attack, there are added, in an advanced civilization and as a matter of conscience and reminder, other methods destined to avoid possible future crimes, thus rendering punishment unnecessary in the long run. Hence, Ferri calls them *penal substitutes*. They would constitute a body of *physical*, *individual*, and *social* correctives against their corresponding factors. As examples of substitutes we may mention: " *Free trade*, which prevents exceptional high prices of food to which are due many criminal agitations; *abolition of monopolies*, which would prevent smuggling and other kinds of offenses; *suppression of certain taxes*, which constitute a constant source of agitation; the *substitution of gold and silver for bank-notes*, for, counterfeit bills being more difficult to detect, it would decrease the number of forgers; *cheap workmen's dwellings; preventive and auxiliary institutions for invalids; popular savings' banks*, which, by bettering the condition of the poor, would cause a diminution of crimes against property; the *construction of wide city streets* and *better lighting*, which render thefts and other offenses more difficult; the *spread of the Malthusian law*, which would lessen the number of abortions and infanticides; better *civil laws* on inheritance, on marriage, on the adoption of natural children, on the

investigation of paternity, on the obligation of making reparation for broken marriage engagements, on divorce, etc., all
excellent antidotes against concubinage, infanticide, adultery,
bigamy, wife murder, and offenses against chastity; better
mercantile laws on the responsibility of the directors of a
company, on the procedure of failures, on rehabilitation, etc.,
thus rendering bankruptcy less frequent; *oversight of the
manufacturing of weapons* in order to reduce the use of these
instruments of destruction; *courts of honor* against duelling;
the *suppression of pilgrimages;* the *marriage of the clergy;*
the *suppression of monasteries;* the *abolition of many holidays;*
physical exercises; public baths; theatres; foundling homes;
the *suppression of immoral publications and accounts of famous
trials; refusing the young admission to police-courts and assizes,"*
etc.

Section 7.   (3)   RAFFAELLE GAROFALO.

Not long after Ferri's " New Horizons," there appeared
Garofalo's " Criminology," [1] which, by its juridical aspect,
becoming a magistrate of the author's caliber, completed the
works of the New Science; works which fall into a spontaneous division according to their different points of view.
With the anthropologist Lombroso, the sociologist Ferri, and
the jurisconsult Garofalo, the school of criminal anthropology
can be considered as fully established.   Hence, one of its
critics has called these three men *evangelists* and their works
gospels.   From that time on they are always mentioned in a
kind of trinity, a little divided at times only by Garofalo's
political and penal conservatism.

The first theory we owe to Garofalo is that of the *natural
crime.*   At the beginning of his investigations, the author
finds this term so much forgotten, that " many, in the presence

[1] *Criminalogia,* Turin, 1885; second edition, Turin, 1889.

of the recent investigations of Despine, Maudsley, and Lombroso, believe them in good faith to be doctrines that will never find their way into legislation. . . . "

In order to correct this neglect, Garofalo states the problem of natural crime as follows: "If, among the crimes and offenses of our modern laws, there are some that have been considered punishable acts at all times and in all places . . . " It would be useless to pretend to make a catalogue of deeds which are universally hateful and reprehensible. Our mind is immediately filled with the sad memories of atavism. But will it be also impossible to define natural crime? In order to succeed we must change method. It is necessary to forego the analysis of acts, mere variable and deceiving forms, and undertake the analysis of sentiments. At this point the author begins a study of the evolution of the moral sense, and, influenced by Darwin and Spencer, he ends with this formula for natural crime: "an offense against the fundamental altruistic sentiments of *pity* and *probity* in the average measure possessed by a given social group." He completes the theory with a table of the natural forms of delinquency and with another of the forms which, in the antinomy that can arise from that appellation, could be called *artificial* or *positive*. "Undoubtedly the legislator must punish both classes of crimes alike, but true science is interested only in the first, namely, the natural forms of delinquency."

The natural crime theory, attained by modern methods but based on old ideas, did not please at first either classical or positivistic scholars. In fact, it reminded one of the old wine in new bottles, or, less metaphorically, of the poet's words:

"Sur des pensiers nouveaux faisons des vers antiques."

It seemed as if old thoughts were being expressed in modern verses. The way in which the question was stated and in

part the method of solving it, has, on account of the vagueness
of Garofalo's artificial or positive crime, more than one feature
in common with the dualism of the Roman *jus gentium* and
jus civilis. Natural crime seems, then, the crime common
to all peoples; while positive crime is that which is peculiar
to each nation. This distinction, flavoring so much of the
classical, resembles that which we find between crimes forbidden because they are evil (*mala in se, prohibita quia mala*)
and those which are evil because they are forbidden (*mala quia
prohibita*). Finally, it reminds one of the *recta ratio, diffusa
in omnes, constans, sempiterna;* and of the innate principles
of justice engraved in the human heart. What makes, then,
classical criminologists oppose a theory of such origin? It
is because, after so many points of contact, the theory proceeds
in an increasing parabola. The old principles of morality
and justice undergo so many amputations that the decalogue
is reduced to only two commandments: *thou shalt not kill*
(pity) and *thou shalt not steal* (probity). Moreover, it is
not God who gives them but it is humanity itself that elabo-
rates them, not at a single time, but through an evolutionary
process. The *recta ratio* ceases to be the patrimony of all men
and becomes the property of civilized men alone.

The positivists on their part reject natural crime, not
because it is a category that does not exist, but because it is
the only one. " Every attack against the positive laws of
a country " (all natural; since what is there of unnatural
or supernatural in nature?) — " just as any obscure lawyer
would say ": such is the modern notion of crime.

Nevertheless, the critique, after having had its say, cannot
help recognizing in Garofalo's theory of natural crime one of
the most interesting productions of modern criminology.

This theory governs all of Garofalo's remaining views.
To it we owe the classification of criminals into two groups:

the *murderers* (offenders against humanity) and the *thieves* (offenders against property). The author has added two others: the *cynics* (for sexual criminals) and the *violent criminals*. We will explain this division by a modern comparison. He refuses to consider the moral sense as a compound of reduced elements. The first three classes are, according to Garofalo, affected by a real *moral Daltonism;* the murderer, the thief, and the cynic are beings deprived of a sense of respect for life, for property, and for the honor of others. The violent criminal, in the confused reaction of his movements, is equivalent to the totally blind.

The cause of both groups is an anomaly, not pathological, — the author is very careful to distinguish anomaly from infirmity — of the moral sense resembling an ethical degeneration through retrogressive selection, which would make man lose his best qualities acquired slowly through a long evolution.

With this as a basis, no one better than Garofalo has worked the hypothesis of the born criminal and of the rejection of individual factors to its last possible conclusions. In his " Criminology " society sees in crime only two elements, without which it could not take place, namely, the opportunity and the victim; the former offering the mere *possibility* of the deed, and never acting as collaborator or protagonist. The chapters devoted to some social influences so hopeful as education, religion, and laws, present education disarmed in the presence of character which, once fixed, remains unalterable like the form and the features; religion powerless to check criminal impulses; the laws exercising a very small influence upon the social body and receiving from it a great deal, so that they become protectors of crime.

The theory of *repression* fills the greater part of Garofalo's book.

This theory is governed by the law of selection, that is, *elimination* in its medium. By this process society must produce by artificial means a selection analogous to that which takes place spontaneously in the biological domain, that is, by putting to death by the hundreds the criminals considered absolutely incompatible with all environment and social group, and by expelling from the country or from a professional or functional group those in whom the lack of pity or probity is less marked. Side by side with this process of elimination applied in its absolute and relative forms, there remains the *reparation* for the harm done, which must be made by the perpetrators of crimes who do not disclose any marked anomalies of the moral sense.

III.

DEVELOPMENT.

Section 8. (1) NATURE AND GENESIS OF DELINQUENCY.

These ideas broke the equilibrium established thirty years ago.

Undoubtedly newness is always a very relative conception; for, from the time of Christ and even before, the human mind has been searching for it on this earth in vain. Yet, it is not the less real, if we consider it as the unfolding of germs planted in times immemorial. It is like the reappearance of things which were believed extinct.

As we open one of the books on criminal law published after 1880, and compare it with a not much earlier one, we detect indeed something new. A peculiar technique established before by older sciences makes its meaning unintelligible to those who, until then, had attained renown in the subject of crime and punishment. Its pages contain prints and engravings, all the graphic apparatus which was believed to be the legitimate monopoly of natural sciences. "Who would have thought," says Ferri, "that the travels and the discoveries made in wild countries; the first studies written by Camper, White, and Blumembach on skull measurements and the human skeleton; the investigations of Darwin on the origin of species; those of Häckel and of so many other naturalists in embryology; and Laplace's hypothesis of the nebulæ," all of which having found applications in criminology and furnished points of view for the "New Horizons of Criminal Law," were to find some day, together with their illustrations, a place in these books as did before them the pictures, maps, and all the apparatus of modern social physics.

Thus, a simple indication on the title-page of a book, announcing illustrations in the text, can serve as a sufficiently sure sign of the novelty of its spirit and contents. In fact, that indication points out, according to our way of looking at the matter, what is the common characteristic of the modern theories in comparison with the old. It points out that crime is conceived as the product of *all the forces of the Universe*, those of the inorganic or preorganic world as well as those of the organic, physical, and social world; the product of *physical or cosmic, anthropological or individual, and social factors* as they are called from that time on, and consequently showing the intervention and the collaboration of all *sciences* in one which, until then, existed on mere conceptions.

This same characteristic determines at present the natural division of the modern theories of criminology; for, as soon as these were formulated, the relative value and conception of each group of factors were looked upon by investigators from different standpoints, so as to produce two great tendencies. The one, by affirming the preponderance of anthropologic factors was called Criminal Anthropology; the other, leaning toward social factors, took the name of Criminal

Sociology. The physical or cosmic factors did not produce a third school, which might have been called *Criminal Meteorology* or *Judiciary Astrology;* but they were the cause of the polemic between anthropologists and sociologists. The influence of these factors, however, is considerable; and, at times, it seems dominant. Still, Kropotkin exaggerates this influence when he writes in his " Prisons ": [1] " By the statistics of previous years one could foretell with astonishing exactness the number of crimes to be committed during the following year in every country of Europe. Through a very simple mathematical operation we can find the formula that enables us to foretell the number of crimes merely by consulting the thermometer and the hygrometer. Take the average temperature of the month and multiply it by 7; then, add the average humidity, multiply again by 2 and you will obtain the number of homicides that are to be committed during the month." $H = t \times 7 + h \times 2$; the operation is not so easy nor so safe.

This polemic completely fills the history of the modern theories of criminology. Is the criminal born so, or is he a product? This is the question, which, after all, is nothing but the problem of human personality.

The division into anthropological and sociological has been criticized as being artificial, when in reality it is so only in as far as all divisions are, as if they inherited an original sin. It would be more than artificial if we looked at it as an irreducible and constant dualism, forgetting, as is often done, that the function of limitation which intervenes in everything is not only to divide and isolate, but also to correlate and unite the elements of any order of things for which nature never gives any solution of continuity, since it hates the void and never advances by leaps.

[1] *Les prisons*, Paris, 1890.

Whether the question is understood this way or not, we seldom find an investigator who does not adopt the proposed classification, and does not use it with more or less success. Does not Ferri himself accept four unilateral biologic and social theories, basing upon them his own, the only double bilateral one? [1] And yet, Ferri complained so much against the critics who " in order to give themselves the easy pleasure of opposing the ideas of the positivistic school, accuse it of representing crime, now as an exclusive product of environment, now as the product of the biologic factor."

Here follows Ferri's classification which has appeared again in the fourth edition of his " Criminal Sociology ":

Crime is a

Normal	{ Biological (Albrecht) } phenomenon.
	{ Social (Durkheim) }

Biologic abnormality due to
- Atavism. Organic and psychic (Lombroso). Psychic (Colajanni).
- Pathology
  - Neurosis (Dally, Minzloff, Maudsley, Virgilio, Jelgersma, Bleuler).
  - Neurasthenia (Benedikt, Liszt, Vargha).
  - Epilepsy (Lombroso, Lewis, Roncoroni).
- Defect of nutrition in the central nervous system (Marro).
- Defect of development of the inhibitory centres (Bonfigli).
- Moral anomaly (Despine, Garofalo).

Social abnormality due to
- Economic influences (Turati, Battaglia, Loria).
- Juridical unadaptability (Vaccaro).
- Complex social influences (Lacassagne, Colajanni Prins, Tarde, Topinard, Manouvrier, Raux, Baer, Kirn, Gumplowicz).

Biological and social abnormality (Ferri).

It may be that the introduction of the conception of normality and abnormality to distinguish the various theories is artificial. The question was raised first by Albrecht at the Congress of Rome,[2] and then by Durkheim in his " Rules for

[1] *Le crime comme phenomène social* (p. 411, second volume of the *Annales de l'Institut international de Sociologie*, Paris, 1896).

[2] *The morphological position of man among mammals; Human criminology from the point of view of comparative Anatomy.*

Sociological Classification." [1] After a short period of surprise, the question, if not forgotten altogether, was at the most relegated to a very secondary position, but it was to produce a greater effect when coupled with another great principle.[2]

Puglia [3] sums up in a few words the nature of the two schools which we consider the most important. Sociology, according to him, considers crime a social phenomenon both as to its causes and as to its manifestations; while anthropology finds only the expression of crime sociological, its roots are to be found in biology.

Once, the two schools had local names, and we hear of an *Italian* and of a *French* school of criminology.

Undoubtedly, the origins of the Italian school are characterized by the following four features, which being so clear and distinct could not help being remarked by all investigators:

(a) the great importance attributed to *individual factors*, whose clear outlines somewhat overshadow the social factors;

(b) the affirmation of a *born criminal;*

(c) explained by *atavism;* and

(d) forming a type determined *anatomically.*

So that the critics of those days could say with Tarde: [4]

[1] *Les règles de la méthode sociologique,* Paris, 1895.

[2] Albrecht considers the criminal a normal being; for, like the greater part of organisms, he acts through selfishness. Durkheim, on the other hand, advocates the social normality of crime because he sees it indissolubly linked to society, forming a factor of the public safety and an integral part of any healthy social body. And this because: (a) it collaborates in the work of selection of the sentiments, preserving them in the malleable condition necessary to gain new and more delicate strength; and (b) it permits necessary changes and transformations, and reduces them to opportunities. Lombroso has taken advantage of these ideas in order to write " Les bienfaits du crime " (in the *Nouvelle Revue,* 1895).

[3] *Le crime comme phenomène social* (p. 455 of the same book, *Annales,* etc.)

[4] *Les Actes du Congrès de Rome* (in the *Archives d'Anthropologie criminelle,* January 15, 1888).

" This school, intoxicated with the wine of natural sciences, lacks the dry, substantial bread of historic and social sciences." It was in the name of the latter that they arose against the school.

When the second Congress of Anthropology was held in the capital of France instead of Italy, the French seized the opportunity of persistently pointing out the earlier errors and defects of the Italian school. It was at the stormy Congress of Paris that the battle was fought between French and Italian criminalists, with Manouvrier and Lombroso as the chief champions.

These local names have become less marked. On the one hand, other countries took up the discussion; and on the other, both French and Italians, especially the latter, have modified their former characteristics by attenuating them. Ingegnieros makes a happy remark on this point when he says: " In order to prove the little value that ought to be attached to the names of Italian and French school for anthropological and sociological school, it suffices to remark that one of the fundamental works of the Italians (Ferri's) is entitled " Criminal Sociology," and that the most important publication of French criminalists (edited by Lacassagne) is called " Archives of Criminal Anthropology." [1]

Section 9.   (A) Anthropological Theories.

Considering them from the point of view of the nature and genesis of crime, anthropological theories can be classified as follows:

a. Atavistic theories;

b. Theories of degeneration;

c. Pathological theories.

[1] *Nuevos rumbos de la Antropología criminal*, in the *Archivos de Psiquiatría y Criminalogía*, which he edits (VI year, 1907).

It is almost impossible to keep these theories apart; because not only, as with Lombroso and his followers, they appear knitted together with more or less incoherence, but chiefly because the three phenomena blend together, and touch and cross one another. On one hand the degenerative influences determine atavistic regressions; and on the other, where can be found the boundary line between degeneration and infirmity?

It has already been stated that the anthropological theories developed, above all, in Italy. " The Archive of Psychiatry, Penal Sciences and Criminal Anthropology for the Study of the Male Offender and the Insane," [1] was founded by Lombroso in 1880, and constitutes the memorial of the school. The features of his method can be seen in the book entitled " Legal Psychiatric Expertism, Methods of Procedure, and Penal Casuistry," [2] consisting of: 1. A first part, in which the Turinese professor gathers and arranges more than sixty studies giving estimates of criminals and due to the pen of Agostini, Antonini, Bertini, Bianchi, Cainer, Carrara, Caterino Stefani, Codeluppi, Cogneti de Martiis, D'Abundo, Frigerio, Gurrieri, Jentsch, Marzocchi, Mingazzini, Ottolenghi, Pelanda, Roncoroni, Seppilli, Tamburini, Virgilio, Lombroso himself and his daughter Gina; 2. A second part which discusses the technique of valuation to be employed in the study of the criminal; 3. Various appendices: (a) on the application of *mental tests* procedure in legal-medical practice, by Dr. G. Guicciardi; (b) on Ganzer's symptom and simulation, by Lombroso; (c) an alphabetic glossary of the most common terms used in criminal anthropology, by Dr. Leg-

[1] *Archivio di Psichiatria, Scienze penali ed Antropologia criminale, per servire allo studio dell 'uomo alienato e delinquente.*

[2] *La perizia psichiatrico legale coi metodi per eseguirla e la casuistica penale,* Turin, 1905.

giardi Laura; a work which had been preceded by Rossi's "Alphabetic Glossary of Criminal Anthropology and Legal Medicine for Jurisconsults." [1]   Moreover, we may mention the bulky and premature conclusions reached in Angiolella's "Manual of Criminal Anthropology," [2] and also Antonini's "Fundamental Principles of Criminal Anthropology." [3]   The lengthy and well documented "Beginnings of Criminal Anthropology," [4] by Zuccarelli, advance, on the contrary, very slowly.

Outside of Italy, the progress of anthropology is equally intense in Germany, but it assumes a decidedly anti-lombrosian note.

From the very beginning, Lombroso found one of his most active supporters in Hans Kurella, who, together with Fraenkel, translated his work and the choicest Italian and foreign criminological literature.   Considering these theories as "general hypotheses of great value to science and progress," Kurella attempted to adapt them to the Germanic spirit, presenting them in a revised form, perhaps not very exact, which constitutes his most important work.[5]

But he does not seem to have met with success.   His work was followed by Baer's "The Criminal," [6] in which, with all the patience characteristic of his race, he analyzes every page of Lombroso's work and reaches a conclusion antagonistic to the investigations of the Italian scholar.   Näcke in his numerous publications, and Aschaffenburg in his "Crime and its Prevention," [7] repeated the attack.

[1] *Glossario alfabetico per l'Antropologia criminale e Medicina legale pei giuristi*, Turin, 1883.

[2] *Manuale di Antropologia criminale*, second edition, Milan, 1906.

[3] *I principi fondamentali dell 'Antropologia criminale*, Milan, 1906.

[4] *Istituzioni di Antropologia criminale*, Naples, 1900.

[5] *Naturgeschichte des Verbrechers*, Stuttgart, 1893.

[6] *Der Verbrecher*, Leipzig, 1893.

[7] *Das Verbrechen und seine Bekämpfung*, Heidelberg, 1903.

German criminology develops between these two tendencies, and becomes dominantly anti-lombrosian. At this
stage, the Germans, the solidity of whose science is proverbial,
criticized with severity not only the theories themselves but
also the method employed to obtain them. The eminent
psychiatrist Flechsig wrote the following opinion, which
was repeated later by Näcke: "There is no doubt that in
our days, when scientific investigations ought to be carried
out with severe precision, Lombroso's method deserves
indeed the qualification of *atavism*." [1] The great pathologist
Virchow expressed the same opinion when, in a lecture given
at Spreyer, August 6, 1896, he compared Lombroso and Gall,
with the difference that the former treats only of anomalies:
"In a few years nobody will consider his wrong and insufficient observations and deductions." [2] Without justification,
some one made so much of this prophesy, that Kirn felt
himself authorized to say in the twenty-fifth meeting of the
Congress of German psychiatrists at Karlsruhe, November,
1893: "To-day we can consider the type of the born criminal
as absolutely destroyed."

But, according to Sommer [3] even if there be no criminal
type in the Lombrosian sense, it does not follow that there
does not exist a born or *endogenous* delinquent, as the Germans
have called the individual or anthropological factor of the
Italians. Therefore, both Sommer and Bleuler can say that
Kirn, Baer, Koch, Näcke, and later Aschaffenburg, in refuting
the ideas of Lombroso, have placed in relief the basis of that
doctrine which rests on the endogenous origin of crime.

[1] *Die Grenzen geistiger Gesundheit und Krankheit*, Leipzig, 1896.
[2] *Ausberger Abendzeitung*, August 8, 1896. See Lombroso's answer
in his *Archivio*, XVIII (Virchow, Sernoff and Criminal Anthropology).
[3] *Die Criminal Psychologie;* at the session of the Society of German
alienists of September 23, 1895, in Dresden; *Zeitschrift für Psychiatrie*
fas. 51.

The German contributions appear in three important publications: the *Archiv für Kriminalantropologie und Kriminalistik*, edited by Gross; the *Monatschrift für Kriminalpsychologie und Strafrechtreform*, edited by Aschaffenburg; and the
*Zeitschrift für Kriminalanthropologie, Gefängniswissenschaft
und Prostitutionswesen*, edited by Wenge.*

In Denmark, Geill has also conscientiously opposed Lombroso's conclusions. In general, we have Havelock Ellis' " The
Criminal," in England; [1] Paulina Tarnousky's " Anthropometric Studies of Female Thieves and Prostitutes," and
" Murderesses," [2] and Kovalewsky's " Criminal Psychology," [3]
in Russia; Winkler's " Studies in Criminal Anthropology," [4]
in Holland. In the United States, where MacDonald
published his " Abnormal Man " and " Criminology," [5] criminologists proceed always more cautiously, although influenced by Lombroso. In South America, the most important
publications are found in the " Archives of Psychiatry
and Criminology," [6] edited by the Argentine, Ingegnieros.

And now we will examine the different anthropological
tendencies according to the proposed classification.

Section 10. (a) *Atavistic Theories.*
From Bordier to Ferrero.

We have already pointed out their appearance in Lombroso's early works. Almost simultaneously with him,
Bordier, in France, sketched the hypothesis of criminal atavism
by comparing the skulls of murderers at Caen with Broca's

[1] *The Criminal*, London, 1890.
[2] *Etudes anthropométriques sur les femmes voleuses et les prostituées*,
Paris, 1890. — *Jenchtchini Oubiytsi*, St. Petersburg, 1902.
[3] *Psychologie criminelle*, Paris, 1903.
[4] *Jets over Criminele Antropologie*, Haarlem, 1896.
[5] *Abnormal Man*, Washington, 1893. — *Criminology*, New York, 1906.
[6] *Archivos de Psiquiatría y Criminalogía.*
* [Discontinued after vol. I.]

series of the cave of the *Dead Man*.[1]   At the same time,
Benedikt, a Viennese psychiatrist, in studying the brains of
beheaded criminals, detected their deviations from the normal
type, and their resemblance to the brains of the great quad-
rumana and of the wild beasts; so that, with these data as
basis, says Orchansky,[2] he imagined an atavistic theory,
according to which there existed among sane people some
persons whose cerebral organism is inferior to the average
and represents the heredity of the savage and of the primitive
man.   The unfortunates who possess a similar neuro-cerebral
organism would form, according to Dr. Benedikt, the rear-
guard of humanity.   Their intelligence and moral sentiments
must be likewise inferior.   Men possessing a psycho-physical
organism so badly developed cannot adapt themselves to the
conditions of their social environment, and are fatally destined
to succumb in the social struggle.   Crime and pauperism
await them.

Atavism, then, considers the criminal as a retrograde.
Phylogenetically, he has been detained in the human or even
prehuman evolution; ontogenetically, his arrest has taken
place in childhood, granted the parallellism between the
evolution of the individual and that of the species according
to the law of F. Müller or of Häckel.   Lombroso has taken
advantage of this in his accessory theory of criminal childhood.
According to the latter, as the child in its organic development
in the womb presents somatologic characteristics which in the
adult would appear as monstrosities, so in the first years of
his life he goes through a period of initial perversity — an
ontogenetic relic of the primitive immorality of the species —

[1] *Etude anthropologique sur une série des crânes d'assassins*; in the
Revue d'Anthropologie, 1879.
[2] *Les criminels russes et la théorie de Lombroso*, in the *Archivio di
Psichiatria*, vol. XIX, 1898.

which is overcome or not afterwards according to the education received. From this point of view, the born criminal, in whom the primary instincts have not been subdued, continues anomalously in a state of childhood, preserving psychological traits of the child, like impulsiveness, want of foresight, instability, etc.

Granting the metamorphic hypothesis upon which modern anthropology is based, the theory of atavism becomes for nearly all those who accept it prehuman and human as well as organic and psychic. Nevertheless, Colajanni, in his "Criminal Sociology," [1] eliminates from the atavistic interpretation all the organic or physical element and reduces it to the simple moral element. According to him, the ethical characteristics would be the only ones to form the retrogressive hereditary transmission, and the criminal would be, morally and not physically, a kind of neo-savage, the relic of times when crime was a physiological state, which turned very slowly into a pathological one.

But, to use Ferrero's words, "while some affirmed with a great display of documents that the primitive man was a murderer, a thief, a ravisher, and an incendiary; others, with no less stock of information, answered by citing cases of savages gentle as lambs, virtuous as Cato, romantic in love as Don Quixote." In examining and revising the resemblances of the criminal and the primitive man, investigators became confused; when archeologists were consulted concerning language, religion, law, and art, all agreed in declaring our ancestors endowed with piety, justice, kindness, industrious activity, bravery, and honesty; [2] geographers, ethnologists, and travellers like Reclus, Kropotkin, etc., when called upon

[1] *La sociologia criminale*, Catania, 1889.
[2] Tarde, *L'atavisme moral*, in the *Archives d'Anthropologie criminelle*, vol. IV, 1888.

to testify, multiplied the instances of *good savages*, as Spencer says; and, finally, the works of Lubbock, Espinas, Forel, Houzeau, Brehm, etc., on animal life, testified to the kind coöperation, mutual assistance, heroic abnegation to be seen among simian families and even among bees, ants, etc.

Yet, the atavistic theory has not disappeared. The vitality of the idea and its deep roots appear in the new form which it has assumed, a more delicate, less rude and material form, corrected, in short, in no different a manner than a product of art or industry.

This corrected form is found in the theory of *atavism through equivalents*, stated in a section of the still unpublished work " Social Progress " by Guglielmo Ferrero.[1]

Which are the characteristics that distinguish the savage from the modern civilized man? Certainly, ferocity of customs is not one; for, when humanity was still in its infancy, we find those simple and tame tribes thus leading people to believe that crime is rather a poisonous fruit of civilization's first steps. These characteristics are rather a ready impulse, inertia, and a physio-psychic excitability, " three characteristics always so intimately connected that we are led to admit the existence of a psychological relation among them, an indissoluble relation of cause and effect." From the full exposition of facts and documents accompanying each of these characteristics the author deduces a new conception of criminal atavism.

" The atavistic trait in the criminal's character is not his propensity to commit a certain crime; it is rather the psychological state that incapacitates him for work, to which,

---

[1] *La morale primitiva e l'atavismo del delitto*, in the *Archivio di Psichiatria*, vol. XVII, 1896. The book " Social Progress " has not been published; but the theory of atavism through equivalents has gained much ground. F. Ortiz declares to have followed it intentionally in *Hampa afro-cubana : Los Negros Brujos*, Madrid, 1906.

through an organic connection, we must add that ready
impulse so common to the criminal that I do not need to
adduce new proofs. The murderer, the thief, the born swindler, are atavistic beings because they are unable to adapt
themselves to the somewhat brutal uniformity and regularity
of human labor in our civilizations. They cannot earn their
living in any other way except through the periodical activity
of hunting and fishing, which sums up the work of the primitive man. The criminal, then, stands apart from civilization,
to which he cannot adapt himself except through indirect
and special means which constitute the crime. On one hand,
his inability to work renders him rebellious to the severe
moral discipline which destroys impulse; thus making impossible in him the building up of a solid moral conscience in
which ethical motives might gain a sufficient mutual strength,
and he becomes the prey of his own tumultuous passions
which, at certain moments, can lead him to very violent acts.
On the other hand, since with all the needs created by civilization a man cannot live only by hunting and fishing, the
criminal, unable to work, enters upon a systematic war,
crime; so that, if on one side he offends through impulse, on
the other, he does so through necessity in order to gain the
means of subsistence and of enjoying life."

(b) *Theories of Degeneration.*

Section 11. (a) Generical.

From Magnan to Dallemagne.

We have seen how the theory of degeneration was stated
by Morel. At present, however, we find that it has undergone
a radical change in thirty years. The degenerate is no longer
the man who has departed from Adam, but " the being who
finds himself in comparison with his most recent ancestors

constitutionally weakened in his psycho-physical resistance, and realizes only in an incomplete measure the biological conditions for the hereditary struggle for existence. This weakness, which manifests itself by permanent stigmata, is essentially progressive except in the case of uneven regeneration, and causes with more or less rapidity the extinction of the species." [1]

In studying the development of this conception, our attention is called to its extraordinary growth. The merit of establishing the unity of the class is due to Magnan, who, in his "Investigations on Nerve Centers," [2] gathers into a compact group the types which had been imperfectly seen by his predecessors.

What are the relations that exist between criminality and degeneration? Besides Laurent and others, the following have attempted to establish them: Magnan, in " Morbid Criminal Obsession "; Féré, in " Degeneracy and Criminality "; Corre, in " Criminals," and " Criminal Ethnography "; Marandon de Montyel, in " Contribution to the Clinical Study of the Relations between Criminality and Degeneracy." [3] In fact, nothing would be easier than to call every criminal a degenerate; for the appellation implies finality. " Beginning with the works of Magnan and his school," says Laurent, " the domain of degeneration has become so vast, that one cannot tell when it begins and when it ends."

---

[1] Vaschide y Vurpas, *Qu'est ce qu'un dégénéré ?* (in the *Archives d'Anthropologie criminelle*, vol. XVII, 1902).

[2] *Recherches sur les centres nerveux*, Paris, 1893.

[3] Magnan, *De l'enfance des criminels dans ses rapports avec la prédisposition naturelle au crime*, in the *Records of the Congress of Paris; L'obsession criminelle morbide*, in the *Records of the Congress of Brussels.* — Féré, *Dégénérescence et criminalité*, Paris, 1888. — Corre, *Les criminels*, Paris, 1889; *L'ethnographie criminelle*, Paris, 1895. — Marandon de Montyel, *Contribution à l'étude clinique des rapports de la criminalité et de la dégénérescence*, in the *Archives d'Anthropologie criminelle*, 1892.

Dallemagne expresses himself in like manner: " Degeneration and criminality," says he,[1] " are two ideas conceived and
defined in very different ways; while the latter tends to
become more and more precise under the influence of the
Italian school, the former tends more and more to disappear."

The undeniable fact which constitutes the cornerstone of
the theory of degeneration is the reality of the progressive
disappearance of races and species through successive and
hereditary degradations, occurring, at times, with the most
subtle and delicate marks of psychic anomaly scarcely perceptible, and, at other times, showing even the extinction
of functions indispensable to racial and individual life. Degeneration is a general phenomenon that can be detected
everywhere.   But, side by side with it, and showing that
its evolution is not fatal, there exist regenerations and regen-
erating heredities. The phenomenon of criminality has many
points of contact with degeneration. As degeneration represents the struggle between the individual and the physical
and social environment for the preservation of the individual,
so crime represents man struggling against the factors which
support order and the progress of societies. Criminal predisposition overlaps degenerative predisposition, the two
varying only in degree and manifestations. Each degenerative
state presupposes a certain dose of predisposition and of
casual intervention; so each crime reveals factors that belong
to the individual and influences coming from environment.

In order to explain this relation, various hypotheses have
been set forth. In the first place, the writer rejects the identification of the two phenomena; for, in many cases, they
become involved only in a short measure, and in others they
exclude each other. Degeneration has also been considered
a factor of criminality, going so far as to prove that a degen-

[1] In a paper read before the Congress of Geneva.

erate can become a criminal. But these proofs do not suffice
to make of degeneration a constant factor of crime, and to
establish between them the relation of cause and effect; for,
frequently, the result of degeneration is opposed to criminal
manifestations.

Certainly, there is degeneration in criminality and criminality among degenerates; but, what is their relation? According to Dallemagne, degeneration and criminality are
only symbols, terms which are used to group under the same
rubric deeds that are bound by the same doctrinal tie. Neither
of them exists as a natural and irreducible process subject to
invariable laws in continual evolution. The objective reality
is the existence of degenerates and criminals. They alone
must be studied, avoiding generalizations and hasty statistics.

In his " Anatomical, Biological, and Psychologic Stigmata
of Criminality," [1] he bases upon this principle the discussion
on the value of the various stigmata.

Section 12. (β) Specific.

The ambiguities of the hypothesis of degeneration seem to
disappear with further explanations.

Defect of nutrition of the central nervous system: Marro. —
In " The Characters of Criminals," and " Puberty in Man and
Woman," [2] Marro attributes the origin of crime to a defect
of nutrition of the central nervous system. Lombroso calls
Marro the De Jussieu of criminal anthropology. It would be
better to say that while Lombroso, according to his own
confession,[3] liked to work with the microscope in initial
investigations, Marro uses the microscope alone with the

---

[1] *Les stigmates anatomiques, biologiques et psychologiques de la criminalité*, Paris, 1896.

[2] Marro, *I caratteri dei delinquenti*, Turin, 1887. — *La Pubertà studiata
nell 'uomo e nella donna*, Turin, 1898.

[3] *L'Anthropologie criminelle et ses progrès*, Paris, 1892 (p. 7).

utmost patient labor, which, although less brilliant, is certainly more safe.

Defect of development of the inhibitory centers: Bonfigli, Kovalewsky. — Bonfigli, in his "Natural History of Crime," [1] by localizing more, finds the injury in the inhibitory centers. Kovalewsky, in his "Criminal Psychology," [2] reaches the same conclusion, starting with Meynert's anatomo-physiological law of permanent antagonism between the cortical layer and the subcortical nuclei. The activity of the former dominates the latter in normal physiology. Pathologic occurrences can invert the potentiality of either and produce crime as the effect of this inverted activity.

Moral insanity: Galton, Virgilio, Ribot, Bleuler, etc. — The conception of moral insanity persists in England, its birthplace; Galton,[3] representing the criminal with sane intellectual faculties, but with deeply perturbed affective faculties, approaches very much this conception. In France, Ribot seems to follow this explanation in his "Psychology of the Emotions." [4] Virgilio, an Italian and a contemporary of Lombroso, in "Passanante and the Morbid Nature of Crime,"[5] explains crime by a criminal neurosis resembling very much the above explanation. Dally, Bleuler, Koch, Jelgersma, and Minzloff, refer also to similar neuroses. Thus, the phenomenon is again reduced to the former vagueness of moral anomaly as was expounded first by Despine and then by Garofalo.

Näcke has distinguished himself by his keen criticism of this conception. According to him, the conditions for a diagnosis of moral insanity are:

1. An innate pathological character or an extreme

[1] *La storia naturale del delitto*, Milan, 1893.
[2] *Psychologie criminelle*, Paris, 1903.
[3] *Inquiries to the human faculty*, London, 1883.
[4] *Psychologie des sentiments*, Paris, 1896.
[5] *Passanante e la natura morbosa del delitto*, Rome, 1888.

eccentricity, accentuated with equal strength in the moral aspect;

2. Immorality as the decisive trait.

But all this is extremely obscure and difficult. Who can be considered normal and harmonious? Character and intelligence form two complex groups. Their factors cross one another always in perplexing lines, which in the pathologic subject are still more intricate. A defect is not like a mountain in the middle of a plain, but like a mountain among other mountains more or less high. Science would require in each case an analysis of the various elements; but, in our days, this cannot be done with our psychological methods. The little that is being done is very incomplete; as, for instance, Toulouse's work on Zola. Moreover, the criterion for the normal type must be found by means of strict observations of normal individuals from the same environment and of the same sex, race, culture, etc.; a work not less impossible. The most diverse estimates are often presented by experts, even in respect to the grade of intelligence in each individual case. For instance, they all say, to-day, that it is impossible to trace the boundary line between imbecility and idiocy.

On the other hand, speaking of morality, we must know what we mean by that term. Ideas of this nature evolve and differ among civilized peoples, even in our days. There is an inferior morality (not bad, but minimal — a "moral minimum") and a superior morality. At this stage, perhaps the only thing which is innate is the anatomo-psychological substratum, perchance hereditary; a state in which the good germs mingle with the bad. We are all, then, more or less latent criminals. The evil seed takes root and comes to the surface under the influence of circumstances, passions, etc.

The coupling of great perversity with great intelligence is frequently seen, as in the case of the depraved men of the

Renaissance, upon whom a barbarous environment had so much influence. Luigi il Moro, Cesare Borgia, Malatesta, Cellini, were surely not imbeciles. On the contrary, we can easily find moral goodness coupled with obtuse intelligence. One does not need much intelligence to understand the Decalogue; the difficulty lies in putting it into practice. This depends upon the will, which sins, at times: (a) through lack of energy; (b) at other times, through its faulty quality; both defects can be either innate or acquired through lack of development and education, lack of stimulus, or lack of pressure from the environment. Such are, then, the elements of a differential diagnosis, which remains always an arduous process.

But, in the elements called " degenerative states," to which, according to Näcke, moral insanity belongs, there exists a perversion not only of the will but also of the intelligence. The example of a moral insane with normal intelligence, as cited by Bleuler, is very rare. In the cases of pure imbecility as well as in those of strict moral insanity we must distinguish between active and passive characters. The imbeciles are not necessarily dangerous (as in the case of innocent childishness). The dangerous passive characters do evil through omission (through egotism, or through weakness of sentiments, of purpose, of attention and reflection, etc.). Among the active characters, we must separate the inoffensive from the dangerous, children of an impulsive tendency, often if not always unintentional.

Only these imbeciles or actively dangerous degenerates, who are often so impulsive as to harm themselves without the check of egotism, can be called *morally insane*.

But it may be that we ought not even to preserve the name.[1]

---

[1] F. Giner, *La locura moral, según Näcke*, in *Anales del Laboratorio de Criminalogía*, I, 1899–1900, Madrid, 1900. — Cf. in the same publication the note by Simarro: *Concepto de la locura moral*.

c. Pathologic Theories.

Section 13. (a) Epilepsy.

Roncoroni, Ottolenghi, Perrone Capano, Lewis, etc.

The epileptic theory has been extensively spread in Italy, from the time when Lombroso coupled it with atavism in the explanation of delinquency. Roncoroni, Ottolenghi, Tonnini, and Cividalli, follow this tendency. Perrone Capano, in " Anarchy and Anarchists," [1] applies the theory to anarchistic criminality. He makes the persistency of the epileptoid state responsible for the strange impulse to criminal hatred, proceeding from extreme sensibility, lofty altruism, and pity, which characterizes the purest types; [2] an impulse which at times — we may add, wonderful miracle! — reverts again to the state of pity. [3]

Outside of Italy, the epileptic theory is accepted by Lewis. [4]

Section 14. (β) Neurasthenia.

Benedikt.

In Germanic countries prevails the neurasthenia theory

[1] L'Anarchia e gli Anarchici, Naples, 1901.

[2] Bourdeau (cf. the word Anarchie in the Dictionnaire d'Economie politique, by L. Say and J. Chailley Bert) skilfully points out this contrast when he says that the greater part of anarchists belong to the class of " philanthropic assassins." The anarchist Randon himself said (Revue Anarchiste, November 15, 1893): " We end by hating some by dint of loving the others." On the question of this contrast, consult our study: Psicología del crimen anarquista, in the review La Reforma, August, 1905.

[3] An interesting example of this was seen in the attempt against Alexander II, in 1881: " The Emperor lay bleeding upon the snow, abandoned by all his following; everybody had disappeared. Only the cadets, who were returning from the parade, lifted him from the ground, covered his trembling body with a cloak and put a cap on his uncovered head. The terrorist Emilianoff, with a bomb wrapped in a paper under his arm and at the risk of being seized and immediately hanged, ran with the cadets to the aid of the wounded man. Human nature is full of similar contrasts " (Kropotkin's Memoirs of a revolutionist, part VI, number 8).

[4] The genesis of crime, in the Fortnightly Review, 1893.

suggested by Benedikt,[1] and taken up by Liszt and Vargha.

What characterizes Benedikt's theory and makes it original is not the primitive atavistic hypothesis which has been alluded to before, but the interpretation of the criminal by means of an *innate neurasthenia*, a nervous and native psychic debility, and consequently, a rapid exhaustion in all work whether it be physical or mental. Aversion to continual work, frivolity, thirst after low pleasures, and debility in moral struggles, are the result of this state, which is as different from madness as it is from the normal individuality. It is the old *Beard's disease*, which Beard himself thought peculiar to the Americans,[2] and which afterwards has been considered as the result of the intellectual and physical overwork in the struggle for life of our days. Previous works describing this state go back to Hippocrates; but, now, like moral insanity, it invades the entire field of Psychiatry, becoming with Moevius the binding web of degenerative states, and allowing anomalous reactions of the organism, which resolve themselves, at times, into crimes.

No better example can be adduced than the sexual excitement under the stimulus of blood, called " Sadism " after the sadly famous Marquis de Sade (1740–1814), who offered an example of it, although perhaps not the most perfect one.[3]

---

[1] *Exposé des titres des travaux scientifiques du Prof. M. Benedikt, avec des courts compts rendus*, Vienna, 1896.

[2] *A practical treatise on nervous exhaustion*, New York, 1880.

[3] In his study on a case of Sadism (in the *General Review of Legislation and Jurisprudence*, 1907), MacDonald has compiled a large part of Sadism bibliography. We notice, however, the absence of Dühren's work, *Der Marquis de Sade und seine Zeit* (1901). The recent studies by Vaschide on the relation between motor impulse and genital action (*La psico-fisiología del impulso sexual*, in the *Archivos de Psychiatría*, by Ingegnieros, 1906) seem to throw a certain light on this problem of the taste for blood,

Section 15. (γ) Various Psychopathic States.
Ingegnieros.

While others pretend to find the root of crime in a final and single state, whether it be called neurasthenia, epilepsy, moral insanity, etc., Ingegnieros,[1] without undertaking a similar task, still very premature, classifies and arranges the psychopathic states connected with criminality as they are pointed out by clinical process.

Accepting the theory of criminal factors more after the German school (endogenous and exogenous) than the Italian (individual, physical, and social), Ingegnieros believes that these factors may be found combined in variable proportions, according to the variety of criminals.   The following drawing shows this varied influence applied to Ferri's classification:

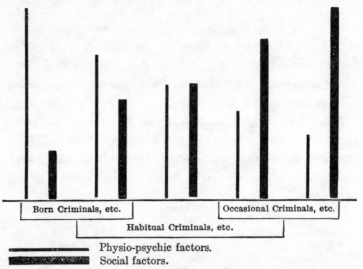

Physio-psychic factors.
Social factors.

which, under the action of morbid or degenerative states, is capable of becoming a stimulating motor image of sexuality; since, according to Vaschide himself, " Sexual life is due to the evolution and tendency of the motor centers to discharge."

[1] *Nuevos rumbos de la Antropología criminal*, in *Archivos de Psiquiatría y Criminalogía*, 1907.

On the other hand, recognizing the necessity for criminal anthropology to study the morphology as well as the psychopathology of criminals, he emphasizes the latter to such an extent that " if one could speak of schools to designate scientific tendencies," the one he would follow — contrary to that initiated by Lombroso — " ought to be called *psycho-pathological school.*"

Finally, on this basis he presents a new criminal classification.

Psycho-pathology of criminals.	Intellectual anomalies (*Dysgnosias*).	Congenital: Criminals through constitutional insanities. Contracted: Criminals through contracted insanity. Transitory: Drunkenness, toxical insanities, etc.
	Volitional Anomalies (*Dysbulias*).	Congenital: Impulsive epileptic criminals. Contracted: Impulsive chronic drunkards. Transitory: Emotional impulsive criminals, emotional criminals.
	Moral anomalies (*Dysthmias*).	Congenital: Born criminals or moral insane. Contracted: Habitual criminals or moral perverts. Transitory: Occasional criminals.

Section 16.   (B) Sociologic Theories.

According to the sociologic theories, crime is only and always due to agencies of such nature and of such power that, at times, far from the intervention of an individual predisposition, the individual, though refractory, is overcome by them. " How many French soldiers and French peasants," says Tarde, in his monograph " The Duel," " have fought duels against their will! How many Italians and Spaniards have murdered one another with a frown on their brow! How many Japanese have stabbed themselves without the least enthusiasm! All of them have borne testimony to the divinity of social environment, the social Moloch, the anonymous autocrat!" [1] This same monograph, when compared with any other of the Italian criminalists, Ferri's "Homicide," for instance, strikes the keynote of the position which criminal sociology holds in relation to criminal anthropology. In vain we might look in the former for the inevitable zoölogic array that precedes the latter; but, instead of natural history, how much human history it does contain! We also see in the former the change of physical and biological causes into the most intimate social factors, and consequently, the solid critique which has enriched modern criminology.

The problem and the difficulties that arise from the presence of anthropological data and stigmata in criminals are solved in two ways by criminal sociology.

First, after the cutting of the Gordian knot, by suppressing or excluding, more or less purposely, from delinquency the pathologic cases. Examples of this method are numerous, so deep-rooted is the idea in the social conscience. Incidently, we may quote Impallomeni's words: "In whatever degree we enter the field of medicine, we remain outside the domain of criminal law." [2] That belongs to the hospital and not to the prison, say many others.

The second way of solving the problem consists in considering the physical and the anthropological not as factors but as symptoms or marks of the social factor which alone exists. It is a case of economic misery resolving itself, in the long run, into physiological misery and degeneration. Interuterine life, even when suspended in fecundation, is equivalent, from this standpoint, to a first acceptation of quintessential and refined social environment, the same as in the reverse and analogous sense anthropologists say that education is the prolongation or the continuation of heredity.

---

[1] *Etudes pénales et sociales*, Paris and Lyons, 1892.
[2] *Il Codice penale Itialiano*, vol. I. p. 173.

It is a question, then, of anthropological states with social bases, or, if preferred, of individual marks of the social state. Colajanni offers an example of these interpretations when, against the general opinion, he maintains that drunkenness is not the cause of poverty (anthropological factor producing a social condition favorable to crime), but that poverty is the cause of drunkenness (social factor converting itself into an anthropological state or mark); for, workmen through lack of means to nourish body and mind, are obliged to recur to alcohol, which serves physiologically and psychologically as a substitute.

A similar interpretation is given for the so-called physical or cosmic factors. In the already classical tripartition of criminal factors, we have said that the physical factors did not produce a new school, but that they gave rise to the polemic between anthropologists and sociologists. We have already mentioned Quételet's thermic law; but, while anthropologists like Ferri explain it upon physical grounds, as climate; sociologists like Tarde, after attenuating it in the same measure as in criminal maps, bring it back to social reasons, like the march of civilization from North to South, so wisely and ingeniously developed by Mongeolle in his "Statistics of Civilizations." [1] The anthropologists, including Ferri, answer that, in spite of all, it is the thermic law that determines the direction of progress, and that civilization, like cold climate, may be a racial sedative. But Tarde and the sociologists reply that: " What we really know is the opposite. The peculiarity of real civilized life is to overexcite the nervous system, while rural life calms it and feeds the muscles at the expense of the nerves. Civilization, in this sense, acts not as a colder climate but as a warmer one. Therefore, the terms of the question are altered and the solution that must be

[1] *Estadística de las civilizaciones.*

sought is other than that of the Italian criminalists." [1] This new solution is already known; it is found in the social factors, by which Tarde and other sociologists explain even the calendar and the hours of delinquency, which were established, in the first moments of ingenious safety, by the partisans of meteors and stars.

The division of the social theories can be stated thus:

a. Anthropo-social theories.
b. Social theories.
c. Socialistic theories.

Section 17. (a) *Anthropo-Sociologic Theories.*
Lacassagne, Aubry, Dubuisson, etc.

The spirit of this first direction is summarized in two typical phrases which marked the deviation from Lombrosian orthodoxy at the Congress of Rome. There, Lacassagne, borrowing a simile from micro-biology, said: " Social environment is the heat in which criminality breeds; the criminal is the microbe, an element of no importance until it meets the liquid that makes it ferment" ; and again: " Communities possess the criminals whom they deserve."

When stripped of the metaphor, the meaning of these not so obscure phrases is that delinquency is produced by social excitations of individual states. An example that throws light on this theory is found in the *thefts caused by the display counters of great department stores.* The mechanism of these thefts is the following. The store, with all its scenery to attract the customer, acts as an aperient for crime in certain persons predisposed by all the neuroses and physical disturbances of which kleptomania is an eloquent sign. It is not, therefore, a question of the classical theory of opportunity; for, a larger number of persons in whom the sense of probity

---

[1] *La criminalité comparée.*

is deep-rooted do not feel the temptation, while others who feel it resist and overcome it. The victim, on the other hand, carries always the mark, however imperceptible, of a special morbid state. But this also would not suffice to produce the crime, if the social environment did not excite it. Moreover, the motive of gain required by jurists is often lacking. Woman, *the eternally sick*, monopolizes the statistics of this crime, which seems expressly made for her. According to Doctor Dubuisson,[1] pregnant, hysterical, and neurasthenic women, those addicted to the morphine and the drinking habit, etc., lose their mind in the movement that exists in the *Louvre* and the *Bon Marché*. Among men, one meets fetiches, bibliomaniacs, and collectors of all kinds. But both sexes steal only in similar places, and not where a weaker irritation is unable to awaken in them the morbid predisposition.

Moreover, this predisposition, far from forming a state of well determined boundaries, distinct from a state of preservation invulnerable to the solicitations of the display or of the shop-window, possesses a whole gamut of shades and modes which enter and mingle with the moral action. By the side of the kleptomaniac, and as the analogous and reverse counterpart, psychiatry describes, for instance, the oneomaniac, that is the buying maniac, a victim of a like morbid obsession and fed by the same factors. This " kleptomaniac who pays," as Féré ingeniously calls him, is in juridical speech called the *prodigal*, guilty of crime against his own property.

P. Aubry also, in the most interesting of his books, " Murder Contagion," [2] develops a conception much like Lacassagne's phrase. The subject of the book is the *contagion of murder*, a topic which in pre-Lombrosian literature is discussed in

---

[1] *Les voleuses des grands magasins*, Lyons, 1903.
[2] *La contagion du meurtre*, 3d edition, Paris, 1895.

Morel's " Moral Contagion . . . , and the Danger which the Accounts of Crimes in Newspapers Constitutes for Morality and Public Safety," [1] and in Moreau's " The Contagion of Suicide, in view of the Present Epidemic." [2]

" Long before the discovery of the nature of virulent diseases, it was known that two elements were indispensable for a man in good health to catch cholera, for instance, directly or indirectly from a patient. There was needed a virus — microbes we would say to-day — ; but neither the virus nor the microbes can always act. Members of the same family may be subjected to the same régime of life for several days, and yet two, three, four of them will be infected, while the others will not, although exposed to the same causes and to the contact of their ill or dead relatives. Why is this? It is because the virulent element has not found in them a prepared soil in which to develop and thrive; while in the others the soil was of the most favorable, and the germs multiplied and soon caused more or less serious disorders. When it is a question of moral contagion, crime for instance, do things happen otherwise? Not in the least. We shall find the same process, with the only difference that we can analyze the noxious elements instead of examining them under the microscope or cultivating them in gelatine."

By the side of heredity, which would be the chief means of transmitting crime, sufficient in itself from the anthropological point of view, Paul Aubry finds that contagion is the product of morbid psychology whose main elements are *suggestion* and *imitation*. With numerous examples taken from contemporary criminal history, the author describes

[1] Morel, *De la contagion morale . . . du danger que présente pour la moralité et securité publique la relation des crimes donnée par les journaux*, Marseille, 1870.

[2] Moreau (de Tours), *De la contagion du suicide, à propos de l'épidemie actuelle*, Paris, 1875.

epidemics like that of *vitriol throwing*, of *criminal mutilation* (upon which we possess treatises by Lacassagne, Ravoux, Nina Rodriguez), of *incineration*, etc. In his opinion, the agencies that prepare the ground are: (a) direct heredity; (b) unbalanced nervous system; (c) certain anatomical deformities or conformations still badly defined. The agencies that transmit the contagion, either singly or combined with one another, are: (a) home education (guilty family); (b) prison; (c) reading of novels and periodicals containing accounts of crimes; (d) the spectacle of capital executions.

There is a relic of the Lombrosian style of thinking when the writer mentions anatomical deformities, or conformations still badly defined; a relic that perhaps is found again in that very homogeneous group of scholars who form the *Lyonese school*, Lyons being the center where, around Lacassagne and Martin, it is founded; although at present, together with the " Archives of Criminal Anthropology " which they publish, it seems to have become a school of Medical Jurisprudence.

b. Social Theories.
Section 18. (a) Failure in Adaptation.
Vaccaro.

The *lack of adaptation of the individual to social environment* is the idea set forth by Vaccaro in " Genesis and Function of Criminal Laws " and in " Critical Essays on Sociology and Criminology." [1]

His starting point is the struggle for existence; but tending to prove " that the Darwinian laws of selection and of the survival of the fittest, although applicable to human society, have been until now, are still, and will be for a long time

---

[1] *Genesi e funzioni delle leggi penali*, Rome, 1889. — *Saggi critici di Sociologia e Criminalogia*, Turin, 1903.

applicable with such restrictions and attenuations, that in most cases, together with a progressive and ascending selection, one meets a reverse process, that is, a descending and retrogressive selection, a true degeneration."

As a result of this struggle, crime appears to Vaccaro as an act which the winners who constitute the ruling power consider dangerous to their own interests; the criminal appears as a rebel against the complicated system of domestication by which the winners try to develop only the aptitudes of the domesticated which they can better utilize for their ends; and punishment appears as one of the forces used by them, until, fear having taken root in the nervous cell, it sufficed to substitute the *threat* of physical pain for the permanent physical correction.

For Vaccaro, then, everything is reduced to relations between conquered and conquerors, considered from a different aspect from that of other sociologists and criminalists; because, while for Garofalo this relation produces the selection of the best, from Vaccaro's standpoint it only leaves the multiple degenerations of the weak, of the coarse, and of the pliable, who have succeeded in adapting themselves to a life of intellectual and physical degradation. Hence for Vaccaro the phrase *legal defense* used by the classicists sounds better and is more real than that of *social defense* used by the positivists; because criminal laws have never aimed to defend the *entire social body* as the interests of favored people of whom public order is constituted. Crime can always be an offense or a violation of *positive* and constituted law; but, in most cases, it cannot be an attack on the true *social* interests which concern the entire social body. As for the criminal, he is always a degenerate through *social* causes, even when showing *physical* marks. Is there, then, anything more natural for the rebels than " after having struggled with poverty and privations, to show unmistakable signs of degeneration, either through paralyzation of development, or through atavistic retrogressions due to the hardships of life or to diseases contracted during hardships in gestation or after birth? " " And, in fact, society is greatly interested to know the number of men who offend through inability to adapt themselves to the unfortunate environment in which they live; for, in this case, it is useless to trust in the efficacy and severity of punishments: what is needed is to do the utmost in bettering the environment itself. If, in the struggle for existence among men, the fittest were always victorious, the artificial selection which the new school proposes would be in some measure justified; but since men do not struggle under equal conditions nor with the same weapons, it often happens that the fittest, physically and morally, succumb and the mediocre or the unfit triumph, favored by wealth or by other casual circumstances."

Section 19. (β) Segregation.
Aubert.

Aubert's " The Social Center " [1] develops with great originality the opposite idea.

In his opinion, far from separating himself from the center, the criminal exaggerates the characteristics of the human center and constitutes himself a center for the combined action of *phobias* and *psychoses* which represent the mutual action and reaction between the individual and the environment, granted in the former an exhausted or shattered nervous system. For Aubert, phobias are mainly: the feeling of frustrated life, and the fear of poverty and ignominy. In the obscure terminology of this writer they are called respectively: *lipothymia*, *penyaphobia*, and *ascrophobia*. In their turn,

[1] *Le milieu social*, Paris, 1902.

the *psychoses* refer to: gambling, acquisition of wealth, quarreling, exterior honors.

When the criminal is thus differentiated from the center (*apothenosis*), there follows the rearrangement of a life hostile to it (*enantibyosis*), in which he still distinguishes the *protero-delinquency* (delinquency of the young without precedent) from the *deutero-delinquency* (in two successive forms: relapsed criminals, and professional ones).

Section 20. (γ) Parasitism.
Max Nordau, Salillas.

Max Nordau, in "A New Biological Theory of Crime," [1] explains parasitism as the combination of the initial unadaptability of the criminal and a posterior anomalous readaptation.

"For me," he says, "crime means human parasitism, using the word in the analogical and not in the purely biological sense. The condition of the natural and normal existence of man, like that of the other species of somewhat superior animals, is to derive his sustenance from nature, excluding his own species. Wolves do not eat one another, says a proverb which expresses a true biological law. We find very few species among which cannibalism does not appear other than as an exceptional or visible pathological aberration.

"Man is not a cannibal by nature. Even in the savage state he is never so in his own tribe, although he eats, occasionally, his dead relations. Anthropophagy is only practiced with the enemy, who, by an opportune fiction, is not considered as forming part of the same species. Man takes advantage of the animal and vegetable resources which Nature offers him. He works for his living and does not beg it of his neighbor. . . .

"As civilization advances and man is removed from his

[1] *Une nouvelle théorie biologique du crime*, in *La Revue*, 1902.

primitive condition, his relations with Nature and with other men become more complicated. He can no longer rely altogether on Nature for his subsistence. Nature has been confiscated by occupants who utilize it for themselves. Those who own neither land nor water can obtain provisions only by personal recourse to the usurpers of the land. The division of labor begins. Men organize themselves economically, and production is differentiated and specialized. The family, the tribe, the nation, the entire species becomes a coöperative society in which each member works for all, and in his turn receives from the common production what he needs. Men depend on one another, living thus, a smaller number as usurpers of the soil and a larger one as dispossessed.

" But this relation does not constitute parasitism; because, with coöperation, there is mutualism. This is the law of the *do ut des;* what I ask of my neighbor I pay by an equal conventional value. Parasitism begins only when, in this coöperative society, there appear men who wish to take without lending anything, and who take away from others the fruit of their labor without their consent and without any compensation. In short, they are men who treat other men as raw material from which they may satisfy their needs and appetites. And the criminals are the ones who precisely fall under this parasitism."

This idea had been set forth before by Salillas, in a volume of his work "Hampa," [1] of the suppressed series "The Spanish Criminal," in which the author calls it the "fundamental theory of crime."

"Mateo Alemán," writes Dorado [2] (to the memory of

---

[1] *Hampa*, Madrid, 1898.

[2] On Salillas' *Hampa*, cf. the volume: *Estudios de Derecho penal preventivo*, Madrid, 1901. Salillas summed up this theory in a paper read before the International Congress of Medicine, which met in Madrid, in 1903.

whom Salillas dedicates his book), " with an exact knowledge of the national Spanish constitution, states that *poverty and knavery come from the same quarry.*" This means that the same causes which make the poor man poor make the criminal a criminal. Poverty is due to the scarcity of the means of subsistence, a deficiency of the internal as well as external basis of nutrition; delinquency is the product of the same deficiency. " Knavery," says Salillas, — and when he says knavery we can read crime — " follows a basal deficiency of the nutritive basis of subsistence."

Thus, Salillas to the diagnosis (parasitism) adds the ætiology of the evil (nutritive injury). But, does that diagnosis fit the whole phenomenon of crime? Can it be applied, for instance, to political crime? Both Max Nordau and Salillas, more or less tacitly, agree in limiting it only to professional or habitual delinquency.[1]

Section 21. (c) *Socialistic Theories.*

Turati, Loria, Colajanni, etc.

From the social theories we reach the socialistic theories. Emphasizing the importance of the economical factor over

---

[1] Thus restricted we have applied it in the study, *La mala vida en Madrid* (Madrid, 1901). Criminality,* prostitution, and pauperism, we said, are manifestations of the same phenomenon, namely, of parasitism. But the kind of reaction which society employs against each manifestation is different; hence the different place assigned by society to its parasites. The character of each parasitical function in relation to the social organism is the following:

Criminals = *enemies.*
Beggars = *guests.*
Prostitution = *mutuality, symbiosis.*

Franchi recognizes the superiority of our explanation over that of Nordau (cf. *La questione della genesi e natura della delinquenza,* in *La Scuola Positiva,* vol. XII, 1902).

* Meaning habitual delinquency, the class of professional offenders.

other social factors — as it becomes the doctrine of historic materialism — they charge the economical system of bourgeois society with having produced delinquency, which will almost completely disappear with the advent of the socialistic régime. The principle of class struggle — very important in socialism — reappears in criminal socialism when the latter considers the present penal justice as a system to defend the class interests of the usurpers of power.

The most perceptible application of socialism to criminology has been made in Italy, under the influence of the theory of the born criminal and of the predominance of the individual causes of crime. Both of these have been affirmed by Lombroso, Ferri, and Garofalo, the three leaders of the school, offspring of Darwinism and of Spencer's social philosophy. The Italian writers of Marxian scientific socialism, Colajanni, Loria, Turati, Prampolini, Zorla, have opposed them and still do so, forming in their turn a criminal theory essentially social with the exception of a few important points.

The polemic between anthropologists and socialists seems to have been settled chiefly in Italy by the fusion of both parties. " Marx complements Darwin and Spencer, and together they form the great scientific trinity of the nineteenth century."

This symbolic phrase belongs to Enrico Ferri, the same who started the dispute, and who was obliged to continue it against socialism in his " Socialism and Criminality." [1]

Dorado gives the history of this debate in " Criminal Anthropology in Italy."

" The polemic began," says he, " by Turati's pamphlet ' Crime and the Social Question,' [2] which was provoked by Ferri's ' Education, Environment, and Criminality.' It was

[1] *Socialismo e criminalità.*
[2] *Il delitto e la questione sociale*, Milan, 1883.

kept up by Ferri's 'Socialism and Criminality,' Colajanni's 'Socialism and Criminal Sociology,' Zorli's ' The Penal Question and the Social Question,' Garofalo's ' Criminology,'[1] and by other productions."

Turati's argument is in substance as follows: Granting that crime be the product of three classes of factors: cosmic or natural, individual or anthropological, and social; granting the five criminal classes enumerated and studied by Ferri — insane, or semi-insane, born incorrigibles, emotional criminals, habitual criminals, and occasional criminals, — it is evident that the first three, in which the individual factors predominate, could not offend if there existed only physical and social factors, which exercise the main influence in leading the last two classes to crime. Well then, setting aside the influence of the cosmic factors, which, in as far as they form the ordinary environment, cannot, according to Turati, be considered as criminal factors, and which, at any event, exercise only a minimum influence, and that on the *quality* rather than on the *quantity* of real delinquency; setting aside also the crimes committed by insane criminals and by those who obey emotional impulse, who, according to Ferri himself, " are, after all, the least numerous, and represent a ratio which, in spite of the uncertainty of data on the subject, can be calculated approximately at five per cent. of the total criminality in general,"[2] it follows that the greater number of crimes are those due to social causes and influences. In fact, if the crimes due to a predominant individual element reach forty per cent., we

[1] Ferri, *Educazione, ambiente e criminalità;* in the *Archivio di Psichiatria,* vol. IV, p. 26, ff. — Ferri, *Socialismo e criminalità,* Turin, 1883. — Colajanni, *Socialismo e sociologia criminale,* I; *Il Socialismo,* Catania, 1884. — Zorli, *La questione penale e la questione sociale,* Milan, 1884. — Garofalo, *Criminalogia,* part II, ch. III.

[2] *Nuovi orizzonti,* p. 255.

must deduct many exceptions from this figure, and Turati rightly does so, reducing the ratio to about ten per cent. From this the writer deduces that the maximum of criminality, represented by habitual and occasional criminals, is due to social environment; and that, therefore, " when this environment is modified, when the iniquitous bourgeois society is overthrown and the socialistic ideal is realized, then misery will end, and the motives for crime will be wanting, education ending by turning men into angels " (Zorli). He believes that, once modified, the social environment which makes the citizen, even the small minority of insane and semi-insane criminals, of born criminals, and of emotional criminals will slowly and gradually disappear, because of the better social order, reign of justice, culture, material welfare, and natural selection aided and not hindered.

Ferri's " Socialism and Criminality " was written with polemical intention. The long prelude contains a number of things and observations more or less connected with the subject, but always interesting. There he discusses even the word " socialism," the classification of socialists, whether society is to progress through evolution or revolution; he states that the division of men into honest and dishonest is due, in thought and practice, to the ingenuity of an Italian minister, and even vindicates the Spencerian conception of sociology. Then he studies in as many chapters the main questions which form the subject of Turati's book. We will give a short summary of his argumentation. After referring to the doctrine of the three classes of criminal factors, he says that the socialists consider only one of them, that of the social factors, and that, through a psychological process (the counter-reaction against individualism) and propaganda strategy. They attribute all the evils and therefore all the crimes to society, overlooking the power and influence of the individual factors. Criminal sociology comes to reëstablish the equilibrium between the two exaggerated currents, assigning to the individual and to society the rôle that belongs to them. Even under a socialistic régime, there would be a social environment, the cause of crime. Setting aside a number of crimes which have nothing to do with the economical social system, as those against honor, insults, etc., of the great categories of crimes — crimes of blood and against the person, crimes against chastity, and those against property — the first two, far from diminishing, increase with economical welfare, and the third could not disappear altogether, since there would never be lacking the kleptomaniacs, the envious of the property of others,.and the lazy, who, to avoid the effort of going to the common store-house, would rob their neighbor. In order to gradually overcome crime by bettering the social element, we should make use of the preventive measures of the positivistic school, called *penal substitutes*. Education, from which socialists expect so much, is of no value and helps only average natures; for, it is useless for those who are bad by temperament, and superfluous for the good. The socialists deceive themselves when they believe that under the new economical system of the society which they dream the political and juridical order will be changed; for, if the latter is bound to the former, it is also certain that the former is the effect of the latter, since there is relation in everything, and it is a narrow criterion that looks at things only from one side as socialism does.

But from the time Dorado wrote this summary, Ferri's thought has not remained stationary. On the contrary, going beyond the " sterile boundary of sociology," he has been able to " free himself from a paralysis of development, reaching the practical and fruitful side of socialism." The exposition of these doctrines which Turati and Prampolino

were making around him; the study of Karl Marx' and
Loria's works, the latter being "permeated with Marxian
theories and saturated by a flood of scientific erudition,"
completed his education and hastened the development of
a germ which Colajanni had already seen mature. Immediately, Ferri testified publicly to his socialistic ideas in a
lecture given in Milan, on Labor Day of 1894. Being a
convinced Darwinist and a Spencerian, he felt it as a duty,
for the tranquillity of his science and his conscience, to prove,
as we have said, "that Marx complements Darwin and
Spencer," and that "together they form the great scientific
trinity of the nineteenth century."

This is the object of Ferri's "Socialism and Positive
Science," [1] in which, while a new edition of "Socialism and
Criminology" appears, he resumes his position of criminal
anthropologist and of socialist, answering thus by his example
those who, like Loria (The Economic Bases of the Social
System), [2] still repeat the contradictions between socialism
and criminal anthropology.

"That with socialism will disappear each and all forms of
crime, is an affirmation due to a generous sentimental idealism,
which is not based upon strict scientific observation."

It is known that against Virchow's statement that "Darwinism leads straight to socialism," the ruling opinion has
thought of seeing such an open incompatibility between the
two that it has been able to state that: "Darwinism will
destroy socialism." Häckel has lent his authority to this
opinion, basing it on three main contradictions: (a) Socialism
proclaims the chimerical equality of men, while Darwinism
explains the organic reasons for their natural diversity;
(b) Darwinism teaches that, in the struggle for existence,

---

[1] *Socialismo e scienza positiva.*
[2] *Les bases économiques de la constitution sociale*, Paris, 1894.

only a small minority wins, while socialism pretends that
nobody must succumb in it; (c) The struggle for existence
assures the survival of the fittest, giving rise to an aristocratic
process of individualistic selection instead of the democratic
levelling of socialism. Ferri answers these three arguments
with much ingeniousness and perspicacity. His answer can
be thus summed up: (a) It is true that the differences among
men are real; but, there is an element of equality, which
socialism affirms, and that is: that all are men; (b) The
number of winners in the struggle diminishes prodigiously
when passing from the vegetable to the animal world, from
the first to the highest steps of the zoölogic scale, from this
to the animal kingdom, and in the animal kingdom itself as
civilization progresses; (c) Like Vaccaro, he affirms that
in the struggle for existence among men, it is not the fittest
that survive, but those who most readily adapt themselves.
In saying this, he does not refer to romantic socialism, but
to the only scientific socialism that exists, that of Marx, which
still needs some rectification at the hands of biologic sciences.

What will happen, then?

Modern socialism is the enemy of Utopianism. To the
frequent questions on the programme of life under its régime,
it answers, with justice, that there can be given only a very
general idea, for the same reason that a Catholic cannot
describe life in the other world.[1] Therefore, what can be said
of criminality under a socialistic régime is only this: " When
poverty and the iniquitous disparity in economic conditions
have disappeared, then, through the direct lack of the acute
or chronic stimulus of hunger, through the beneficent and
indirect influence of better nourishment and the absence of

---

[1] For this reason Ferri is right when he calls " lymphatic " and " gro-
tesque " books like Richter's, which pretend to satirize life, " Dopo la
vittoria del socialismo," Milan, 1892.

opportunities for an abusive use of power and wealth, there will be a decided decrease and disappearance of those crimes, largely occasional, which in the social environment have a greater determining strength. But this will not cause the disappearance of crimes against chastity through pathologic sexual aberration and others of the same nature. In conclusion, even under a socialistic régime, although in infinitely smaller proportion, there will always be beings defeated in the struggle for existence in the form of the weak, infirm, insane, neurasthenics, criminal, suicidal; and, therefore, socialism does not deny the Darwinian law of the struggle for existence. But it will have such a superiority that the epidemic or endemic forms of physical and moral human degeneration will be stifled by the elimination of its primordial cause, physical and moral poverty. Under these conditions, the struggle for existence, although remaining the permanent propelling force of social life, will have its course in less brutal and more humane forms, that is to say, intellectual forms and higher ideals. Like physiological and psychic evolution, the struggle will be based on the assurance that every man will receive his daily bread for the body and for the mind." [1]

Colajanni also attributes to poverty and in general to the entire modern economical system, directly and indirectly, the great majority of crimes. Speaking of alcoholism [2] and of delinquency in Sicily (Delinquency in Sicily and its Causes),[3]

[1] While Ferri advances in the path of socialism, Garofalo inveighs against it. According to the latter, the danger of socialism does not come from the working class, whose members with the exception of a few — fanatics in his opinion — have little desire and time to meddle with things so remote from real life as collectivism. The true danger is found in the conviction of a large number of people belonging to the middle class and even to higher classes that socialism means truth, progress, " intellectuality." Therefore, he believes it to be his duty to warn them against the socialistic superstition.

[2] *L'alcoolismo*, Catania, 1887.

[3] *La delinquenza della Sicilia e le sue cause*, Palermo, 1885.

his native land, he sets forth this point of view, which, on account of the polemic we are describing, he was obliged to treat more fully in his book " Socialism and Criminal Sociology." [1] The first part of the book contains the principles of socialism in relation to modern science. The second part has become a voluminous and independent work entitled " Criminal Sociology," [2] in which, with numerous authorities, data, and documents, he studies the entire programme of modern criminology.

This is essentially a critical book. In the presence of the Italian school of anthropology, when he examines its fundamental hypotheses (relation between the physical and the moral, between organs and functions, between cerebrum and intelligence and morality), and notices its contradictions (qualitative, ethnical, historical, and sexual), Colajanni exclaims: " *Ignoramus!* *Ignoramus!* In repeating this sad truth, we do not despair in the struggle for the unknown. Everything leads us to believe that the unknown of to-day will not be so to-morrow. This is the sound doctrine of Italian positivism, which, rejecting Spencer's *unknowable*, plunges into the loftiest investigations, and looks resolutely in the face of the most arduous problems (Ardigó, Bovio, Angiulli, Sergi, Morselli)."

Thus Colajanni, far from stopping on the obscure features of the criminal's nature, and yet not satisfied with Vaccaro's solution, goes beyond socialism and the independent minds which struggle against the environment, and advances one more hypothesis which we have mentioned elsewhere.

He does not share a single idea with other socialists, including Turati and all those who, following Fourier, admit the natural goodness and the loving charms of the first men.

[1] *Socialismo e sociologia criminale*, Catania, 1884.
[2] *La sociologia criminale*, Catania, 1889.

His doctrine, on the contrary, is atavistic; an atavism whose new traits are: its application to psychical and moral characteristics, and the fact that the regression which it includes, instead of having the immovable and always even issue of the primitive man and the savage, is movable and accompanies in its movement the evolution of culture. " Psychic atavism is the reappearance in men of a determinate race, of psychical characteristics peculiar to phases of past evolutions"; a formula more exact than that of Mantegazza, which calls it a " sudden regression of very ancient psychical characteristics in men of a superior race." Why must they be very ancient? And why in a superior race? Every race has its psychical retrogrades in various degrees and with various characteristics.

This theory is followed by a long examination of the function attributed by the school of criminal anthropology to anthropological (age, sex, civil state, heredity, race) and physical (latitude, altitude, instability of climate, rain, cold) factors. " People who do not go beyond the surface of things will think that the greater part of this study is of a thoroughly negative nature, intended to prove, above all, *what are not* the true preparatory and determining causes of crime, without considering that every negation has always a *positive side*. My positive side is that it is necessary to search for the ætiology of delinquency, preferably in the social contingencies, because crime is a social or historical phenomenon. . . . That crime is a product of the social system has been maintained for a long time. This is not a recent discovery. Puttmann clearly says: *leges ineptæ criminum causa* (Magri). Helvetius, Filangieri, etc., repeat the same. J. Mill, Perrier, Laveleye, and many others have declared themselves for the evolution of human society to the detriment of race, climate, geographical configuration, etc. Men like Maudsley, Schüle, and largely Morelli himself, whose competence in similar matters is beyond doubt, when facing phenomena ˹closely connected with delinquency, as mental alienation and suicide, have, in order to explain their oscillations, likewise referred to the *influence of the social factors.* Spencer, the most authoritative expounder of evolution, subordinates more and more evolution to social factors, in proportion to its complexity; factors which, on the other hand, are the only ones that can be removed and modified by us(?) . . . Among the most important of these factors are war, militarism, religion, the environment as a whole, mimicry, etc."

But, without doubt, the most important of all is the *economic* factor.

" It seems impossible that there should be thinkers who doubt the pre-eminence of this factor in social evolution. They are deceived by the complexity of modern life, in which are often seen men who subordinate economical and material necessities to intellectual and moral aims. The illusion is explained by the fact that they pay attention to the individual and not to the species. In these cases, phylogeny illustrates and explains ontogeny, showing that these very noble and admired men are the last product of the entire previous evolution, in which the economical influence was evident and even brutal. . . . Nevertheless, it is an exaggeration to affirm that every social fact — political, religious, æsthetic, or moral — is the *direct* and *exclusive* product of an economical phenomenon (Marx, Loria); because, in certain given moments, the sentiments and passions of some superior men, free from material preoccupations, are communicated to the masses through an irresistible contagion. Yet, one does not err in affirming that the consequences of similar events are almost always *economical;* because, in the complexity of interests which are in constant contact with

one another, it is not possible to influence one without reaching
the others; and because material necessities, assigned for a
while to a secondary position, assume again their natural
pre-eminence."

This having been settled, Colajanni devotes three long
chapters to the *direct* and *indirect* influence of the economical
factor in its *statics* and *dynamics*.

" The economical condition exercises a direct action on the
genesis of delinquency; for, the deficiency of the means to
satisfy the numerous necessities of man is a sufficient stimulus
for him to adopt honest or criminal methods in the struggle
that ensues. These necessities differ according to peoples
and are more numerous among those who have reached a
higher grade of civilization and possess a larger view of life.
Some features of the present economical system give a greater
impetus to immoral activity in some determined social circles.
In some cases, its positive result is greater, and its danger
less than in honorable work. . . . This feature of the *direct*
influence of the economical system on crimes, especially those
against property, is enormous. But the *indirect* influence
is not less evident and powerful. Wars, the present industrial
system, the family, marriage, political institutions, idleness
and vagrancy, prostitution, education, etc., are so many causes
of crime. But each of these in its turn is subject, in a more
or less apparent and determined way, to the economical
factor, according to the unanimous opinion of thinkers belonging to the most opposite schools: from Morgan to
Lacombe, from Marx to Molinari, from Engel to Thulié,
from Spencer down to Schäffle, Gumplowicz, Loria, Vaccaro,
etc. . . . Suppose alcoholism possessed all the criminal
influence attributed to it, to what conditions does this vice
owe its allegiance genetically? To poverty. . . . Poverty
engenders likewise vagrancy and not vagrancy poverty. . . .

As for prostitution, the greater number of its causes can be reduced to one common denominator: poverty; and its clandestine character ' accompanies the necessity of securing the means of avoiding starvation (Fiaux).' . . . The direct relation between poverty, economical misery and crimes against property is easily perceived; but it is not less real than the relation to crimes against the person, especially through the *indirect* influence due to necessity and to the degree and kind of education received. It often happens that crimes of this kind, in order to have full course, are combined with the former. There are, moreover, men who confess crimes that they have not committed, in order to escape the imperious necessity of hunger and to be admitted to a prison, where almost always they find board and lodging not rarely better than that enjoyed by the honest workman. . . . Finally, the doubts concerning the relations between the wealth of a people or of an individual and delinquency disappear when one considers the *dynamics* of such relations; for, one will see that the disturbances in the economical situation are the cause of disturbance in criminal conditions. When the former improves, the number of crimes decreases, and, *vice versa*, when it grows worse there follows an increase in delinquency."

Colajanni could be answered that things are not always thus. Strangely, in the crimes of blood and even in those of lewdness, the curve is reversed, since they decrease during hard times and increase during prosperity.

The relations between the economic factor and criminality are not yet definitely known. Van Kan's voluminous work, " The Economic Causes of Criminality," [1] and Bonger's " Criminality and Economic Conditions " [2] are based more

---

[1] *Les causes économiques de la criminalité*, Lyon, 1903.

[2] *Criminalité et conditions économiques*, Amsterdam, 1905.

on the opinion of the authors than on facts. Many minute investigations are needed, like those in Fornasari di Verce's " Criminality and the Economical Vicissitudes in Italy from 1873 to 1890." [1]

Section 22.   (2) INTERNATIONAL CONGRESSES OF CRIMINAL ANTHROPOLOGY.

" Using Hegel's terminology to explain the aspects of the three Congresses of criminal anthropology," wrote Ferreira Deusdado,[2] " we should say that the first (Rome, 1885) represents the period of *affirmation* or *thesis;* the second (Paris, 1889) that of *negation* or *antithesis;* and the third (Brussels, 1892) that of *composition* or *synthesis.*"

Unfortunately, the comparison used by Ferreira leaves no room for a fourth term; and yet six Congresses have been held, and one is to follow every five years. On the other hand, the terms with which he qualifies the first three are not very exact when submitted to a careful analysis. We should say that, after all, every Congress, no matter how international it may be called, is always a limited meeting of scholars coming from nations, which, through language, race, and proximity, maintain more intimate relations and more frequent contact with one another; and since in everything there rules the maxim of international law by which *locus regit actum,* the Congress of Rome assumed the character of Italian science as we have seen, and that of Paris that of the French school. The last Congresses held in Brussels (1892), Geneva (1896), Amsterdam (1901), and Turin (1906), were more neutral in science, with a slight emphasis on the anthropological side in the last, on account of the place and of the celebration of Lombroso's scientific jubilee. It ought to be remembered that

---

[1] *La criminalità e le vicende economiche d'Italia dal* 1873 *al* 1890, Turin, 1894.

[2] *A Anthropologia criminal e o Congresso de Brusellas,* Lisbon, 1890.

Lombroso and his followers did not attend the Congress of Brussels, in which was seen an act of protest against the hostility with which they were received in Paris.

Here follows an account of the last two Congresses held in the time intervening between the first and the second edition of this work.

The 5th Congress was held at Amsterdam from the ninth to the fourteenth of September, 1901.

A good number of Italians hastened to the Dutch city. Three of Lombroso's family were there: Cesare, Ugo, and Gina.   There were also Ferri, Sighele, Tenchini, Romiti, Carrara, Eula, Ferrari, Antonini, Frigerio, Treves, Mariani, Murgia, Squillace, Parnisetti, Scapucci, Zimmerl.

On the other hand, the absence of noted French and German criminalists was remarked.   No Spaniards were present.

Italians and Dutch were in the majority; and since not a few of the latter, beginning with Van Hamel, look with favor upon the tendencies of the former, the 5th International Congress of Criminal Anthropology was considered a triumph for the Italian school of criminology.

The programme was as follows:

A.   General Questions.

1. Anatomical and physiological characteristics of criminals. Descriptive studies.

2. General psychology and psycho-pathology. — Criminals and madmen. — General considerations. — Practical measures.

3. Legal and administrative application of criminal anthropology. — Directive principles. — Preventive measures. — Repressive measures.

4. Criminal sociology. — Economic causes of crime.— Other causes of delinquency. — Delinquency and socialism.

5. Criminal anthropology and comparative ethnology.

B. Special Questions.

Alcoholism. — Juvenile delinquency. — Senile delinquency. — Hypnotism. — Sexuality. — Criminal psychology in literature, etc.

As usual, time failed to take up so many questions. Many important communications were not discussed.

After the inaugural address by Van Hamel, Lombroso's paper on "The latest investigations of Criminal Anthropology" served as introduction to the business of the Congress. The paper was a kind of index of the main works produced since the Congress of Geneva. He mentioned the studies of Pellizzi on " The disorders of the stratification of the nervous cells of the cerebral cortex in epileptic idiots "; those of Carrara on the " Frequency of progressive characteristics in criminals "; those of Favaro, Modica, and Audenino on " Determined anatomical and physiological peculiarities "; the studies of Fano on the " Hindoo fakirs "; those of Mariani on " Russian criminals "; those of Ottolenghi on " Tattooing "; those of De Blasio on " The hieroglyphics of Neapolitan *camorristas* "; those of Laschi on " Banking delinquency," etc. A very incomplete memoir on psychological and social studies ended by referring to the conception of the *symbiosis of crime* (social utilization of criminal instincts), the last word of the school.

Anatomy and physiology of criminals. — Tenchini, in his own and in Zimmerl's name, spoke on " A new abnormal process in the human presphenoid, observed mainly in various skulls in the Craniological Museum of the Insane Asylum of Reggio-Emilia."

Parnisetti presented a fine album with various drawings of " Anomalies of the Willis' arterial polygon (circles of Willis) in criminals."

Treves emphasized the value of " Functional Stigmata,"

which are, perhaps, more important than somatic anomalies, either as a trait of degeneration and vital insufficiency; or, being too difficult to detect, it is to be presumed that they exist in a greater number of cases than observed thus far.

Cesare Lombroso undertook to answer the question: " Why criminals of genius do not show the criminal type? " His opinion, as we have already seen, is that this type appears mainly in atavistic criminals, like ravishers, murderers, highway robbers, etc.

Other works sent to the Congress were:

Romiti, "Anatomical characteristics in the corpses of criminals."

Giuffrida Ruggeri, " The asymmetry of pentagonoid skulls."

De Sanctis, Toscano, Cortini, and Gay, " Contribution to the anthropology of the hand of degenerates: finger-nails, digital marks."

De Blasio, "Right-handedness in Neapolitan thieves." Zuccarelli, " Frequency of the Wormian fossa."

Criminal Psychology and Psycho-pathology. — The Congress turned its attention mainly to the subject of collective criminal psychology.

Sighele, in a paper on " Collective crime," summed up the theories fully developed in his books: " The Criminal Couple," " Sectarian Delinquency," " Mob Crimes," and " Positive Theory of Complicity."[1] He considers suggestion as being at the bottom of collective crime, from that committed by two, the criminal couple composed of the active and the passive — the incubus and the succubus of the ancient enchantments — to the most complicated social aggregation: the sect and the

[1] *La coppia criminale*, second edition, Turin, 1897. — *La delinquenza settaria*, Milan, 1897. — *I delitti della folla*, second edition, Turin, 1902. — *La teoria positiva della complicità*, Turin, 1894.

mob, in which impersonality, unconsciousness, and mental minority, even in a mass of selected persons, reach their limit.

Carrara, in order to fill a gap left by Sighele, spoke of " The criminal couple and the principal and accessory in crimes of blood."

Bouman reported " An important case of psychic infection," which had occurred in Aspellern (Holland), a region where religious questions are being revived. A man suffering an abnormal hallucination expresses delirious ideas of condemnation against all those who approach him. One of his brothers is immediately infected; and, one day, excited by the caresses of a girl who had come to him for exorcism, kills a servant whom he thought had shown her little respect, mutilates the corpse, and tramples upon it. Twenty-seven persons, acting by suggestion, affirm under oath that the victim fell struck by divine fire.

Andreotti read a paper on the " Psychology of provoked crime."

On the whole, the Congress appeared little favorable to the doctrines of modern collective psychology.

In his paper on " Some observations concerning the psychology of crowds," Jelgersma criticized the mystical conception of the soul of crowds, showing how it must be understood in order to free it from that defect.

Steinmetz and Benedikt criticized the abuse of the conception of suggestion.

Dechterew answered with other objections.

Sighele and Carrara undertook a reply.

Benedikt presented the only paper on individual criminal psychology, entitled " A fundamental psychological formula and its relations to criminology." Let M stand for each manifestation of the life of an organism; N for the congenital qualities; E for the evolution (including all the influence of education, environment, climate, vicissitudes of life, infirmities, etc.); O for the occasional irritations which each manifestation of life requires, and we shall have the following formula:

$$M = (\pm N, \pm N', \pm E \pm O).$$

Portigliotti read a report on " Tattooing as a psychologic trait."

Miss Delfine Poppée read a paper on " The handwriting of criminals," which gave rise to a discussion on graphology.

In reference to psycho-pathology, the Congress busied itself mainly with the relations between degradation and criminality and with the proper measures against the insane criminal.

Gina Lombroso reported " Two clinical cases of acquired criminality in old age."

Ferri referred to another case.

Frigerio reported four other clinical cases, by which he wished to demonstrate that we ought to reduce the penal responsibility of degenerate criminals without delirium.

Antonini brought forward a communication on " Degeneration and criminality among people affected with pellagra."

A discussion on degeneration followed. Henri Martin, one of Lacassagne's followers, remarked appropriately that if we say with the Italians that criminality is sometimes the product of envirenment and at other times the product of degeneration, we do not depart from the epoch of Morel.

Crocq, Baer, Albanel, Dechterew, and Ferri took part in the discussion.

Lewis and Kurella also referred in their papers to two problems of criminal psycho-pathology. The former spoke on " The influence of psychopathy on the production of crime "; and the latter on " Criminal degeneration as a symptom of the variability of the type."

The following important papers were sent to the Congress on the subject of criminal insanity:

Dedichen, " What measures shall we adopt concerning criminals declared insane by the experts, when their crimes are not considered sufficiently dangerous as to compel us to send them to insane asylums? "

Meijer, " Assistance for criminal lunatics."

Deknatel, " Trial and treatment of border-cases in civil and military communities."

Näcke, " What is the best method of disposing of criminal lunatics? "

Antonini, " Casuistry of criminal insanity."

Renda and Squillace, " Criminal madness in Calabria."

Zuccarelli, " An epileptoid mental invalid who from a suicidal impulse experiences an homicidal one, and is acquitted by the Tribunal of Chieti, Abbruzzi."

The question was somewhat neglected for lack of time. The Congress only discussed Dedichen's paper, in which he suggests a mining colony in Norway; and that of Meijer, who prefers the Prussian system of sanitariums connected with prisons. Antonini, on the other hand, advocated separate sections in criminal asylums.

Legal and administrative applications of criminal anthropology. — This very important question was also neglected by the Congress.

The following papers were read:

Ferri, " The symbiosis of crime."

Dorado Montero, " Is punishment, properly speaking, compatible with the data of criminal anthropology and sociology? "

Gaukler, " The necessity of separating in the penal system the measures which aim to punish the criminal and those which aim to correct him, and of putting at the disposal of the judge distinct penal measures, some for punishment and others for correction."

Clark Bell, " Indeterminate sentence in New York."

Zuccarelli " Necessity and means of preventing the reproduction of individuals in a serious state of degeneration."

Morel, " Prophylaxis and treatment of relapsed criminals."

Miss Robinovitch, " The duty of the State in reference to the origin and prevention of crime."

Cutrera, " Preventive measures against crime in Italy."

Moteri, " Criminal anthropology in its legal applications."

Franchi, " Penal procedure and criminal anthropology."

Lacassagne and Martin, " Positive and irrefutable results produced by criminal anthropology in the enactment and application of laws."

Ferri spoke on the symbiosis of crime, or rather on how should the criminal be utilized in cultured society, when the diffusion of scientific theories on the natural and social genesis of crime allow a state of peace between criminals and judges.

After that Gauckler's paper was discussed. It is impossible to support a double entry system of criminology, that is, half corrective and half punitive. Undoubtedly, some members of the Congress accepted it as a matter of course.

Van Hamel lamented the absence of Dorado, whose paper aimed at pointing that out.

Miss Robinovitch's paper showed a more modern spirit than Gaukler's. She presents as model the famous Elmira Reformatory of New York, and ends by declaring that in sociology as in medicine the principle of prophylaxis is bound to win.

Due to the absence of the authors, the Congress did not discuss the other papers, among which were some as interesting as that of Bruno Franchi, " Criminal procedure in relation to criminal anthropology."

Criminal sociology. — The social causes of crime were expounded by Tarde, Denis, Colajanni, and Veroni.

The first sent a paper on " The economical causes of criminality."

The second and the third on " Socialism and criminality."

The fourth on " Delinquency among the upper social classes."

In the absence of all, only Colajanni's conclusions were read, which are the following: 1. Even if not admitting that socialistic propaganda and socialism cause a diminution of criminality, it is certain, however, that they do not increase it; 2. Criminality varies according to social conditions; 3. Socialistic ideals contribute in the measure of their realization to a decrease of crime, without determining the inverse order of crimes against the person and against property, which would condemn humanity to despair of its moral reform.

Comparative ethnography. — Steinmetz, who was present at the Congress, had sent a well documented study on the relations between criminal anthropology and ethnography, which was not discussed.

Among other papers sent to the Congress were the following:

Turco, " Delinquency in Calabria."

Schiatarella, " The delinquency of the Hebrew Prophets."

Sutherland, " The disappearance of the convicts in Australian society."

Special questions. — The notion of crime, juvenile delinquency, senile delinquency, political crimes, alcoholism, sexuality, criminals in art.

Piepers discussed " The notion of crime from the point of view of evolution."

Bombarda brought forward a communication on " Crime among animals," recommending systematic observations that may lead to a true biological animal history.

The following works on juvenile delinquency were presented to the Congress:

Baer, " Juvenile murderers."

Garnier, " Juvenile criminality."

Carrara and Murgia, " The delinquency of the young and its preventive measures."

De Sanctis, Tosanio, Cortini, and Gay, " Physical, physiological, and psychological factors in the conduct of children."

Arie de Jory, " False testimony of children."

Bérillon, " The pedagogical dispensary of Paris."

Struelness, " Some considerations on criminal childhood, and some measures adopted in Belgium for the prevention of its development."

Various speakers referred to the constant growth of crime among the young. For instance, according to Dr. Garnier, murder in France is six times more frequent among minors than among adults.

Bérillon, the advocate of hypnotism, spoke of its application to the education of vicious and degenerate children.

After juvenile delinquency the question of senile delinquency was taken up in the way of contrast and analogy.

Wellenbergh summed up his conclusions on " Senile delinquency," stating that the mental changes caused by age deserve particular attention by legislation. In fact, the latter ought to set senility at the age of seventy-two, and order a special procedure for the old without criminal record, who might not have offended until then.

The Congress announced two communications on political crime: one by Niceforo on " The utility and necessity of political crime "; and the other by De Bella on " The high-priests of criminal anthropology." The absence of the authors prevented their discussion.

The relation between alcoholism and criminality was discussed in the following papers:

Legrain, " Relapsed drunkards in the presence of the law."

Garnier, " Alcoholism and criminality."

Luzenberger, " Alcoholism in Italy."

Only Legrain read his paper.

Furthermore, Eula spoke on the causes of frustrated psychopathic heredity in some drunkards of his country.

The subject of sexuality was one of the novelties of the Congress. As always, some were scandalized and spoke of suppressing it. But they were unsuccessful and Aletrino was able to read his paper on " The social condition of sexual perverts." Moll and Viazzi sent also papers, the former on " Sexual perversion," the latter on " The legal defense of female chastity."

Finally, on the subject of criminal anthropology in art, Teschich presented a work entitled " Criminal types according to Dostoyewsky."

The Congress passed the following resolutions:

On the proposition of Miss Robinovitch, it was resolved: " That the 5th International Congress of Criminal Anthropology, meeting at Amsterdam, expresses its grief for the attempt on McKinley's life and the consequences that may result, and affirms the necessity of continuing the scientific investigations of methods to fight crime and put an end to its causes, moved only by a desire of attaining a higher appreciation of humanitarian ideas and a more efficacious and equitable social defense."

On the proposition of Doctor E. Martin, it was resolved: " That in the opinion of the 5th International Congress of Criminal Anthropology, the biological examination of the guilty ought to be added to the ordinances on all criminal matters."

On the proposition of Mr. Albanel, it was resolved: " That the Congress is of opinion that, in every country, juvenile delinquents be examined by a competent physician, preferably before coming to trial, and that those who give signs of degeneration be placed in a medico-pedagogical institution for their mental and moral reform."

On the proposition of Dr. Garnier, read by Dr. Boncour, it was resolved: " That the Congress advocate the monopoly of the production and the sale of alcohol in order to prevent the increase of criminality."

The 6th Congress was held at Turin, beginning on the 28th of April, 1906.

The programme appeared in a new form. The following topics were to be discussed.

1. The treatment of juvenile delinquency in criminal law and in penitentiary discipline, according to the principles of criminal anthropology;

2. The treatment of female delinquency;

3. The relations between economical conditions and criminality;

4. Equivalents between criminality and the various forms of sexual psychopathies;

5. Criminal anthropology in the scientific organization of the police;

6. The psychological value of the witness;

7. Prophylaxis and therapeutics of crime;

8. Institutions for life detention of criminals declared responsible through mental defect.

Around these questions were to be grouped all the free communications that might be presented.

The discussion of all these topics fills a large volume of more than 600 pages with fine illustrations. We will give an account of its contents, excluding the memoirs which do not deal directly with criminology, even when they treat of auxiliary sciences as general anthropology (Chio, " The blood of the orang-outang has more affinity with that of man than with that of non-anthropoid apes "; J. Marro, " Normal and pathologic anatomy of the pituitary body, anomalies of the zygomatic arch, two new arrangements of the internal orbital walls, the cocygeal foveola "; Niceforo, " The anthropology of the poor "; Robinovitch, " The genesis of genius and sex "; Viola, " Anthropometry as a basis of classification for individual constitutions "), psychology (Aly Belfadel, " Mental tests of touch, taste, and smell "; Audenino, " Right-handedness, left-handedness, and ambidexterity "; Bianchi, " The language zone and the frontal lobules as organs of thought and personality "), psycho-pathology (Audenino, " Consciousness in epileptic fits, skull and cerebrum of an idiot "; Burzio, " Investigations of cretinism "; Frassetto " Diagnosis and significance of degenerative characteristics "; J. Marro, " Parietal division in the idiots, the medical occipital fossa in the insane "; Tenchini, " The morphology of the thyroid glands in the insane "), and medical jurisprudence (Clark Bell, " The use of poisons in embalming "; Vicarelli, " Common methods in criminal abortions ").

Omitting the above, the works that will engage our attention fall into three groups:

1. Anthropology.
2. Sociology.
3. Penology.

Some works being too descriptive cannot be summarized. Of such we will mention: Antonini and Zanon, " Anthropology of the insane and the criminals of Friuli "; Audenino, " Unilateral mimic pareses in the normal, the insane, and the criminals "; Bellini, " Anthropological notes on a melancholic murderer "; Cherie-Lignière, " Further remarks on the sources of the second branchial arch in normal adults, the insane, and the criminals "; Clark Bell and Eckels, " A case of homicide by chloroform "; Falciola, " Contribution to the experimental method in the legal-medical study of aliena- tions "; Frigerio, " Cases of criminal sexuality "; Gualino, " The *prominentia squamae occipitalis* in the normal, the crimi- nal, and the insane"; Lattes, "Contribution to the study of the cerebrum of the female offender "; Levi Deveali, " Comparison of criminals' handwriting with that of the insane "; Mar- gnani, " The skeleton of a pseudo-political insane criminal "; J. Marro, " The malar division in the criminals and the in- sane, cranial variations in the insane, division of their nasal bone "; Panseri, " Three skulls of criminals "; Pighini, " Crime in precocious dementia "; Roncoroni, " Histo-morphological anomalies in epileptics and criminals "; Tovo, " The transverse palatine suture in criminals."

Of the remaining works we shall begin with Sommer's " The application of new methods of investigation in criminal anthropology." He claims that the psychological methods of investigation employed thus far must be perfected pro- gressively according to the principles and the development of experimental psychology (motor and graphic methods, ob- jective judgments of valuation, association of ideas, time of reaction). Thus it will be possible to reconstruct the epilep- toid type, so important in criminology, especially in violent and sexual crimes. By this consideration of epilepsy, Sommer is a Lombrosian, a rare example in Germany, where, in gen- eral, they reject the equality between epilepsy and criminality, contrary to what is found in Italy. But, even granting this premise, *that all epileptics and born criminals do not present the type as such*, Audenino answers this question which is asked as an objection to the Italian doctrines. In his opinion, we must distinguish between epileptics and born criminals

properly speaking and those who have become so in consequence of illness, intoxication, or traumatism. Certainly, the
latter cannot show the exterior somatic type of their class;
but, since the author himself admits that among those of the
first class there are individuals who do not show it, the question remains as unsolved as before. Del Greco, freer from Lombrosian influence, presents a formula of the *criminal character*.
Its main traits are combativeness and rebellion, dominating
his social sentiments. Levi writes sympathetically in his
" Observations on the philosophical range of the Lombrosian
theory."

More important than all these generalizations, still so obscure, are some studies on certain classes of criminals and
determined forms of criminality. Perhaps the most interesting is Marro's " The psychic hyperaesthesia of homicide."

The painstaking teacher believes that the determining
cerebral condition of the murderer is essentially a psychic
hyperaesthesia, now morbid now physiologic, which renders
some subjects so sensitive to the impressions touching their
personality that it is impossible for them to tolerate them
without a sudden and violent reaction against the person from
whom they proceed. The unfolding of puberty, the effect of
heat and alcoholic intoxication mainly favor so dangerous an
hyperaesthesia.

Treves' attention is called to a special form which crime
takes occasionally, and proposes to call it " labyrinthic or
paranoeidal crime." Its morbid nature is so complex and
inextricable, that the criminal himself cannot explain it, or
the reasons he gives are so strange, absurd, and paradoxical,
that the confession loses all resemblance to truth.

The same writer discusses in another paper " The criminality of emotional geniuses," dealing especially with Ben-
venuto Cellini. The lamented Angiolella discusses the same

question in " Genius and criminality." The three cases which
he studies are Cellini, Aretini, and Mirabeau.

Judge Ryckère summarizes his studies on " The criminality
of female servants," which, in his opinion, is distinguished by
its simple, brutal, unimaginative, misoneistic, monotonous
character, like the minds that produce it. The two military
physicians, Colonel Ferrero and Lieutenant Consiglio, are
the authors of a well documented monograph on professional
criminality, entitled " Military criminology." Then come
two communications on juvenile delinquency, one by Miss
Faggiani, " Considerations on juvenile delinquency "; the
other by the Spanish professor of medical jurisprudence,
Valenti, " Precocity in criminality." Both make no new contribution.

Under the title " Simulators," Charpentier relates three
good cases, the last being of a twenty-two year old degenerate female thief who simulates kleptomania. In conclusion, he admits the difficulty of finding a convenient treatment for these cases.

Another group of communications do not deal exactly
with criminals, but with prostitutes and sexual perverts. Ascarelli's " Digital prints in prostitutes " shows,
as the most important conclusion, that the anomalous forms
of the line texture of the tip of the fingers are more frequent
in prostitutes than in normal women, and that the more
primitive the drawing the more accentuated is the difference.
Gualino treats of the means of detecting homosexuals. Finally,
Lombroso traces a parallel between homosexuality and congenital criminality. This parallel, sufficiently superficial,
shows that in childhood there is a transitory criminality even
in those who will be later normal beings, as well as a kind of
transitory homosexuality, a moral hermaphrodism, even in those
who will be normal sexual beings; that as there are true

born criminals and occasional criminaloids, so there are born and occasional perverts; that there exists a type of sexual pervert as there is of born criminal, and that it will surely betray itself occasionally; and, finally, that the ætiology of both phenomena is analogous if not identical.

Then come the works on criminal sociology, that is, those that treat of criminality and not of individual criminals.

First we will mention Roos' " Investigations on the causes of the increase of thefts in winter and of crimes against the person in summer." Is the phenomenon due to physical or to social causes? To explain the frequency of thefts in winter, the length of the nights has been adduced as an important factor; while for the increase in crimes of blood in summer the rise in temperature or the organism's effort of adaptation to the summer heat has been proposed (Corre). But, since in the case of thefts we cannot overlook the increase of the needs and misery of winter, and, in crimes of blood, the greater contact which takes place among peoples in summer, it follows that in both groups of crimes there intervene both classes of factors, without our being able to define exactly their respective rôles.

" The fascination of criminality," which forms the topic of Masini's study, points out the suggestive influence which great criminals and great crimes have upon the masses, to the point of producing complete imitations.

Tovo and Rota discuss a " Law of criminal development," according to which criminality, as it passes from light forms to serious ones, shows proportionally slower and more uniform variations; for instance, in the number of murders there is less variability than in that of homicides, and in the number of robberies less than in that of small thefts, etc.

Another group of communications refer to local criminality in determined regions. Angiolella investigates " The ethnical

and psychologic origins of the *Camorra* and of highway robbery "; Slingenberg speaks of " Criminality in relation to class
struggle in the Lower Countries." Of the same nature is
Herz' communication on " Criminality and the working
classes," referring to the present conditions in Austria. In
general, according to him, the increase in the modern trade
agitation causes an increase of criminality among working
men; but, contrary to the observation made by Niceforo some
years before, he claims that the increase of industrial activity
among women does not involve an increase of criminality
peculiar to the sex, even though it may lead to the dissolution
of the family and to laxity among young people. Minovici's
paper treats of " The female offender in Roumania."

Penology follows. Lombroso's daughter, Mrs. Gina Ferrero, speaking of the rôle played by " Pity in Justice," asks that
the latter be complemented by the former as an expression and
a synthesis of the entire complicated labor of the human mind,
through which we may see and foresee the consequences
which a painful event can have in the life of men.

The sentimental aspect is complemented by the scientific
aspect presented by Mount Bleyer in his " Treatment of
criminals." " To instruct ignorant criminals, to reform the
corrigible, to prevent the incurable from offending, are the
duties which the State must fulfil with loyalty and zeal. When
science, constantly applied by a prolonged number of generations, will have removed the causes of crime by repressing the
too rapid growth of population, by respecting the laws of
heredity, by reorganizing the family and social life and scientifically instructing the individual as a member of the community, then the criminal type will disappear or will remain
only as an historical record."

Happy optimism! Nevertheless, " Æthoiatry, science and
art of reforming minor and adult delinquents," to which Dati

devotes a short note, does not fail. Brück-Faber treats of
" Neuro-electricity in the service of penitentiary work."
For incorrigibles, who are rebellious to corrective action, it
is necessary to employ an exogenous action sufficient to produce useful results in spite of and without the intervention of
the criminal's will. This action must aim at the cerebral
organs, the instrument of psychic functions, and through the
neuro-electrical medium of a suggester.

Two criminal groups deserve special attention: the insane
and the minors. For the first we have: Antonini's " The law
on insane asylums in Italy and the criminal insane "; Del
Greco's " The moral treatment of the criminal insane ";
and Garofalo's " The establishment of asylums for the perpetual confinement of certain criminals declared irresponsible."
For the second we have: Brück-Faber's " Treatment for
young criminals in the Grand Duchy of Luxemburg "; Kahn's
"Treatment of young criminals in criminal law and in the penitentiary discipline, according to the principles of criminal
anthropology "; that of Van Hamel on the same subject; and
Albanel's " Practical organization of juvenile criminal prophylaxis."   Kahn's communication is conspicuous for the
eleven clinical cases of young criminals he discusses, as that of
the fourteen year old girl who writes verses in praise of
the *apaches* and of the bloody dagger! Van Hamel's communication is also remarkable for the precision of his conclusions
in favor of the scientific treatment of young criminals, a treatment which " can and must be " a prototype of that employed
for adult offenders.

Finally, the volume does not lack studies on criminal procedure.

In reference to general scientific prosecution, Niceforo has
a paper on " The police," and Ottolenghi one on " Criminal
anthropology and the scientific organization of the police."

The identification of criminals is discussed in Gasti's " Dactyloscopic identification and the system of classification in Italy," in Locard's " The present services of identification and the international catalogue," and in two communications by Reiss on the " Word portrait." Reiss has also a third communication on " Some new applications of photography in judiciary investigations." The value of testimonial evidence, a delicate question, is discussed in Claparède's " Collective experiments on testimony and cross-examination," in Mariani's observations on " The psychology of witnesses," and in Brusa's " The psychological value of testimony." President Maynard discusses the " Modern judge," claiming that he ought to be the defender of equitable justice against juridical justice, a true " social plague."

The Congress passed the following resolution: In reference to the treatment of the so-called incorrigibles, resolved " that, in order to protect society against dangerous abnormal individuals, it be necessary to place them in a special asylum, where no other severities be employed than those necessary for vigilance and discipline.

" This confinement will be indeterminate; but there will be a provision for freedom when the temperament or the instincts of the criminal have changed to such a degree that no doubt remains of his moral reform.

" The regulating measures which set forth that criminals acquitted on account of insanity be kept in separate wards in the asylums, will be modified so as to substitute for the juridical criterion of acquittal the clinical criterion of the diagnosis of the form of criminality."

As for the penal treatment applicable to minors, the Congress adopted the following conclusions:

1. In order to prevent and fight juvenile delinquency, it is necessary to adopt penal and penitentiary prophylactic meas-

ures, based upon educative principle.

2. The prophylactic measures recommended are:

a. Supervision in the family, the school, and the shop;

b. The judicial deprivation of parental power;

c. The placing of children in honorable families, preferably outside the city;

d. The establishment of special houses of detention.

3. As for the penal and penitentiary treatment, the traditional distinction of a fixed classification of penalties must be abandoned, and the Judge must be given the power to choose, with unlimited freedom and according to the exigencies of the individual case, from a series of measures modelled in their general features upon domestic discipline. They should consist in:

a. Repression;

b. Small fines paid by the culprit himself out of his own wages;

c. Short detention in an educational house of discipline;

d. Conditional sentence;

e. Placing the offenders at the disposal of the Government for their systematic and professional education in a State or private institution till they reach majority, or placing them in families inspected by the State with conditional freedom as a test measure.

4. Every measure concerning young criminals or near criminals must be necessarily preceded by a medico-psychological examination of the individual and information concerning his ancestors. In the course of the treatment, the authority of the psychologic physician must be thoroughly recognized in order that he may prescribe, if necessary, a distinct medico-pedagogical treatment, especially in the case of undeveloped children.

5. Both in theory and in practice the treatment of young

criminals must serve as a prototype for the treatment of adults.

6. It is desirable that the prosecution of the young receive the least publicity possible.

On the subject of the investigation of crime, the Congress expressed the desire that " Governments should collect the objects confiscated from criminals in a museum for the progress of legal studies and of the scientific investigation of crime."

On Lombroso's proposition, the Congress resolved " that the magistrates, lawyers, and other judiciary officials acquire a medico-psychiatric education that may enable them to know in what cases competent physicians ought to be summoned in order to avoid judicial errors."

The resolution ends by the announcement " that in the next Congress the following question will be taken up as the order of the day: To determine what studies must be taken up by committing magistrates and police officers so that they may impart in the future a justice more in accordance with the dictates of criminal anthropology."

3. CRIMINOLOGY IN SPAIN AND IN SPANISH AMERICA.
A. Spain.
Section 23. (a) Beginnings.

On account of its western location and scientific seclusion, the modern ideas of criminology were late in reaching Spain.

We find a few popular treatises in juridical and social reviews; but this expository presentation is not faithfully and systematically carried out until the publication of Dorado's " Criminal Anthropology in Italy," [1] written on the ground.

After that, the expository and popular presentation of the subject continues uninterruptedly. Among the publications of this kind, excels Ruiz' " Criminal Anthropology," [2] and

[1] La antropología criminal en Italia, Madrid, 1889.
[2] Martinez Ruiz, La sociología criminal, Madrid, 1889.

notably the first part of the work, in which he treats of the growth and sources of the new science.

Section 24.   (b) Contributions.

Spread of criminality. — It seems that Spain was one of the first countries to take a census of its criminality; for—according to a writer [1] — " in a decree of January 4th, 1729, Philip V. charged all tribunals in the capital and elsewhere to report through his Council all pending and disposed of cases. Charles IV., in 1792, sanctioned the practice of drawing up annual summaries of the civil and criminal business dispatched the previous year. The famous Cadiz Constitution, article eleven, refers to this practice. . . .

" In spite of all these decrees," the writer continues, " the service of criminal statistics did not begin, even partially, until 1884, when it was only possible to present them for the years 1843, 1859, 1860, 1861, and 1862. . . . [2] From 1882, the work continues regularly. . . ."

It must be added that the plan of the work was influenced more by bureaucratic than scientific aims; and we are justified in suspecting even the scrupulousness of its process.

The first *Criminal Statistics* collected by the Department of Justice (1838, 1843, 1859, 1860, etc.) are preceded by a ministerial report, a practice which, from 1882, is not renewed until 1900, with the publication of a report by Minister Montilla. This report is preceded by a lengthy summary of the spread of criminality in Spain, and is based on official documents.

These documents form a necessary basis for the studies that follow. But, the studies on the spread of criminality in Spain are few and deficient.

[1] D. Pazos, *Reseña de la organización y trabajos de la Estadística oficial en España;* in the Madrid review *La Administración,* 1898.

[2] Pazos forgets the criminal statistics for 1838.

The seventh volume of the " Memoirs of the Royal Academy of Moral and Political Sciences " [1] contains a few pages headed by the following suggestive caption: " *Criminality in Spain* from 1848 to the present day. To determine the causes for the increase or decrease of criminality, taking into account the influence of the character and customs of the inhabitants of each region, their industry, their degree of education and culture, their political institutions, and their laws, especially those relating to the administration of justice in criminal matters." These are the records of a discussion held in the Academy during 1887, 1888. The men who took part were: Colmeiro, Figuerola, and the Marquis de Reinosa y Cos Gayón. The debate proved of tiresome insignificance. The hopes which the above caption suggested were defeated.

After that time, the works that can be cited are:

An arid and insignificant memoir by Jimeno Agius, entitled " Criminality in Spain." [2]

A few pages and drawings in C. Silió y Cortes' " The Crisis of Criminal Law " [3] and " Criminality in Spain " [4] by the same author.

A study by Dorado on " Criminality in Spain during the period of regency (1885–1902)," [5] was inserted later in his " Criminology and Penology." [6] Undoubtedly, this work is much superior to those that preceded; only, we must discard Dorado's personal equation, his tendency to muddle up matters.

[1] *Memorias de la Real Academia de Ciencias Morales y Políticas.*

[2] *La criminalidad en España;* in the *Rivista de España,* vol. CVI and CVII, 1885.

[3] *La crisis del derecho penal,* Madrid (no date).

[4] *La criminalità nella Spagna;* published in *La scuola positiva,* vol. II, 1891.

[5] *La criminalidad en España en el período de la regencia* (1885 *to* 1902); published in *Nuestro Tiempo,* May, 1902.

[6] *De Criminalogía y Penología,* Madrid, 1906.

Finally, we must add the works of some foreigners, who have made valuable contributions to the study of criminality in Spain. Among these are the pages in Ferri's " Criminal Sociology " [1] and " Homicide in Criminal Anthropology" ; [2] those in E. Tarnowsky's " The spread of Criminality in Western Europe"; [3] and, finally, Augusto Bosco's latest work, " Criminality in various countries of Europe," [4] in which he devotes an entire chapter to Spain.

The period studied is between 1883 and 1899.

Bosco remarks, above all, that delinquency in general, including minor offenses, has not met with a considerable increase; on the contrary, it remains stationary, at least as far as crimes are concerned.

Crimes in Spain preserve their primitive character and are little susceptible to influences which in other countries modify their manifestations. The frequency of crimes against the person, especially homicides, continues to be one of the main features of Spanish criminality; and although the number of persons convicted of homicide has not increased, Spain still remains one of the countries in which this crime is more frequent. Infanticide, on the other hand, numbers few cases. A decrease in wounding is noticeable, but it has not continued in later years. However that may be, says Bosco, the physical, ethnical, economical, and historical conditions, emphasize, as a psychological characteristic of the Spaniards, a few moral traits, which, if on one hand constitute their dignity, on the other, lead them to crimes against the person.

Insult and calumny seem on the decline, although

---

[1] *Sociologia criminale;* fourth edition, Turin, 1900.

[2] *Omicidio nell'Antropologia criminale*, Turin, 1895.

[3] *The spread of criminality in western Europe;* published in the *Review of the Department of Justice*, Saint Petersburg, 1899.

[4] *La delinquenza in vari Stati di Europa*, Rome, 1903.

statistics do not give us definite information on the subject, nor is it possible to well estimate the causes of the phenomenon.

Assaults and insults against authority and public function-aries increased until 1908; but they diminished soon after, as if to the stimulus of rebellion there was opposed a traditional resignation to domination.

As for crimes against honor we may suspect that it is not customary to recur to criminal justice, so few and insignificant are the data at hand.

Of the crimes against property, thefts and robberies are the most frequent, while frauds and swindles are the less nu-merous. Professional criminality is not wanting in the cities, nor are thefts in the country. The distress among the people, grown worse in late years, stimulates crimes against property, although conditions in Spain prevent their increase. The slow growth of bartering and trade, the slow introduction of new methods of commerce and credit, explain the relatively small number of convictions for swindling, bankruptcy, and falsification.

In short — apart from the combined circumstances which do not enable statistics to state the true situation — Spain has, in general, a constant criminality of grave and violent nature, and a minimum one of minor offenses, which swell the statistics of the most civilized nations. Only in those provinces where the growth of industry introduces new habits of life, we find statistics analogous to those of other European countries.

This, then, is the general condition of criminality in the country.

Now, we will point out the works that treat of some specific aspects of criminality.

The author of this book has made a study of the " Criminology of the Crimes of Blood in Spain."[1] Statistics show that criminality of blood leads all other forms in intensity. Below is a table giving the ratio of homicides of all degrees for every million inhabitants:

Mexico	1,000[2]
Chile	340
Argentine Republic (maximum in the State of Tucuman)	230
United States of America	120[3]
Italy	95.1 to 98
Spain	74.1 to 77
Hungary	74.1 to 77
Roumania	38.1 to 47
Portugal	23.1 to 26
Ireland	23.1 to 26
Austria	23.1 to 26
France	14.1 to 17
Belgium	14.1 to 17
Switzerland	14.1 to 17
Russia	14.1 to 17
Denmark	14.1 to 17
Sweden	11.1 to 14
Germany	3.1 to 11
England and Scotland	5.1 to 3
Holland	5.1 to 3

This intensity affects mainly the impulsive forms of the crime; but it is distributed with extraordinary irregularity over the country: from a maximum of 17.60 crimes of blood for every 100,000 inhabitants in Logroño to a minimum of 1.60 in Orense. The irregularity is generally due to racial distribution. Thus, in the Northwestern provinces of Lugo and Oviedo, where the brachycephalic (eurasian) type prevails, there is a minimum intensity of crimes of blood; while in the

[1] *Criminalogía de los delitos de sangre en España*, Madrid, 1906.

[2] These figures must be lowered to 180, according to the Mexican criminalist C. Roumagnac (cf. our study " El homicidio en America," in the volume " Figuras delinquentes," Madrid, 1909).

[3] Bosco: *L'omicidio negli Stati Uniti d'America;* in the *Bulletin de l'Institut internationale de Statistique,* vol. X, 1897.

regions mainly inhabited by dolichocephalics (eurafricans), including the upper plateau of Castile, the lower Ebro, the eastern slope and the elevation of Andalusia, there is a maximum intensity, especially in the second and last places.

But, what is the cause of this distinct criminal disposition of races?

In order to answer this question we must consider the physical and social environments which mould ethnical stocks.

The influence of culture and of the density of population is sufficiently noticeable in the distribution of criminality; but, what determines it better are the natural factors, like temperature and humidity.

Taking humidity, for instance, whose influence can be more easily detected, we find that the rainy Asturias and a portion of the Basque provinces and the very rainy Galicia and another portion of the Basque provinces experience the minimum intensity of criminality of blood; while in the drier zones (province of Almería) the contrary takes place. The reverse relation between humidity and criminality of blood can offer no better example than the great intensity found in the province of Logroño, which belongs to a zone of normal humidity, and which preserves in sufficient purity the ancient impulsive and violent Iberian race. It seems, therefore, that with the humid and sedative environment of the Atlantic climate, the race loses its tendency to violence; while the contrary takes place in the dry environments of bright sunshine.

The influence of the winds — if it could be studied — might also explain some features in the distribution of this form of criminality.

The rôle which minors play in the criminality of the country has been studied by E. Cuello Calón in his " Child and Juvenile

Criminality in certain Countries." [1] He makes the following observations:

1. The decrease of this form of criminality both in quantity and in gravity (a strange phenomenon of contrast with what happens in other countries, where the increase is so continuous, constant, and noticeable, that Niceforo considers it one of the features of modern criminality); [2]

2. A possible increase of crimes which imply cunning;

3. Predominance of crimes against property: thefts in preference to other forms;

4. The high figures of convictions for wounding, second only to that for thefts;

5. The diffusion of crimes against property in thickly populated cities, especially of those not accompanied by force, and the almost absolute absence of violent crimes.

There are few monographs dealing with territorial, provincial, or local criminality. M. Jimeno Azcárate is the author of one entitled " Criminality in Asturias," [3] written with a certain apparatus extremely modern (maps, diagrams, tables of statistics), but full of commonplace repetitions. Yet, it would be desirable to have more such monographs dealing with local criminality.

The author of this book, in collaboration with Llanas Aguilaniedo, has discussed criminality in the capital in "Low Life in Madrid." [4] The work belongs to the large body of writings on dangerous classes in cities, to which contributions have been made by Niceforo, Sighele, Caggiano, Cutrera, De Blasio, Alonghi, Cuidera. M. Gil Maestre, the author of " Criminality in Barcelona and

[1] *La criminalidad infantil y juvenil en algunos paises;* in the *Revista general de Legislación y Jurisprudencia,* vol. CVIII, 1906.

[2] *La transformación del delito en la sociedad moderna,* Madrid, 1902.

[3] *La criminalidad en Asturias,* Oviedo, 1900.

[4] *La mala vida en Madrid,* Madrid, 1901.

other great centers," [1] had already preceded the author by his " Criminals of Madrid." [2]   In all these works, little use is made of the statistical method, which has been entirely subordinated to the psychological point of view.

The phenomenon of moral degeneration, limited to a definite surrounding, has been fully considered in " Low Life in Madrid."

The authors consider the man who has broken away from social discipline and from his class, the so-called *golfo* (outlaw) among us, as the protoplasm of criminal life. A product of vagabond temperament, of early neglect and social decadence, the *golfo* lives as a parasite of the social organism, devoting himself to theft, prostitution, and beggary. We find in him the aptitude and, at times, even the practice of these three phases of life, which he combines according to caprice or convenience.

Certain individuals of an extreme erratic and restless nature remain indefinitely in this state; but oftener, with the approach of puberty, the *golfos* evolve into a more differentiated state.

Thus it happens that, adopting as a definite occupation one of the said modes of life and practicing it habitually, they become identified with delinquency, prostitution, or criminality, producing the delinquents, the prostitutes, or the beggars.

This state is noticeable by the loss of a number of erratic tendencies, characteristic of the *golfo*. When they become settled in any of these differentiated states, they experience also a series of changes and transformations related to the adaptation to the new mode of life; that is, they lose the

---

[1] *La criminalidad en Barcelona y en las grandes poblaciones*, Barcelona, 1886.

[2] *Los malhechores de Madrid*, Gerona, 1889.

characteristics which may hinder them and develop those
that may prove useful. Undoubtedly, the differentiation
is never so complete as to atrophy altogether the primary
aptitudes for every kind of parasitism. Then, there appears
what is called by naturalists the phenomenon of *mimicry*,
by means of which, obeying the instinct of preservation,
biological species abandon or hide the characteristics for
which they are persecuted and imitate others in order to
mask themselves. Therefore criminal life often imitates the
tolerated social types.

The differentiation of species is determined by various
factors. Now it is heredity or education that causes children
to follow the occupation of their parents; now it is temperament that leads the more impulsive to criminal life and
leaves the weak of body and mind to a life of pauperism; at
times, it is the sex that leads women to prostitution and men
to crime; at other times, it is the union of exterior circumstances, which, arriving at the opportune time, allow an easy
exploitation.

Society reacts against these forms of delinquency in different
ways; hence the different place which it assigns to its parasites.
The delinquent whose attack is keenly felt is persecuted; the
beggar is tolerated through confused reasons of superstitious
pity; and finally, with the prostitute society makes an exchange of service: *do ut facies*.

We believe, therefore, that in relation to the social organism
the characterization of each parasitical function is as follows:

> Criminals   = enemies;
> Beggars   = guests;
> Prostitution = mutualism, symbiosis.

Nevertheless, in spite of his hostility toward us, the criminal
is the superior type in low life. The struggle in which he is

obliged to live has endowed him with a capital of energy and activity which is not to be seen in the prostitute and in the beggar.

The last two form the inferior class in low life. Two important facts lead us to this belief. In the first place, of the different classes in low life, the weakest and the most useless are those who tend to pauperism; and in the second place, when age or disease determine in criminals and prostitutes a regressive evolution, both of them break down and fall back on pauperism, the last refuge of parasitical life.

The general theory is followed by monographs on delinquency, prostitution, and pauperism, the last two showing marked deficiency of treatment.

The local delinquent types, which the authors have called " criminal fauna of Madrid," are classified into genera, species, and varieties.

Two genera of delinquency give rise to five species. One, in which force is used, produces the *robbers* and the *ruffians;* the other, in which skill is employed, produces *thieves, forgers,* and *swindlers.* Their varieties are many. The *robbers* are subdivided into *cutpurses, house-breakers, footpads,* and *highwaymen.* The *ruffians* include the gambling house and the brothel *bouncers,* etc. The *thieves* are subdivided into *pickpockets,* and *tricksters.* The *forgers* include the varieties of *confidence men;* and the *swindlers* include the *sharpers.*

The classification is better seen in the following table:

```
                           ⎧ Against ⎧ Articles  . . .  Cutpurses.
                           ⎪ things  ⎩ Houses    . . .  House-breakers.
              ⎧ Aggression ⎨ Against  ⎧ In the streets   Footpads.
Delinquents who ⎪          ⎩ persons  ⎩ On the highway  Highwaymen.
  employ force ⎨  Protection extended to forbidden and immoral resorts.
              ⎩                   Gambling house and brothel bouncers.

                        ⎧ Simple abstraction . . . .  Pickpockets.
Delinquents  ⎧ Organic  ⎨ By causing to disappear or by
who employ   ⎨          ⎩   substitution . . . . . .  Tricksters.
   skill     ⎩ Psychical ⎧ Forgery  . . . . . . . .  Confidence men.
                         ⎩ Suggestion . . . . . . .  Sharpers.
```

Authorities fix the number of habitual offenders at nearly three thousand.

The ratio of the species is obtained by another approximate calculation.

The various species of thieves constitute the bulk of delinquents. The figures are so high, that, together with their varieties, they constitute half the total.

The other half is unevenly taken up by robbers, forgers, and swindlers.

The first of these are the most numerous; but the species tends to disappear not only because, being the most dangerous, the city tries to eradicate it with greater energy; but also because, in the internal evolution of criminality, which especially in urban environments develops cunning and fraudulent forms, it represents an archaic form which is being abandoned and which is preserved only by virtue of that tenacious persistency that clings always to primitive and inferior systems.

Forgers are less numerous; but they tend to develop by virtue of the evolutionary movement just mentioned.

Finally, a study is made of criminal association and of how delinquency is related to prostitution and pauperism, especially to the former.

Causes of crime. — Insanity has been studied by Salillas. In his " Criminal Lunatics in Spain," [1] he reaches the two following conclusions:

a. The development of insanity in Spain is considerable;

b. Criminal insanity meets with little interest both on the part of public opinion and on that of courts of justice.

The scarcity of documents, the vagueness and the errors of diagnoses, forbid the author to pass a judgment on other

[1] *Los locos delincuentes en España;* in the *Revista de Legislación y Jurisprudencia,* vol. XCIV, 1889.

questions, as, for instance, on the peculiar nature of hallucinations in Spain.

The influence of alcohol on the degeneration of the race and on criminality, is studied in a few general monographs, like J. Gómez Ocaña's "Life in Spain,"[1] and Salillas' "Alcoholism";[2] or in more localized ones, like J. M. Llanas Aguilaniedo's "Alcoholism in Seville."[3] Jimeno Azcárate's "Criminality in Asturias" contains also some interesting documents.

Crime is also influenced by some anthropological coefficients.

The greater part of the course on "The fundamental theory of crime" given by Salillas in the Madrid Atheneum (1902–1903), dealt with the development of the physiological age in crime among a total of 110,727 Spanish criminals. This part of the course had been preceded by a lecture on "Age and Crime in Spain."[4]

Salillas, finding the maximum intensity which in criminal statistics corresponds to each of the five ages distinguished in the penal code (younger than 9 years, older than 9 and younger than 15, older than 15 and younger than 18, older than 18 and younger than 60, older than 60), defines the type of each as follows:

1st *age*. — Delinquency having a nutritive significance.

2nd *age*. — Delinquency having a nutro-generative significance.

3d *age*. — Generative delinquency with its homologue, delinquency of blood.

[1] *La vida en España*, Granada, 1900.

[2] *El Alcoholismo*, Barcelona, 1903.

[3] *El alcoholismo en Sevilla;* in the *Actas del IX Congreso internacional de Higiene y Demografía*, Madrid, 1900, where other statistics on alcoholism in Spain may be found.

[4] *La edad y el delito en España*, published in the *Revista de Legislación y Jurisprudencia*, vol. C, 1902.

4th *age.* — Delinquency of unadaptability or rebellion.

5th *age.* — Psychic delinquency.

All these terms must be interpreted through his fundamental bio-sociological theory. His theory is based on facts already pointed out. Theft appears from the very first ages. Woundings follow. Robbery comes later, and still later come swindling and fraud, which rarely appear in the age of puberty.

Sex is another biological coefficient that has been studied.

Using a diagram based on data taken from the " Penitentiary Annual " for 1889 and published by the Department of Justice, the author of these pages observes the following characteristics in female delinquency: [1]

a. Female delinquency is always less than the male;

b. This difference oscillates according to age, from a minimum of one half to a maximum of more than the twentieth.

c. The greatest approximation between the criminality of the two sexes is found in the first age (till the age of eighteen) and in the last (over seventy);

d. The spread of crime according to age shows almost a perfect parallelism in the two sexes;

e. It is to be noticed, however, that the process of decrease is more brusque and accentuated in male delinquency than in the female, due to the change of life in women, which in Spain takes place about the forty-sixth year, the age when the definite decrease of crimes occurs.

If the equivalence between prostitution and crime is admitted in this study, then female delinquency assumes a character determined essentially by sex.

In fact, before the period of puberty, delinquency, still insignificant, is not much greater in the male than in the

---

[1] *Carácter de la delinquencia feminina;* in the *Revista ibero-americana de Ciencias Médicas,* March, 1903; and in the volume: *Alrededor del delito y de la pena,* Madrid, 1904.

female. When puberty is reached, we find a natural condition which predisposes to delinquency, as has been fully shown in the works of Marro and of Stanley Hall. Instantly, male delinquency increases rapidly in ascending disproportion to that of the female, until it reaches the maximum of twenty times greater in the third age (the twentieth year).

Female delinquency also increases. During the entire period of menstruation, which, according to Gutiérrez' figures,[1] lasts about 31 or 32 years (from 14 to 46), criminal activity among women increases in the form of prostitution and delinquency, especially in the former.

The differentiation between prostitution and delinquency having been established, the spread of the latter is as follows:

During the sexual period, especially from the twenty-fifth year, female delinquency reaches the maximum and maintains it with a certain fixity. This is due to the fact that at this age woman is subject to organic disturbances, like menstruation, pregnancy, and nursing, which, poisoning the blood, produce acute neuroses and increase her disposition to delinquency. This organic factor may be the reason, or one of the reasons, for the phenomenon observed by Prinzing, namely: that conjugal life acts upon the two sexes in a different manner; it increases the criminality of women and diminishes that of men.[2]

Finally, the change of life arrives. Criminality decreases as well as prostitution, and the equilibrium between the criminality of the two sexes, altered from the age of puberty, is reëstablished. Male delinquency, which was more than twenty times greater than the female, becomes only double,

---

[1] Estadística sobre la vida sexual de la mujer en España ; in the Revista ibero-americana de Ciencias Médicas, 1901.

[2] Der einfluss der Ehe auf die Kriminalität des Mannes y Die Ermeherung der Kriminalität des Weibes durch die Ehe ; in the Zeitschrift für Socialwissenschaft, 1889.

through the extinction of prostitution as a substitute for crime.

Characteristics of the delinquent. — A few anthropometrical data on Madrid delinquents are found in the book " Low Life in Madrid."

The average cephalic index among 119 delinquents of the capital, measured by the anthropometrist Díaz Sánchez, is 78.53, which is very near the normal index in Madrid (77.87, according to Olóriz). The series is analyzed thus:

	AVERAGE INDEX
10 Dolichocephali	73.73
71 Mesocephali	77.44
36 Sub-brachycephali	81.53
2 Brachycephali	87.80

The following inedited table is based on the data found in Olóriz' memoir, " Cephalic Index in Spain," [1] and in Díaz Sánchez' memoranda:

CEPHALIC INDEX

JUDICIARY DISTRICTS	Normals, measured by Olóriz		Delinquents, measured by Díaz	
	Number measured	Average Index	Number measured	Average Index
Avila	40	77.40	18	77.47
Arenas	22	77.99	22	78.34
Arévalo	16	79.32	15	78.40
Barco	16	75.80	9	77.68
Cebreros	23	77.50	14	78.62
Piedrahita	21	77.26	10	77.55
Madrid	697	77.87	119	78.53
Alcalá	44	78.78	18	72.91
Colmenar	10	78.35	13	79.43
Chinchón	44	79.76	18	78.34
Getafe	23	77.94	15	77.04
Navalcarnero	10	77.03	6	77.50
San Martin	13	78.39	4	78.63
Torrelaguna	12	75.90	9	78.18

As it has already been observed, this table shows a general tendency to emphasize the ethnical type.

[1] *El índice cefálico en España*, Madrid, 1894.

"Low Life in Madrid" contains also some information concerning height, which, according to Olóriz and Hoyos, is smaller in delinquents than in law-abiding citizens. This is only true in offenders belonging to the lowest classes of large centers.

Another investigator, J. J. Arráez y Carriás, has studied some peculiarities of Andalusian delinquents.

First, he has studied the *skin and the hair of Andalusian delinquents*,[1] by comparing 150 convicts with as many persons having no penal antecedents. Arráez finds nothing peculiar in the color of the skin; except in some, who have a certain greenish-yellow tint, due, perhaps, to the bile. He notices that wrinkles are more frequent and premature in the delinquents than in the honest. He finds the zygomatic wrinkle, called by X. Francotte "the wrinkle of vice" and the "characteristic of delinquency," in about 58 per cent. of delinquents and in about 11.5 per cent. of normals. In the examination of the hair, he remarks that the black predominates among delinquents, and that their beard is thin and scanty. Almost 17 per cent. of delinquents had no beard against 2 per cent. of the normals.

His second study is on *the ear of Andalusian delinquents*.[2] The comparison is made between 150 convicts and 150 persons having no penal antecedents. His observations can be stated thus:

	Delinquents	Normals
Regular external ear	23 per 100	61 per 100
Sessile ear	29 " "	17 " "
Darwin's tubercle	16 " "	14 " "
Ear with adhering lobule	3 " "	5 " "
Prominent anti-helix	13 " "	4 " "

[1] In the *Actas de la sociedad española de Historia Natural*, vol. XXV.
[2] In the *Actas de la sociedad española de Historia Natural*. vol. XXVI.

He also remarked in delinquents the incomplete helix and the atrophy and hyperthropy of the lobules. In short, more and more anomalies.

Then, we reach the psychic characteristics.

The psychological point of view predominates in Salillas' series of works entitled " The Spanish Criminal."

In the volume " Hampa, Picaresque Anthropology," [1] the author studies the conditions of Spanish environment, from which he derives his criminal type; and especially the poverty of the soil, which determined the classical Spanish knavery, according to Mateo Alemán's remark that *poverty and knavery come from the same quarry.*

An exaggeration of this national characteristic is illustrated by the criminal *hampa* in its two rôles of valor and knavery. A foreign element comes to swell these types, namely, the gypsy, to whom the author devotes one of the most interesting sections of his work.

In a second volume of the series, entitled " Language, a Philological, Psychological, and Sociological Study, with two Slang Vocabularies," [2] Salillas studies criminal slang. His point of view differs from Lombroso's theory, which considers the obscure prattle of delinquents as a philological archaism depending on and corresponding to the organic and psychic atavism of the criminal; nor does he explain it, like Niceforo, as being only a means of defense employed by criminals to hide their plans and thoughts. The author reaches a definition of a true anthropological character: " We can say that criminal slang is the language employed by bullies, robbers, ruffians, and the like, and is composed of *words adapted to the life and thought of this people.*"

[1] *Hampa, Antropología picaresca,* Madrid, 1898.
[2] *El lenguaje, estudio filológico, psicológico y sociológico, con dos vocabularios jergales,* Madrid, 1896.

The interpretation of these words reveals a most genuine criminal psychology, that is, it reveals the criminal mind's way of understanding, feeling, and associating.

The work ends with two slang vocabularies: one taken mainly from Hidalgo's " Dictionary of Criminal Slang (*Germania*)," [1] and the other being an unedited collection of phrases of criminal slang (*caló*), which represents to-day the lexicon of the delinquent world.

" Ruffian Poetry," [2] a less important work, belongs also to the series " The Spanish Criminal."

" Low Life in Madrid " treats also of the psychic characteristics of professional criminals in large centers.

The authors think that the psychic basis of the offender is analogous to that of the stratum of society from which he comes. Thus, " the soul of people leading a low life is, in short, the common soul, having no other peculiarity than the modifications caused by two chief factors: the *wandering* character, and the *professional deformities*."

The first is generally the result of degeneration or of perverted education.

The second are the result of parasite life which determines always atrophies and retrogressive metamorphoses. This deformity causes the loss of moral reactions, purity, dignity, and remorse. Alcohol often intervenes to realize these inhibitions.

The expression of the offender's life is found in what the authors call " stigmata of low life," revealing marks of his condition. Of these stigmata, the following are being studied:

a. The *nicknames* which delinquents receive from their companions;

b. The *slang* used by habitual criminals in large centers.

[1] Juan Hidalgo, *Vocabulario de Germania*, 1609.
[2] *Poesía rufianesca;* in the *Revue Hispanique*, 1905.

This is composed of a limited number of words taken from the criminal slang (*caló*), sufficient for their usual proceedings and mingled with the corrupted forms of ordinary, gross, and nasty language;

c. *Tattooing*, considered as a bodily ornament as well as a personal souvenir of love, vengeance, etc. It must be traced on one's own body, and with delinquents it is of an obscene, trivial, or bloody character;

d. The *traumatic and pathologic scars*, especially the venereal;

e. The *alcoholic type*, especially in reference to the so-called " drunkard's mark; " and

f. The *professional type*, which tends always to reproduce and at the same time to destroy itself through the need of mimicry, and which, at times, leads to the opposite characterization, like the prostitute of modest appearance and the worthy and bashful beggar.

The various types of professional criminals have their corresponding psychological portraits. Another series of psychological portraits of old and famous Spanish criminals appears in our pamphlet " Criminal Faces." [1]

Moreover, some psychological traits of Castillian vagrants have been pointed out by J. Diaz Caneja in his work: " Castillian Vagrants." [2]

The most original and modern section of his work is that dealing with the graphic signs used by vagrant beggars among themselves.

Díaz Caneja dedicates a study to the slang and games of vagrants, one to the typical vagrant, and one to a vagrant family.

Finally, an anthropological study on the criminal sentenced to hard labor with all his needs and miseries appears in " Penal

---

[1] *Figuras delincuentes*, Madrid, 1909.

[2] *Vagabundos de Castilla*, Madrid, 1903.

Life in Spain," [1] the first and chief of Salillas' works. Of
great interest is the part devoted to "La Casa Galera," a
good study of female prisoners and of the sexual affinity
between prisoners of both sexes.

Special reference to penal life is made in "Low Life in
Madrid," in the pages devoted to the subject of prisoners;
there a description is given of scenes of life in the so-called
Model Prison and in the prison for women.

Section 25. (c) Critique.

After a careful selection, the following works on the subject
can be mentioned: Aramburu's "Modern Penal Science"; [2]
F. Vida's "Penal Science and the Italian Positivistic School," [3]
a very dogmatic work; and a few pages by Concepción
Arenal which are not always to the point. [4] Nevertheless,
she understood criminology in its fathomless contents. "The
man who has offended," she said, "is like the center from
which issue rays touching all moral and intellectual problems."

Section 26. (B) Spanish America.

Less influenced by tradition, the peoples of the other hemi-
sphere offer less resistance to innovations. Only in American
countries the text of judicial sentences contains fragments
by modern criminalists, upon which the judgments are based. [5]
Mexico and Argentine have made an important contribution
to the science.

In Mexico, the first memoir on the criminality of the

[1] La vida penal en España, Madrid, 1888.

[2] La nueva ciencia penal, Madrid, 1887.

[3] La ciencia penal y la escuela positiva italiana; in the Memorias de la
Real Academia de Ciencias Morales y Políticas, vol. VII, 1893.

[4] Consult, for example, "Clínica criminal," in the discontinued review
"Nueva Ciencia jurídica," vol. I, 1893, where that idea is opposed.

[5] Tarde, Philosophie pénale, Paris, 4th edition, 1895.

country is Macedo's " Criminology in Mexico." [1] Then
comes Guerrero's important work " Genesis of Crime in
Mexico," [2] a study dealing mainly with environment for
which the characters are furnished by Roumagnac's " The
Criminals in Mexico," and " Sexual and Emotional Criminals." [3] Worthy of mention is also Martínez Baca y Vergara's
" Studies of Criminal Anthropology." [4]

The Argentine Republic, as soon as the movement became
general, saw in its capital a *Society of Criminal Anthropology*,
due to the initiative of Drago, Pinero, and Ramos Megía,
editors of a " Bulletin " in which were published the first
studies. This was followed by the review " Modern Criminology," greatly influenced by anarchistic and socialistic
elements. Later appear the excellent " Archives of Psychiatry and Criminology," edited by Ingegnieros and still in
existence.

We have already spoken of the ideas of this prolific writer.
We must not forget his extensive treatise " Simulation of
Insanity," [5] in which he treats of criminal simulation. Drago is
the author of " Men of Prey," [6] a natural history of the most
fearful criminal variety. Moyano Gacitua's " Delinquency in
Argentine according to some Figures and Theories " [7] gives a
thorough estimate of the criminality of the author's country.
De Veyga's " Medico-legal Studies," [8] and Arreguine's " Legal
Studies " [9] contain also interesting monographs.

[1] *La criminalidad en México*, Mexico, 1897.
[2] *Génesis del crimen en México*, Mexico, 1901.
[3] *Los criminales en México*, Mexico, 1905. — *Crímines sexuales y pa-
sionales*, Mexico, 1906.
[4] *Estudios de Antropología criminal*, Puebla, 1893.
[5] *La simulación de la locura*, Buenos Aires, 1903.
[6] *Los hombres de presa*, Buenos Aires, 1888.
[7] *La delincuencia Argentina ante algunas cifras y teorías*, Córdoba, 1905.
[8] *Estudios médico-legales*, Buenos Aires, 1879.
[9] *Estudios legales*, Buenos Aires, 1879.

Smaller countries have also made some good contributions.

In Cuba, F. Ortiz' " The Delinquency of Cuban Negroes," and " Negro Sorcerers " [1] are important works and first of a series on " Afro-cuban *Hampa*." In Costa Rica, A. Alfaro's " Criminal Archeology " [2] gives a revision of old trials with allusions to the modern bearings of criminology. In Venezuela, we have F. Ochoa's "Studies on the School of Criminal Anthropology." [3] In Uruguay, Miranda has a monograph on " Climate and Crime." [4] In Chile, we find Newmann's " Stray Pages on the Death Penalty ";[5] Galdames' " The Struggle Against Crime ";[6] Braudau's " Repressive Criminal Policy ";[7] some writings by the late Luis Ross, etc.

[1] *La criminalitá dei negri in Cuba;* in the *Archivio di Psichiatria.* — *Los Negros Brujos,* Madrid, 1906.

[2] *Arqueología criminal,* San José, 1906.

[3] *Estudios sobre la Escuela penal antropológica,* Maracaibo, 1899.

[4] *El clima y el delito,* Montevideo, 1907.

[5] *Notas sueltas sobre la pena de muerte,* Santiago, 1896.

[6] *La lucha contra el crimen,* Santiago, 1903.

[7] *Política criminal represiva,* Santiago, 1909.

CHAPTER II

CRIMINAL LAW. — PENITENTIARY SCIENCE.

I. ORIGINS.

Section 27.

IN later years, the field of history has been considerably enlarged. The ethnographical studies of savage peoples allow us to cast a retrospective glance beyond the limit of ancient legal ideas, which were sought until not long ago in India or in Egypt, in heroic Greece or in primitive Rome. Thus we have been able to reach indirectly the origins of humanity stripped of all that civilizations have added,— the primitive man just as he was in the world.

At that epoch, as Steinmetz remarks,[1] punishment is " an outburst of passion, the first whom it met becoming the victim, even when nothing in the latter rendered him particularly responsible for the act committed. Originally, punishment is aimless; only much later it becomes disciplined and organized."

The time came, when, according to Hamon,[2] *reflex action* (instinctive) became *reflective action* (intelligent). Then, becoming conscious of itself, it produced as its last florescence the biological phenomenon, that is, the juridical phenomenon. D'Aguanno declares that " the feeling of right and wrong appeared at the end of the quaternary age," [3] that is, at a

[1] *Ethnologische Studien zur ersten Entwickelung der Strafe,* Leyden and Leipzig, 1894.

[2] *Déterminisme et responsabilité,* Paris, 1898.

[3] *La génesis y la evolución histórica del derecho civil.*

period of the formation of the earth's crust when, with the present knowledge of things, it is not fully demonstrated that man existed. No matter how vast the extension of these prehistoric ages may be, to set a definite period in them for such an event throws suspicion even on what there remains of exactness; but, in spite of this, it has the positive value of contradicting with anthropological and ethnical data the opinion of others who put it further back.

From that period, the mental effort directed to the inhibitory discipline of the impulsive force of social reaction is being exercised against crime, and has been called punishment.[1] But, in reality, the history of human thought raised to the position of science begins, if not absolutely at least perceptibly to the eye, in very recent times, namely, toward the end of the 18th century. We find it so near our period, that between the two there intervenes only the space of a century. Nevertheless, however little may be covered by a hundred years of history, penal science has been established during this time under the double action of criminal law and penitentiary science, in a dualism which only lately has been terminated by their fusion.

Section 28. (1) CRIMINAL LAW.
Beccaria and Röder.

" The mass of opinions which a large part of Europe honors with the name of laws are nothing but legislative remains of

---

[1] Cf. Makarewicz' study " *L'évolution de la peine* " in the *Archives d'Anthropologie criminelle*, vol. XIII, 1898. It is taken from the book " Einführung in die Philosophie des Strafrechts auf Entwicklungsgeschichtlicher Grundlage," Stuttgart, 1906, which describes the different aspects of the old penology until the creation of the modern State. Makarewicz insists upon the necessity of distinguishing between the reaction of those directly offended by the crime and the reaction of the social group, which is the true punishment. Westermarck is of the same opinion (cf. *Der Ursprung der Strafe*, in the *Zeitschrift fur Socialwissenschaft*, 1900; and his *Origins of Moral Ideas*, London, 1906).

an ancient conquering nation, compiled by the order of a prince who ruled twelve centuries ago in Constantinople, mingled later with barbarous customs, and wrapped in an entangling farrago of obscure commentaries. Even to-day, the spirit of routine, as fatal as it is general, sets down one of Carpzovio's opinions, an old practice advocated by Claro, or a torture invented with barbarous complacency by Farinacio as principles to be safely followed by those who ought to tremble when deciding on the life and affairs of their fellow-citizens " (Beccaria).

Such was the situation at the end of the 18th century. But, under the already dying barbarous institutions there throbbed the spirit of reform. The Encyclopedists were preparing by their sayings, deeds, and writings a new criminal law; [1] and there, in Milan, a remote disciple, Cesare Beccaria (1738–1794), voiced their mind in the small pamphlet " Crimes and Punishments." [2]

This work was the true germ of our criminal law. Ellero remarks that of the eighty more or less radical practical propositions which it contains, more than seventy have been adopted in our common laws, beginning with the abolition of torture and of capital punishment.[3] When the memorable selection from the punishments accumulated by history was realized, and their number was reduced to the minimum needed for social defense, thus assuring the individual against the excesses of society, then began the decadence of established penology.

In the meantime, a more radical transformation was being

---

[1] On this subject, cf. Overbeck's " Das Strafrecht der französischen Encyclopadie," Karlsruhe, 1902.

[2] For the writings and works of the famous Milanese, cf. Cantú's " Beccaria e il diritto penale," Florence, 1862.

[3] Quoted by Ferri in " L'opera di Cesare Lombroso e la giustizia penale," in the volume in honor of Lombroso, Turin, 1906.

prepared. Karl Röder (1806–1879) begins, in 1839, a series of writings aiming at bringing the conception of penology back to the universal law of tutelage over deficient beings.[1]

At the basis of this doctrine we find, on one hand, the state of the will out of harmony with justice, pointing out the crime in the delinquent; and, on the other, the consequent necessity of a tutelage — as in any other abnormal state of the individual, even exercised in the way required by each, — " not only in its restrictive sense of decreasing the criminal's exterior freedom, so as to diminish the stimulus and the opportunities that cause him to persist in his condition, to relapse, and to grow worse; but also, in its positive sense — which is always the first — of protecting the development of his freedom, the repression of his will, the regeneration of his conscience, the restoration of the sense of justice in his soul, and his energy and strength in the realization of his deeds."

To quote from one who has best interpreted the author's thought, " this restriction of the delinquent's freedom which removes all the elements that might induce him to persevere in his degradation; this educative discipline of his reason; this true medicine for the patient, whose affliction counteracts in him and in all the normal course of the juridical life, is what Röder means by *punishment*." Thus we can understand why at the beginning of his scientific work he could ask himself whether *punishment was to be an evil;* although, according to Carnevale, his real question was whether *punishment ought to be a punishment.* " Whether the delinquent will consider this punishment — this tutelage — as an evil or as a blessing, will depend only on the state of his mind. The moral temper of his sentiments will make him capable

[1] Röder's first memoir is entitled "Commentatio an poenam malum esse debeat," Gisae, 1839. On the personality and works of this penalist, cf. F. Giner's " Karl Röder," in the *Revista general de Legislación y Jurisprudéncia*, 1880.

or incapable to know his true interest, his aversion from the remedy being always in inverse ratio to that inspired by his crime. To consider punishment an evil for the delinquent, would be the same as to agree with the patient when through ignorance he detests the medicine, or with the child when he cries because forced to go to school."

Modern criminalists have taken offense at this illustrious thinker. His name seems forgotten, and his doctrine badly understood. Tarde's " Penal Philosophy " does not mention him once; while it devotes entire pages to writers without whom penal history would not suffer in the least. Others, like Garofalo, speak of " the absurdities of the reformistic school " without being acquainted with it.[1] It is to Röder that we must trace the beginning of the movement of penal transformation, which, changing punishment into tutelage, makes of it a branch of reformatory education, *Etoiatry* as De Sanctis [2] proposed to call it.

Section 29.   (2) PENITENTIARY SCIENCE.
Howard.

This reformation could prosper but little in a juridical, dogmatic, and conventional environment. In fact, it would have probably failed if the accepted distinction between penal and penitentiary function had not been allowed to spread in a beneficent and moral atmosphere.

---

[1] Cf. *Criminalogia*, p. 162 of the Spanish edition, and the corresponding note of the translator which rectifies it. It is well known that Karl Röder, Krause's disciple, has exercised a certain influence in Spain through the so-called *Krausist generation*. His works were translated by Romero Girón and F. Giner. On the solicitation of Don Nicolás Salmerón (1873), Minister of Justice, Röder edited for our country several reports on penal and penitentiary reforms, one of which can be found as an appendix to his work: *Las doctrinas fundamentales reinantes sobre el delito y la pena en sus interiores contradicciones*, Madrid, 1877.

[2] *L'Etoiatria, le carceri e i riformatori*, in the *Rivista di discipline carcerarie*, 1907.

While Beccaria and the philanthropists of the end of the 18th century, aided by the avenging arm of the French revolution, were causing the radical transformation in penal legislation from which have come our present codes, the Englishman John Howard (1726–1789) was beginning his penitentiary reform.[1]

The origins of penitentiary science are characterized by more sentimental traits than those of the reform of penal laws and prosecution. The journey over the " geography of grief," to which Howard devoted the best portion of his life, and which caused his death — for often one dies for what he lives — means the daily practice of a work of charity if not of asceticism. More personal and intimate than "The state of the prisons in England and Wales (1777)," the " Diary " of his activity reveals in every page both features. Penitentiary reform is not, in its origin, a work of *justice* nor one of *science* — Howard detested the latter, as in the case of geological investigations — but one of *charity* and *mercy*.

It was only later that the reform assumed the characteristics of the first two. International Congresses began to be held. After those of Frankfort (1846 and 1857) and Brussels (1847) there followed:

    I.   London, 1872.

    II.   Stockholm, 1878.

   III.   Rome, 1885.

   IV.   Saint Petersburg, 1889.

    V.   Paris, 1895.

   VI.   Brussels, 1900.

  VII.   Budapest, 1905.

[1] The principal work on the life and work of John Howard is that by R. W. Bellows, published in the volume " Prisons and Reformatories at home and abroad," London, 1872. The International Penitentiary Congress of Saint Petersburg (1889), which coincided with the centenary of Howard's death, was a continual commemoration of the famous man

The movement gave rise to national societies, like the "Howard Association" in England; "The General Prison Association" in France; and the "American Prison Association" in the United States. Reviews were founded, like the "Revue Pénitentiare" in France, the "Rivista di Discipline carcerarie" in Italy, the "Revista Penitenciaria" in Spain, etc.

Of the modern works which give an idea of its progress, we will mention: Cuche's "Treatise of Penitentiary and Legislative Science"; [1] Delvincourt's "The Struggle against Criminality in our times"; [2] Franchi's "Prison Discipline and Institutions before and after Lombroso"; [3] Boise's "The Science of Penology," etc. [4]

II. TENDENCIES.

Section 30.

Modern penology, therefore, is the outcome of the two aforesaid currents. In its actual state, three tendencies are noticeable: 1. The traditional; 2. The reformistic; 3. The radical.

Section 31. (1) TRADITIONAL.

Makarewicz.

The traditional tendency might be characterized: (a) by the claim of opposing crime only by means of punishment;

who inaugurated prison reform. The Russian delegate, Galkine Wraskoiy, published an interesting biographical pamphlet, and Professor Spasso-wicht began a series of lectures on the same subject, ending them with the following words: "Is not his memory worthy of veneration in every respect, and even worthy of a kind of worship on the part of modern communities?"

[1] *Traité de Science et de Législation pénitentiaires*, Paris, 1906.
[2] *La lutte contre la criminalité dans les temps modernes*, Paris, 1897.
[3] *Le discipline carcerarie e gl'istituti prima e dopo Cesare Lombroso*, found in *L'opera di Cesare Lombroso*, Turin, 1906.
[4] *The Science of Penology*, New York, London, 1901.

(b) and by understanding the latter as a retribution — without any other aim — of crimes.

We say " might be characterized " and not " is characterized," because most likely this conception does not actually exist in a complete and perfect form. Like extinct fauna and flora, it is no longer of this world.

Nevertheless, it is important to point out some vestige, some atavistic mark which reappears in contemporary writers. Thus, Makarewicz, in his " Evolution of Punishment," [1] writes: " The reaction against crime IS AND WILL ALWAYS BE *malum passionis quod infligitur propter malum actionis*, when the member of a community commits an act detrimental to all." Modern criminalists, those who can really be called innovators — Lombroso, and especially Garofalo, — when treating of the application of remedies to crime, deserve the name of reactionaries more than that of conservatives.

According to Dorado,[2] " the idea of an *intelligent* social defense, which carries with it the conception of punishment as *something good* for *all*, including the guilty, and perhaps more for him than for any other, has not yet entered in a thoughtful way the positivistic school of Italian penology; and this is perhaps its greatest fault."

Section 32. (2) REFORMERS.
Liszt, Prins, Van Hamel, etc.

The reformers are noted for planning a kind of " double entry " penology. They advocate the traditional penal measures for certain delinquents only with a repressive aim, while for others they reserve preventive measures against relapse and imitation, in accordance with the teachings of modern criminology.

[1] *L'évolution de la peine;* in the *Archives d'Anthropologie criminelle* vol. XIII, 1898.

[2] *Problemas de Derecho penal*, Madrid, 1895; vol. I, p. 386.

The reformers are in the majority everywhere. Among the most noted, we may mention the late Tarde and La Grasserie in France; Prins in Belgium; Stoos in Switzerland; Van Hamel in Holland; Liszt in Germany; Zucker in Austria; Fayer in Hungary; Drill in Russia; Typaldo Basia in Greece; Méndes Martins in Portugal; Alcántara Machado in Portuguese America, etc. In some countries, special reviews have been founded, like Liszt's "Zeitschrift für die gesammte Strafrechtswissenschaft"; Stoos' "Schweizerische Zeitschrift für Strafrecht," or "Revue pénale suisse"; and the "Revue de Droit pénal et de Criminologie" in Belgium.

In Italy, from Lucchini to Ferri, from the "Rivista Penale" to the "Scuola Positiva," the various shades of reforms succeeded in giving birth to a group called the "Third School" under the leadership of Alimena and Carnevale. This school represents a movement of reaction against the early exaggerated positivism, which attenuated the existing code by the addition of the innovators' principles. In our days, Manzini could be said to approach this tendency. If we accepted this nomenclature — which has almost disappeared — we should give the name of "Fourth School" to a secluded group, who, under the leadership of Pozzolini, edit the more recent "Rivista di Diritto penale e Sociologia criminale." In fact, aside from Lucchini (who remains alone and unshaken and whose dissidence rather suggests personal animosity) and others impossible to mention, the old teachers, like Brussa, Stoppato, Civali, and the young ones, like Alimena, Carnevale, Rocco, Manzini, Pozzolini, Olivieri, Franchi, Viazzi, Florian, Zerboglio, all show a reciprocal movement, whose different shades of opinions would be difficult to classify.

Finally, in 1889, Liszt, Prins, and Van Hamel founded the "International Union of Criminal Law" for the promotion of reform. The following by-laws were drawn up:

I. The " International Union of Criminal Law " holds that criminality and the means of repression must be examined both from the social and the juridical point of view. Therefore, it aims at the realization of this principle in the science of criminal law and in criminal legislation.

II. The Union adopts, as a fundamental basis for its activities, the following propositions:

1. The mission of criminal law is to combat criminality regarded as a social phenomenon.

2. Penal science and penal legislation must therefore take into consideration the results of anthropological and sociological studies.

3. Punishment is one of the most efficacious means the state can use against criminality, although not the only one. Punishment must never be isolated from other social remedies, nor must preventive measures be neglected.

4. The distinction between occasional and habitual criminals is essential in theory as well as in practice, and must serve as the basis for criminal law regulations.

5. Since repressive tribunals and penitentiary administration have the same ends in view, and since the sentence only acquires value by its mode of execution, the Union considers the distinction which the modern laws make between the court and the prison as irrational and harmful.

6. Punishment by deprivation of liberty justly occupying the first place in our system of punishments, the Union gives its special attention to all that concerns the amelioration of prisons and allied institutions.

7. So far as short sentences are concerned, the Union considers that the substitution of more efficacious measures is not only possible but desirable.

8. So far as long sentences are concerned, the Union holds that the length of the imprisonment must depend not only

on the material and moral gravity of the offense, but on the results obtained by the treatment in prison.

9. So far as incorrigible habitual criminals are concerned, the Union holds that, independently of the gravity of the offense, and even with regard to the repetition of minor offenses the penal system ought before all to aim at putting these criminals for as long a period as possible under conditions where they cannot do injury.

III. The members of the Union adhere to these fundamental propositions.

This seems a creed, a confession of faith, or a decalogue of the Penal Code; for, through a strange coincidence, ten are the propositions devoted to it. The clause of acceptance that follows them must have given rise to some objections and criticisms, most of them against the propositions themselves, others against the presumptuous appellation by which they were baptized, and still others against the right assumed by some of imposing them on the nations.[1]

But an International Union of Criminal Law finds its justification in our days in as much as such activities in great questions break down boundary lines. Institutes, Leagues, Congresses, standing committees, etc., are products of the present state of culture. There was no reason why the struggle against crime was not to find in a Union the strength which it needed, as Foinitzky has pointed out.[2]

On the other hand, the Union hastened to explain the meaning of what might have been considered an exacting dogmatism. It declared in the first Bulletin [3] that its by-laws

[1] Cf. Albérique Rolin's *L'Union Internationale de Droit Pénal, ses bases fundamentales, ses travaux pendant la première session et les novateurs de Droit Pénal;* in the *Revue de Droit International et de legislation comparée,* XXI, 110.

[2] *Juriditzeski Westnik,* Moscow, 1890.

[3] *Les tendences de l'Union;* and *Les deux premières campagnes de l'Union.*

were not the result of a preconceived doctrine, but the basis of the Union's activity and the guide for its task. It was adduced that whoever aspires to a change of legislation must set down his object clearly, plan it, even if it be in rough outlines, and state the reasons for its desirability. It was added that in order to come together and discuss matters certain principles in common were needed, and that, after all, the by-laws could always be revised.

Believing this, the Union soon counted among its members penalists of the most opposite opinions and the leaders of the most hostile schools, from the Hegelian T. A. Berner to the positivist E. Ferri.

Yet, it was found necessary to revise the old by-laws by suppressing the minute enumeration of the propositions and by drawing up a new formula of a general character to which all could freely subscribe. After the discussion held at the sessions of Linz and Lisbon in 1895 and 1897, the second article of the by-laws was made to read as follows:

" The International Union of Criminal Law holds that criminality and the means of combating it must be considered from the anthropological and sociological side as well as from the juridical. Its aim is to pursue a scientific study of criminality, its causes, and the means of attacking it."

This study was to be made at the yearly sessions of the Union. But, since an international legislator is bound to appear always as a phantom, there arose in the bosom of the Union national groups whose activity has proved more efficacious and adequate for the legislations of the various countries they represent.

The Union publishes its Bulletin,[1] and edits a long treatise

[1] *Mitteilungen der Internationalen Kriminalistischen Vereinigung.* — *Bulletin de l'Union Internationale de Droit Pénal.*

of comparative penal legislation which is indefinitely continued by means of supplements.

All this has been accomplished, but the importance of the
Union is declining if not already dead.

In America, on the other hand, a similar institution has
been founded lately. The American Institute of Criminal
Law and Criminology was founded in 1909, in Chicago,
under the presidency of John H. Wigmore, Dean of the
Northwestern University Law School.

Section 33. (3) RADICALS.

Vargha, Dorado, Tolstoy, Solovieff, etc.

This school, like the conservative, constitutes another
minority. It arose under the same circumstances as the
latter and is already on the decline. The radicals repudiate
the double entry penology of the reformers and develop only
its preventive side.

An illustration of this is found in Vargha's " The Abolition
of Penal Servitude." [1] Proposing to study the struggle for
the reform of criminal law, this writer collects them only into
two groups, namely, those that defend and those that oppose
the conception of punishment as an evil and a chastisement.
He also analyzes the evolution of the fundamental ideas upon
which the criminal judiciary bases itself into the following
phases answering to the same contrast:

a. Unlimited vengeance;

b. Limited vengeance as a material compensation for crime,
that is, the law of retaliation, which in itself constitutes a
step in advance;

c. Limited vengeance as a moral compensation;

d. Safety without respect for the personality of the delinquent;

[1] *Die Abschaffung der Strafknechtschaft*, Graz, 1896.

e. Safety with respect for the personality of the delinquent. This is the feature that characterizes criminal law reform. The desire for vengeance meets with no official recognition, and penal servitude is on the point of disappearing. The delinquent's personality is respected; and the penal reaction consists in a mere limitation of the freedom of movement and action of the delinquent who is a menace to society. Thus is fulfilled the double function of protecting society and of guarding the delinquent.

Contemporaneously with Vargha and even preceding him come Dorado's series of persistent works: " Modern Juridical Problems," " Studies on Preventive Criminal Law," " Bases for a new Criminal Law," " New Penal Tendencies," " Medical Experts and Criminal Justice," " Criminology and Penology," [1] all of which were summed up in a paper sent to the Congress of Criminal Anthropology at Amsterdam, and entitled: " Is punishment, properly speaking, compatible with the data of criminal anthropology and sociology? "

Positivism which took form in Italy under the influence of Ardigò and Siciliani, and organic correctionalism which rose in Spain under the influence of Giner have been happily combined by Dorado, thus forming a fusion perhaps never realized until now.[2] " Summarizing our thought in a few

---

[1] *Problemas jurídicos contemporáneos*, Madrid, 1893. — *Estudios de Derecho penal preventivo*, Madrid, 1901. — *Bases para un nuevo Derecho penal*, Barcelona, 1902. — *Nuevos derroteros penales*, Barcelona, 1905. — *Los peritos médicos y la justicia criminal*, Madrid, 1906. — *De Criminalogía y Penología*, Madrid, 1906.

[2] F. Giner's penal ideas are condensed in the following extracts from *Principios de Derecho penal* (written in collaboration with A. Calderón, Madrid, 1873, p. 113): " The compensation for the juridical order disturbed by crime is called *punishment*. Punishment is, then, the reaction of the juridical activity against crime, having for object the re-establishment of violated justice. Since punishment must act upon the cause of crime, its whole aim must be to correct the perverted will of the criminal (as far as possible by exterior means, if it is a question of social law).

words, we can say that the penal system of the future (and even of the present; for, without the efforts of any one, it is gradually being formed thanks to that activity, which to use a paradox, deserves to be called the *wise labor of the unconscious*) must be a kind of fusion of the corrective and the positivistic schools, the spirit of the former imparted to the mass of badly ordered data of the latter. The metaphysical and narrow mold of the corrective school must be widened by the young and active vitality which the positivistic school derives from experimental observation; or, in other words, by the experimental synthesis, the reduction of what were only inspired intuitions of great poets and abstract speculation, into a decided realistic, scientific, philoso-experimental system based on the certainty derived from the observation of facts, their comparison, and the deductions derived therefrom." [1]

Dorado is careful to warn us that according to the penal system he conceives, " severe measures may be used whenever required . . . ; but that they are not punishments, that is, they are not forms of reaction against the crime committed, but a part of the protective system itself." [2]

Therefore, punishment is not an evil as it has been supposed; since it is not an evil to correct the will of the pervert, even if he does not acknowledge and accept it as a blessing. — The basis for punishment is found in the crime through which the criminal has shown his inability to freely guide his own life. Hence the *tutelar* nature of punishment, which is nothing but the exterior action of protection and vigilance employed by the State in order to reassert the will of its members. Punishment, being a reaction against crime always in the form of abuse of freedom must consist above all in an exterior limitation of this freedom of which the criminal does not know how to make a rational use. As long as punishment has this in view, it becomes *a right of the criminal himself*, even if the abnormal condition of his mind does not allow him to acknowledge it, in the same way as tutelage is a right of the child even if he denies and opposes it."

[1] *Problemas de derecho penal*, vol. I, Preface.
[2] A paper presented before the Amsterdam Congress.

At this point, a very radical tendency branches off —
based on the principle of resist no evil by violence — which
excludes all reaction against crime except oral persuasion.
This tendency which favors abolition altogether appears in
modern philosophy at times satisfied with the spontaneous
repressive effects of the natural consequences to which the
offender is exposed through his crime (Wille); at other times
adopting as the only measure a system of publicity which may
strengthen public sentiment against crime (Popper). The
tendency culminates in Tolstoy, who, according to Golden-
weiser,[1] has illustrated in his "Resurrection" the paradox
of considering "Punishment as a crime and crime as a punishment." Clarence Darrow develops the same principle in
"Resist no evil" (Chicago, 1903). The influence of Tolstoy
can be detected also in Molinari's "The Decline of Criminal
Law";[2] and perhaps even in Reich's "Criminality and
Altruism."[3]

Solovieff's article "The penal question from an ethical
standpoint"[4] discusses in a masterly way this ultra-radical
tendency and traces it to its sources.

He claims, in short, that in the presence of any crime we
are moved by two distinct sentiments: profound indignation
against the criminal and great pity for the victim. Yet,
when we consider things in the light of Ethics and find that
every offense is unfailingly connected with a moral injury in
the soul of the offender, then we must agree that through the
fall of the human dignity which the offense reveals in him, he
becomes worthy of as much pity and compassion as the victim
himself.

[1] *Le crime comme peine, la peine comme crime,* Paris, 1904.

[2] *Il tramonto del diritto penale,* Mantua, 1904.

[3] *Criminalität und Altruismus,* Arusberg, 1900.

[4] *La question pénale au point de vue éthique;* in the *Revue internationale
de Sociologie,* 1897.

Solovieff finds two classes of men opposing these ideas. In the first place, there are those who deliver the aggressor as a being deprived of rights and considerations to the defense and vengeance of the offended party; and secondly, those who going to the other extreme sustain that the offender must be brought back to reason by oral persuasion without any other individual or social defense on the part of the offended party.

Taking up the first class, the author examines the historical manifestations of vindictive punishment and proves that it is still in force although on the point of disappearing. Punishment in our days is a deferential and ceremonious vengeance without subsequent complications on account of the solidarity and cohesion of its advocates. Some men in France and Germany believe that the penal function has reached the last degree of its evolution in the *maximum* of its moderation. But, if so, what is the cause of such a unanimous demand for penal reform? Truly, to-day we punish less and with less severity; but, since the selection of sentiments proceeds in proportion to this process of mitigation of punishments, the offense of the former persists in a larger degree and with less injury. "What remains of vengeance and reprisal is still considerable and is being defended with such tenacity by some thinkers, that posterity," says Solovieff, "will be astonished in reading of them as we do to-day when we read Aristotle's ideas on slavery."

The second group exalts the respect due to the person of the delinquent. Changing the ethical point of view to a mystical one by the principle of *resist no evil by violence*, they deny any other repressive and preventive measure except oral *persuasion*. Here Solovieff refers to Tolstoy, for whom this principle is so absolute that he would not stop a mother's arm on the point of taking her child's life. The basis of this doctrine is the *laissez faire* of Providence, whose designs are unsearchable. A man saved from violent death to-day may prove a criminal to-morrow. A more complicated case is the following: A man has been forbidden by force to enter a tavern believing to do him good. But, if he had been allowed to follow his inclination, wine would have excited his sensibility and, on coming out and meeting a dog half frozen by the cold of the night, he would have taken it into his arms and revived it. As he saved the animal from death, in time he would save a little girl from drowning who had been destined to become the mother of a great man. By not allowing that man to enter a tavern, the dog would have died of cold, the little girl would have drowned, and a great man, a genius, would not have been born. But, why not continue the process, asks Solovieff. Perhaps the great man, the *hero*, might have caused great misfortunes to humanity. The doctrine of the unforeseen and the unknown ends by destroying itself.

The ethical principle demands an effective reaction, which, although not expressed in works, will still remain moral. But, the deprivation of liberty by imprisonment is an inferior form of reaction. Some day we shall look upon prisons as we do upon the psychiatric institutions of a century ago. "A *public tutelage* composed of competent men for the correction of the guilty is the only idea of punishment or of *positive* reprisals that the ethical principle can admit. It is only when the penitentiary system shall be based on this principle that it will become more equitable, humane, and efficacious than it is at present."

As a precedent and illustration of this transformation we are often referred to what happened in the treatment of the insane.

We will only quote what Kropotkin says in his " Prisons ": [1]

[1] *Les Prisons*, Paris, 1890.

" In former times the insane were considered as possessed with evil spirits and were treated accordingly.   They
were chained in infected rooms and tied to the walls like wild
beasts.   Pinel, a man of the great Revolution, came and
dared to break their chains and treat them as brothers.   The
guards warned him to be careful lest they should devour
him; but Pinel dared in spite of their warnings and the men
who were believed to be wild beasts stood around him proving
by their attitude how right he was in forming a better opinion
of human nature, even when the mind is darkened by infirmity.

" From that time the cause of humanity was won.   The
insane were no longer enchained.

" The chains disappeared; but the asylums, a new form of
prison, remained, developing within their walls a system as
accursed as that of irons.

" Then, peasants and not doctors of Gheel, Belgium, found
something better.   They said: ' Send your insane to us and
we will give them absolute freedom.'   They received them in
their families, gave them a place at their own table, interested
them in the care of the land and of the flocks, and made them
share in the feasts of the field with their young people. ' Eat,
work, amuse yourselves in our company, run in the fields,
be free! '   This was the system and the science of the Belgian
peasant.

" Freedom produced miracles.   The insane recovered.
Even the unfortunates afflicted by an incurable organic injury
became tractable and docile, members of the family as the
rest.   The infirm brain acted always abnormally, but the
heart was right and nobody found occasion for complaint.

" People cried at the miracle.   The cures were attributed
to some saint or to some Virgin.   But the Virgin was Freedom,
and the saint, the work in the fields and brotherly treatment.

" The system found imitators.   In Edinburgh, I have had the pleasure of meeting Dr. Mitchell, a man who has devoted his life to the same treatment of freedom in Scotland.   He has had to overcome many prejudices and has been opposed with the same arguments used against us; but he has won. In 1886, there were already 2,180 insane in Scotland distributed among families, and scientific commissions highly praise the system.   No medicine can compete with freedom, free work, and brotherly treatment.

" In one of the boundaries of the ' vast space between mental infirmity and crime ' mentioned by Maudsley, freedom and brotherly treatment have done wonders.   Why could not the same happen at the other extreme boundary where to-day we place crime? "

III.   APPLICATIONS

Section 34. (1) RESPONSIBILITY.

Whether criminality is due to atavism, degeneration, or pathology constitutes a question of pure criminal anthropology.   Whatever be the conclusion reached, as long as the phenomenon is due to a cause, we are justified to ask: Where shall we fasten responsibility? And for whom shall we reserve the specific social reaction called punishment?

This constantly debated question [1] is proving unusually troublesome for our contemporaries who have not been able to look at it from the correct point of view.

Before the Congress of the " International Union of Criminal Law " held at Lisbon in 1897, Garraud presented the following

[1] Loening has started the publication of its history, entitled: *Geschichte der Strafrechtlichen Zurechnungslehre*, Jena, 1903. The first volume goes no further than Aristotle.

résumé of the modern theories of the basis of penal responsibility:

Theories of responsibility.
- Classical theory — Moral and social responsibility, based upon the notions of obligation, free will, and personality.
- Modern theories
  - Mere social responsibility.
    - Contract: Fouillée.
    - Based upon the notion of the defense of the social organism.
  - Social and moral responsibility without the suppression of free will.
    - Through real and personal identity, and through social similarity: *Tarde.*
    - Through the normality of the deed: *Liszt.*
  - Social and moral responsibility, but reduced to a simple noumenon.

Garraud forgets the *integrity of intelligence* upon which Ferri looked with favor at the beginning, the *integrity of the whole character* advocated by J. Vida in his " Criminal Responsibility and the Causes that Exclude or Modify it," [1] Alimena's *susceptibility of feeling psychic coercion*, etc. He forgets also the strange theory of semi-responsibility set forth by the jurists against the psychiatrists, and which does not lack the support of some clinicians.[2]

The theories of real identity and social similarity and the theory of the normality of the deed are the two most original attempts to replace the old basis of responsibility, possessing as they do a moral trait which may be perhaps a mere conventionalism.

The first was propounded by Tarde in his " Penal Philosophy." This thinker believes that the affirmation of free will is in contradiction with science. But, it is not less true — he adds — that to deny it is to contradict conscience. What is, then, the basis for responsibility? Not accepting

[1] *La imputabilidad criminal y las causas que la excluyen ó modifican,* Salamanca, 1891.

[2] Grasset, *Demifous et demiresponsables,* Paris, 1907.

the prevailing notion of society as an organism, Tarde does not see in the phenomenon an effect of its irritability as it is generally conceded (Letourneau, Guyau, Hamon, Schiattarelli, Ferri, etc.). On the other hand, he thinks that we need a system having a moral basis and characteristic, animated and strengthened by modern science. This system bases responsibility and the penal function upon the notion of *real* or *personal and social identity*. Puglia has accepted this fully in his " Genetic Principle of the Right to Repress." [1]

" Responsibility," says Tarde, " not only supposes an act hostile to the general utility or will of the co-partners, but also a crime judged from its material aspect. It supposes, moreover, two essential facts: personal identity and social identity. The combination of both positive notions, which are never illusory, affords the complete explanation of both moral merit and demerit. In order that the author of an act injurious and contrary to the wish of others may realize the feeling of guilt, and in order that in its spectators and judges there may arise the corresponding sentiment of indignation, censure, or scorn, the two following conditions are necessary: In the first place, the author of the deed must judge himself or be judged the same at the time he accuses himself or is accused as when he committed the act; in other words, he must attribute to himself with or without reason the act in question, and not because of organic or physical causes outside of his person. In the second place, it is necessary that the man judge himself or be judged as forming part of the *same society* as the judges and the victim; in other words, responsibility exists only when the author of the deed preserves his identity (*real or personal identity*), and when between him and

[1] *Il principio genetico del diritto di reprimere*, in the *Scuola Positiva*, January, 1892.

the social group to which he belongs there exists a sufficient
number of resemblances that will make him responsible.

The working of the system is illustrated as follows:

a. *Irresponsibility. — Through lack of personal identity.—*
Why is the *hypnotized* man irresponsible? Is it because he is
not free? No; he is irresponsible because he has momentarily
lost his identity, and because it is not *he himself* that acts
but *he* altered by suggestion. *Through lack of social identity:*
deaths, devastations, and pillages brought about by a tribe
or a horde against another at the time when social unity,
restricted to the small number of persons that composed it,
caused them to resemble very much one another and differ
much from their neighbors. *Through lack of personal and social
identity :* insanity which alienates, separates, and destroys both
identities. (But, can this principle be applied to *congenital madness*, the often quoted *moral insanity ?* The morally insane
besides being insane can be a man deprived of the fundamental
sentiments of morality, but still *identical to himself from birth*
as writers describe him. Moreover, as Garofalo remarks,
if the criminal who becomes insane loses his identity and
becomes irresponsible, the criminal who was insane before
the crime and continued so afterwards preserves his identity
and would be responsible for his deeds. And once more,
could not the principle of irresponsibility through lack of
identity be applicable to all *emotional* acts and to those
outbursts which are qualified by phrases like *being beside
oneself, being possessed, etc.* Certainly, this interpretation,
which is not very pleasing to Tarde's uncompromising repression, would receive the support of modern mental pathology to which a conception analogous to that of Maudsley's
medial zone explaining the boundaries and relations between
the sane and the insane seems already too limited and rigid.
In short, what can be said of personal identity is that it is

never completely lost, not even in the worst case of insanity; that it fails at every step (normal and abnormal?); and that it is not easier to answer the verdict's question whether the culprit was the same before as after the crime than to say whether he was free or not; although, at bottom, the author thinks that the question has been one of *identity* and not of *free will*).

b. *Mitigated responsibility.* — *Infanticide* is cited as an example of mitigated responsibility; for, " the newly born not participating in the social life of the family, its death is far from producing the same horror as parricide." There is also mitigated responsibility for *international* crimes and misdemeanors.

c. *Aggravated responsibility.* — *Through personal identity.* — " If, in the case of *flagrante delicto*, it has been felt always convenient to become indignant and to punish more severely than when the culprit falls into the hands of justice after a long time, is it not because, in the first case, personal identity is more evident and in its maximum intensity? " (But are we not confusing here the *identification* of the culprit with the *identity* of his psychic personality?) *Through social identity,* like cases connected with the family, namely, parricide, fratricide, etc. (But family identity is not always aggravating. On the contrary, it excuses at times, as in the case of domestic thefts in our Code. It seems that the author forgets here what he so carefully tries to differentiate in the first chapter of " Criminal Law " on *The transformation of the law,* namely, that in the penal function by the side of *vindictive reaction* against foreign aggressors there exists *protection* and, at times, *pardon* for relatives); through *functional identity,* as professional comradeship; through *national identity,* etc.; all of which are aggravated, some through law, others through custom.

The theory of the normality of action, which to-day is advocated by Liszt, appears for the first time with the unjustly forgotten Poletti, a philosopher and a criminalist of noble and refined manner of thought.

In his works,[1] Poletti studies crime and punishment "in relation to the economics of human nature," because on this subject, says he, "we still find ourselves in the times of Grotius and even of the Romans."

Approaching the question from this point of view, crime is recognized by signs that leave no room for doubt. As soon as it is committed, an unusual and spontaneous activity is being displayed. The law which preserves human equilibrium displays a series of movements of defense and resistance by which society and the individual, yielding to a natural impulse, try to repress the offense, harm, and danger caused by the crime, and to erase its sad impression and immoral influence. "The general features that enable us to recognize a criminal action cannot be derived from our sentiments, social interest, or the idea of justice itself, but from something naturally more complex, more vast and at the same time more invariable and certain." The essential feature of crime consists in its opposition to the most intimate and delicate attributes of our nature, "to that wonderful combination of tendencies, ideas, and sentiments found in the individual and in society."

Thence, a conclusion of the greatest interest. The first victim of any crime is the delinquent himself; for, his deed betrays the abnormality of his constitution through lack of

[1] Poletti, *Il diritto di punire e la tutela penale*, Turin, 1863. *La legge universale di conservazione e la repressione dei delinquenti; Il delinquente, cenno d'Antropologia criminale*, Udine, 1875. — *Legge empirica della criminalità*, 1881. — *La persona giuridica nella scienza del diritto penale*, 1886. — *Il sentimento nella scienza del diritto penale*, 1887. — *L'azione normale come base della responsabilità dei delinquenti*, 1889.

"that powerful shield which preserves other men in the tranquillity of their existence," and of "the harmony and equilibrium between effectiveness and the principles which all take as a rule for moral conduct." Shall we attribute this fact to any regression toward primitive humanity? No; "the fine dignity of the legal conscience of modern nations makes us consider, as immoral and criminal corruptions, things which in very remote times nobody opposed or condemned." Is it, then, the effect of pathological conditions of the organism? "Certainly; criminality is neither moral insanity nor impulsive mania; although, in its most salient features, it may often bear some resemblance to them in that it makes it possible for honest people to draw back before actions devoid of sentiments which they possess." But the choice of free-will is not personal either. "Reason is surprised to see the extraordinary number of influences, currents, and premises originating from the combined active volitions that determine the particular value of the deeds of each individual; and, therefore, this phenomenon cannot be considered hereafter as a fortuitous event and as an incidental alteration of the order of things, but as a regular effect of the no less inseparable attributes of human nature, because others besides them oppose to it a prudent resistance."

Thus Poletti succeeds in establishing an empirical law of criminality analogous to Ferri's or Quételet's laws of saturation, and more explicit than either in that it teaches that delinquency advances always in proportion to the sum total of productive, conservative, and juridical activities; because, after all, crime and work, vice and genius derive their vitality from the same sources which, more than normal, are indifferent in their relation to the laws of nature, although when applied to humanity some are abnormal and others remain normal and rational.

" Henceforth, we will not say that man is responsible for
his actions because he possesses a will or because he is free;
but because, having been created by the power of natural
laws which trace for him the way of true humanity, he acquires
in the relations which he establishes and changes through
human intercourse rational and human aptitudes which
make him responsible for all his actions."   " Only the normal
man is responsible for crime because of the fundamental conditions of his being and of his physiological and psychic
development: conditions which he does not meet in nor
receive from society, but carries in his autonomous constitution and inner atmosphere."

But, who is the normal man?   Is the normal the ideal or
the most common?   And in either case, where is the ideal
or the normal?

Section 35. (2) TREATMENT OF DELINQUENCY.

Meanwhile, the discussion of this question does not prevent
the process of the law continuing in full vigor.

In discussing the present condition of the code that is being
formed around the questions of crime and punishment, we
must refer to three interesting publications of a general
nature: " Comparative Penal Legislation," [1] undertaken by
the " International Union of Criminal Law " under Liszt's
supervision;   " A Comparative Exposition of German and
Foreign Penology " [2] by the same author; and " A Sketch
of the Present Penal Code in the Lower Countries and
abroad " [3] by Van Swinderen.   Especially the first is to be
recommended.

[1] La legislation pénale comparée (Liemann's German and French editions, Berlin.   Two volumes already published).

[2] Vergleichende Darstellung des Deutschen und ausländischen Strafrechts.   (Six volumes published).

[3] Esquisse du Droit pénal actuel dans les Pays-Bas et à l' étranger (Gro-
ninga; Noordhoff, editor.   Six volumes already published).

Section 36. (A) Treatment of Minors.

The most prophetical feature of present penology —
besides others of an atavistic nature as we shall see — is the
establishment of a special jurisdiction for young delinquents,
based exclusively on the principle of tutelage. During the
time intervening between the first and the second edition
of this book this segregation has taken place in the United
States of America, where it had been announced long ago.

The history of the Juvenile Courts begins in Chicago,
Illinois, with a law of July 1, 1899. " From that time on " —
says Julhiet in his " Juvenile Courts in the United States," [1]
a work followed by Rollet, Kleine, and Gastambide's " Juvenile Courts," [2] — " Juvenile Courts have spread over the
immense territory of the United States with unprecedented
rapidity." Of the forty-eight States that compose the American Union, the following have established Juvenile Courts:
New York, New Jersey, Pennsylvania, Ohio, Michigan,
Indiana, Illinois, Missouri, Wisconsin, Minnesota, Kansas,
Nebraska, Colorado, Utah, Georgia, California, Washington,
Oregon, Connecticut, New Hampshire, Tennessee, Maryland,
Rhode Island, Iowa; and perhaps others very recently.

According to Julhiet, these Courts have the following features in common:

1. *Extreme specialization of the Court:* A judge well acquainted with child nature, a separate court room, [3] special

---

[1] *Les Tribunaux pour enfants aux Etats Unis;* in the Memoires and
Documents of *Le Musée Social*, 1896.

[2] *Les Tribunaux spéciaux pour enfants*, Paris, 1906.

[3] It is interesting to quote what Judge Stubbs says about this: " I
have remarked that whenever I sat behind a table as in an ordinary court
room, my words produced very little effect on the boy seated on the culprit's bench; but, if I sat near him so as to pass my hand over his head
and shoulders I nearly always won his confidence."

procedure and modes of enforcement, but no Code. These Courts do not trouble themselves with the question of a fixed classification of penalties, this being fully replaced by the necessity of striving to protect the young.[1]

2. *Suppression of imprisonment:* The arrested child is never admitted into the common room of the Police station; the convicted child is never sent to a common prison.

3. *Freedom under surveillance:* In some cases the child is sent to a reformatory, to a penitentiary colony, or to a charitable institution; but, whenever it is possible, the child is returned to the family in freedom subject to supervision. This is the method of enforcement of the American system. We shall meet it later under the name of parole system.

Julhiet forgets, in our opinion, a fourth interesting feature. Not only delinquent children come before the Juvenile Court, but also dependent and neglected children who are on the point of offending on account of bad environment. Thus, in this special jurisdiction, a unique feature of the Penal Code of the future, the repressive and the preventive elements are united under the principle of tutelage.

[1] A kind of free and flexible Code results from the following advices due to the experience of Judge Mayer:

a. *For rebellious and turbulent children,* who throw stones at one another, etc., but who, in reality, are not bad: simple reprehension and freedom on probation for the leaders of the gang;

b. *For children easily tempted,* who, desiring, for instance, a book displayed in a library, resist twice and finally fall: freedom on probation;

c. *For children with bad surroundings,* who join bad company and have careless parents: at times it is necessary to send them to the house of correction;

d. *For children of unworthy parents:* house of correction or a charitable institution;

e. *For children lacking moral sense:* necessarily the house of correction;

f. *For adventurous and vagrant children,* etc.: freedom on probation;

g. *For children born incorrigible:* their number is diminishing since the law compels the parents to pay for their support in reformatories.

h. *For neglected children:* a charitable institution.

Outside of the United States, Juvenile Courts are found mainly in the United Kingdom (England: Birmingham, Bury, Bolton, Manchester, Liverpool, Nottingham, Tunbridge Wells, Swansea, Stockton, Hull, Coventry, York, Southport, Beverley, Scorborough; Scotland: Greenock, Glasgow, Dundee; Ireland: Belfast, Dublin, Cork). Canada has one in Toronto; and Australia one in Adelaide.

Continental Europe has not accomplished as much. A curious state of transition is found in the Draft Code of criminal procedure in Italy, which combines the principle of conditional sentence with that of suspension of judgment in the case of less than 18 year old children guilty of crime and having been sentenced to less than a year's imprisonment (article 324). Although not establishing a special court, this means to exclude children from the ordinary one. Everywhere, if not in connection with the court, at least in the application of the law we find the elaboration of a treatment for minors distinct and even opposite to that for adults. At the same time there is a sensible tendency to extend as much as possible the limit of minority of the penal age in order to apply the treatment to a larger number of cases. The Dutch law of April 1, 1905 — in imitation of which the Congress of Criminal Anthropology of Turin (1906) passed its resolution — offers also one of the most interesting examples.

Section 37. (B) Treatment of Adults.

As we shall gradually point out, the progress made in penitentiary treatment is attained by extending to adults the treatment adopted for minors. How is it, then, that what is being done for children and youths is not done for adults?

Among the incoherent answers that are offered in order to maintain a dualism which the spirit of tradition and mistrust do not wish to forego, another development is already outlined within the uniform treatment of adults.[1]

It seems as if the penal reform episode of the beginning of the 19th century were repeated at the beginning of the 20th. While the statutes of those days adopted the so-called *mitigating and aggravating circumstances*, to-day, two new groups are emphasized which we may call, as they have already been called,[2] *very mitigating and very aggravating circumstances*, corresponding to the *absence of criminal record* and to *recidivism*. The French law of March 21, 1891, called the *law of mitigation and aggravation of penalties*, can serve as a formula for the general tendency of our times. It is as such that we shall present it.

Section 38.   (a) *Persons Without Criminal Record. —*
Pardon.   Conditional Sentence.

Pardon. — In the case of a person without criminal record and of good personal antecedents, who offends through excusable reasons and is not to be feared, why should the law be inflexible?   Why — asks Judge Dumontet in his " Mitigation in Repression " — do we not give the judge the same power of pardoning as is enjoyed by the jury, in spite of the evidence of the charge, the result of the proof, and the confession of the defendant himself?

In the country where the penal code is the most severe, the law of pardon is on the point of being sanctioned through the efforts of the celebrated President of the Tribunal of

---

[1] The idea of special courts (composed of women) for adult women appears in De Ryckère's study, *La criminalité ancillaire*, in the *Archives d'Anthropologie criminelle*, vol. XXI, 1906. The author, who is a judge in Brussels, refers to crimes committed by female servants, discussed in his *La servante criminelle*, Paris, 1908.

[2] Dumontet, *De l'adoucissement dans la repression*. . . . II, *Des circonstances très attenuantes*, Amiens, 1896.

Chateau-Thierry, the " good judge " Magnaud,[1] Congressman Morlot, etc. In the same Draft of Penal Code revision in France, article 66, we read: " In cases when, by virtue of the disposition of criminal law or in consequence of extenuating circumstances, the judge is authorized to impose light fines, he can, if the defendant has not been previously sentenced for crime or offense, waive sentence and warn him not to count on this immunity in case of relapse. The pardoned person will be condemned, nevertheless, to pay the costs, and, if the case requires, to furnish reparation for damages.[2]

Probation system and conditional sentence. — The law of pardon has not yet been fully accepted. But here we have two systems that resemble it. Their common trait is the suspension of the sentence extended to certain offenses according to law. The more the two systems are studied the more distinct they appear. They are known as:

a. The American system of *probation;* and

b. The European system of *conditional sentence.*

For a length of time, treatise writers — and we ourselves have shared in the same error in the first editions of this work — have considered the two systems as distinct species of one genus. To-day, with a better knowledge of the question, they appear as two distinct genera. Guido Bortolotto[3] is right when he says: " According to our opinion, the two systems are different in their basis, form, development, and effects. The conditional sentence, as the name suggests, is a true sentence naming a definite judgment both in quality and

---

[1] Leyret, *Les jugements du Président Magnaud,* Paris, 1900.

[2] *Texte du projet de la Commission du Code Pénal;* in the *Revue Pénitentiaire,* February, 1893.

[3] *El sistema de la prueba en Europa ;* in the *Rivista di Diritto penale e Sociologia criminale,* 1908; from the Spanish translation in the *Revista general de Legislación y Jurisprudencia,* 1909.

quantity; the benefit lies only in suspending the execution of the sentence. On the other hand, the probation system has no element of punishment; there is neither sentence nor judgment. When the period of probation ends favorably, there remains nothing of the procedure, not even the record of the offense committed. If anything remains, it is the healthful reform of the delinquent."

We shall discuss the two systems separately.

Beginning with the probation system, its origins can be traced to Boston, Massachusetts, in the appointment, in 1869, of the *State Agent*, who was soon replaced by *Probation Officers*. The system has gained ground year after year: from the capital it spread over the whole State; from Massachusetts to other States of the Union; thence to Australia and New Zealand; and finally it reached Europe with the English *Probation of Offenders' Act*, in 1907.

In order to give a faithful account of this system we can do no better than continue to quote Bortolotto.

In the probation system — says he — we must distinguish two distinct aspects and periods: a preliminary one which we may call the period of *investigation*, and a supplementary one, that of *surveillance*, also of great importance on account of its highly philanthropic and efficacious nature.

The period of investigation is of a peculiar nature and differs sensibly from the course followed by the police. The investigation is based on new principles. It loses the severe and inquisitorial character and assumes the essential importance of a preparatory act, which is particularly influential in the treatment of the guilty. With the change of principles there comes a change of means; the tools of judicial investigation are supplanted by elements which are more conscious of the importance of their mission and better prepared to understand and apply the new systems which are to guide in the verification of unlawful deeds and in the investigation and conviction of the guilty.

The preliminary inquiries are entrusted not to the police but to persons who do not limit themselves to the discovery and verification of the mere existence of the deed, but investigate the causes, no matter how remote, that have prompted it and the circumstances under which it was committed. Meanwhile, more than a frigid work of information, it is an act of zealous charity exercised by persons who consider crime not so much as an evil deed deserving punishment, but as a symptom of anomalous conditions.

When applied to juvenile delinquency this system gains unusual importance on account of its effects of prevention and correction. The investigator does not come before the judge as a mere witness of the deed and of what he has seen, as in the case of the police officer; but, weighing with calm discernment the elements of the offense, he finds himself in the position of throwing light upon the deficiency of information, measuring his utterances according to circumstances.

We must not forget that the only and true information is that accepted by the judge, who, guided by the principle that society must look more to correction then to repression, decides upon a verdict. But, he does not go so far as to make a final declaration of guilty or to pronounce sentence; this he replaces by a measure which pardons the deed, returns the defendant to society without the stain of a legal punishment, and offers him the opportunity of working out his own redemption under a treatment of protection and tutelage.

This is the preliminary period of the system, which adequately prepares the way for that of surveillance. The probation order covering the first period does not possess the characteristics of a judgment and even less that of a sentence.

No legal measure is applied, no penalty is inflicted, and, above all, in the case of minors, " it is not a question of punishment but one of education." [1]

Judgment and sentence are suspended, and everything is reduced to a personal conviction of the judge who has the power of collecting the data needed for a sentence which he can pronounce whenever the probation does not meet with favorable results.

The probationer must declare that he will submit to surveillance and that he will observe the conditions which the judge imposes upon him and which the circumstances of his case may require. For instance he is prohibited from frequenting undesirable company and places, is asked to abstain from intoxicating drinks if the offense was that of drunkenness or one committed under the influence of liquor,[2] and to follow other rules of good conduct and laborious life.

When the Court issues a probation order, the defendant rarely receives these directions in writing.[3]

With the probation order ends the first period of investiga-

[1] *The Journal of Prison Discipline and Philanthropy*, Philadelphia, January, 1906, p. 19.

[2] In the American system, whenever it is a question of drunkenness or of offenses committed under the influence of liquor, the officer not only watches the behavior of the probationer, but draws also his wages or the product of his work and hands it to the interested family, so that he may not waste it in a saloon (Cf. Reed: *The Reformation of Criminals*, MacMillan's Magazine, October, 1904, *Acts*, p. 308).

[3] The gist of these directions is more or less as follows: " The court, in spite of finding you guilty, places you under probation in order to give you the opportunity of reforming without suffering punishment. You are kept out of jail under promise that you will behave, live in peace with all men, appear before the court whenever summoned, thus avoiding losses to your bondsman, pay the costs if so required, and give your bondsman an account of your conduct at the end of every month of the probation period. — *Special warning:* If you wilfully forget your promise you will be brought back before us who will pronounce your sentence. Your bondsman will answer for you. (Signature)." (Cf. Reed: ibid., *Acts*, p. 303).

tion and begins that of surveillance which constitutes the real period of probation. The method of exercising this surveillance is outlined only in the adopted laws, some of which do not give any directions at all, allowing the probation officers full freedom of action. The officers, guided by the same principles as in the preliminary investigation, aid and advise their probationer, investigate his tendencies, look after his conduct, correct his vicious inclinations, and facilitate the development of his good tendencies.

Thus, the real period of probation includes two efficacious tendencies: true surveillance and the education and betterment of character. The former is very important although of a purely formal nature, while the latter contains all the useful and essential function of the system. For, if environment and vicious and corrupted associations cause and determine the offense, regeneration cannot be attained except through a persistent contact with honesty and righteousness. This, then, is the mission of the officer, who needs to proceed with tact, prudence, and courage [1] that the nature of the delinquent may require, until the aim that society has in view is happily attained.

If this, then, is the important and delicate function of the officers, Hughes is right in saying that " permanent and complete success depends upon the individuals to whom the working of the system is entrusted." [2]

The selection of officers — apart from the question whether volunteers are to be preferred to salaried officers — must be made with the greatest care from among persons who consider surveillance not as a detective but as a humanitarian work, and look upon the suspension of sentence not

[1] Cf. Barrows' " Children's Courts in the United States," p. xiii.

[2] Hughes' " The probation system of America," London, Weilhamer and Co., 1903 (Cf. Barrows, ibid., p. 49).

as a judgment but as a kind measure for the reform of the delinquent.

Therefore, probation officers must have nothing in common with police [1] and jailers.[2] The experience of American legislations has shown that the more probation officers and functionaries are differentiated from other functionaries of inspection and surveillance the better are the results of the system.[3]

All the legislatures that have adopted the probation system provide an adequate salary for officers.

The activity of paid functionaries can be supplemented by voluntary and gratuitous services. The spontaneous coöperation of private citizens, either as individuals or as members of benevolent societies,[4] becomes a valuable auxiliary. It has even been said that " if the citizens themselves do not take the initiative in this new movement there is no reason to expect great things in the proposed direction." [5]

Voluntary service is better adapted to the philanthropic nature of the system. Let no one say that volunteers do not understand their mission.[6] A visit to the Indianapolis Court, says Mrs. Bartlett, suffices to convince one that such an assertion is without foundation.[7] What we need is that

[1] They wear no uniform, are not identified with detectives, and have no connection with the police, except that the latter are obliged to come to their aid if need be (Cf. Reed, ibid., *Acts* p. 303; also Stoppato, " I tribunali speziali per i minorenni delinquenti," in *Rivista Penale,* LXV, 415).

[2] Cf. Hughes, ibid.

[3] Bartlett, *Système de la mise à l' épreuve dans les Etats Unis d'Amérique* (*Actes du VII Congr. pénit. int. Budapest,* 1908; cf. pp. 280, 281).

[4] Stoppato, ibid., in *Rivista penale,* LXV, 415.

[5] Reed, *Actes du Congrès,* quoted on p. 311. — Cf. Trompeo, in *Nuova Antologia,* July 16, 1907, p. 321. — Cf. also Barrows' " *Children's Courts in the United States,*" pp. 156, 159.

[6] " . . . A voluntary officer is sometimes looked upon as a meddler, and is not received with the respect the office should command " (Cf. Barrows, ibid., p. 112).

[7] Cf. ibid., p. 293.

officers be selected with care and that they give proofs of
zeal; once granted to them the same power enjoyed by paid
functionaries, we have reason to hope that they will fulfill
their office successfully.

The duties of the probation officer under the direction and
inspection of the court to which he is assigned are as follows:

a. To visit and gather information concerning the cases
assigned to him at intervals fixed by the probation order or
left to his own judgment;

b. To verify whether the probationer fulfills the conditions
imposed upon him;

c. To report to the court on the conduct of the probationer;

d. To advise, help, and befriend him; and if necessary, to
find him a suitable occupation.[1]

Many American Statutes make no similar provisions. The
officers, free in their movements, display more diligence and
lend their assistance in each case according to their own judgment.

This, then, is the treatment applied during the period of
probation; but the time is not so fixed that the Court cannot
alter it, and, if satisfied with the experiment, release the
probationer from surveillance.[2]

The duration of probation is left to the discretion of the
judge, who can lengthen or shorten it at pleasure. Undoubtedly, some statutes do not permit that the duration
of probation exceed that of the penalty;[3] others prescribe

---

[1] Cf. Probation of Offenders' Act, 1907, art. 4.

[2] Cf. *Probation of Offenders' Act*, n. 5. New York State possesses a
remarkable system. The possibility of imposing the penalty does not
end with the period of probation; for the judge orders the sentence suspended for the length of time covered by the suspended penalty. This is
analogous to the procedure on parole. Cf. *Report of the Probation Commission of the State of New York*, 1906, Albany, Brandon Printing Co.,
1906, p. 5.

[3] California, 1903, ch. 34; Michigan, 1903, ch. 91.

the time in which the judge expects the reform, a period varying from one [1] to three years; [2] and others, which are in general the most recent, have no special ordinance on this point.[3]

On verification of the fact that the offender has not com-
plied with the conditions imposed, the Court can issue a
warrant for his apprehension or for his appearance in Court.

The prisoner, when not brought before the Court that issued
the probation order, can appear before a Judge sitting in
Chambers who can order his detention or release on bail
until able to appear before the Judge interested in the case.

This is the American system of probation. Next we shall
glance at the European system of conditional sentence.

Its oldest precedent is found, evidently, according to
Loeffler,[4] in the canon law; but its actual and immediate
precedent to which is due its expansion in Europe is to be
found in the Belgian law of May 31, 1888, recommended
to legislators by the International Union of Criminal Law at
the meeting of 1889 as the best means of avoiding the great
inconveniences of short sentences.

The progress of its expansion can be better seen in the
following table:

1. Belgium: law of May 31, 1888; and Code of military
criminal procedure of 1900 (for no martial penalties).

2. France: Berenger's law of March 26, 1891, on the mitigation and aggravation of penalties.

3. Switzerland:

a. Canton of Geneva: law of October 29, 1892.

---

[1] Connecticut, 1903, ch. 126; New York, 1903, ch. 613, for minors as
well as for adults.

[2] New Jersey, 1899, ch. 102, for adults.

[3] Minnesota, 1893, ch. 150; 1903, ch. 220; Missouri, 1901, ch. 135;
1902, ch. 212.

[4] *La condannation conditionelle au Moyen Age;* in the *Bulletin de
l'Union Internationale de Droit pénal*, 1893.

b. Canton of Neuchatel: law of March 24, 1904.

c. Canton of Vaud: law of May 13, 1897.

d. Canton of Valais: law of May 23, 1899.

e. Canton of Tessino: decree of November 19, 1900.

f. Canton of Friburg: law of May 9, 1903.[1]

4. Luxemburg: law of May 10, 1892.

5. Portugal: law of June 6, 1893.

6. Norway: law of May 2, 1894; and Penal Code of 1903.

7. Germany:

a. Saxony: order of the Department of Justice, March 25, 1895.

b. Prussia: royal edict to the Department of Justice, October 23, 1895.

c. Würtemberg: idem, February 24, 1896.

d. Bavaria: idem to the Department of Justice, March, 1896; and royal sanction of January 15, 1896.

e. Hesse: decrees of the Department of Home Affairs and of Justice, June 22, 1893; June 29, 1895; and June 25, 1896.

f. Hamburg: circular of the Chairman of the Department of Justice, April 30, 1896.

g. Brunswick: ordinance of March 5 to 22, 1903.[2]

8. Bulgaria: law of January 5, 1904.

9. Italy: decree of June 26, 1904 (Ronchetti law), recast in the Draft Code of criminal procedure, 1905 (articles 462 to 464).

10. Spain: law of March 17, 1908.

Found only in the state of draft are:

1. Greece: Typaldo Bassia's draft (1906).

---

[1] The principle of conditional sentence is set forth in Stoos' *Draft of the Federal Penal Code in Switzerland*, article 50.

[2] The German preliminary Draft of Penal Code also accepts the principle of conditional sentence.

2. Argentine Republic: draft of Penal Code (1906).

3. Japan: revision of the present Penal Code.

Besides Europe, the principle of conditional sentence has been adopted by:

1. Massachusetts: Penal Code of October 1, 1900.

2. Maurice Island: law of 1900.

3. Egypt: Penal Code of February 14, 1904.

The Belgian law of May 31, 1888, authorizes the Courts to pronounce at their own discretion the conditional sentence under the following circumstances: when the penalty, be it principal or accessory or both, does not exceed a term of six months' imprisonment; and when the prisoner has not served any sentence for crime or offense. The term of suspension is for five years, and the sentence is considered as nul unless the offender commits a new crime or offense during this period; in which case the suspended penalty or penalties increase by the addition of the new sentence.

Other laws have imitated this system in the main, with the exception of some details which will be discussed later. Only the Norwegian system deserves special attention.

In Norway, the courts not only have the faculty of conditionally suspending a prison or a fine penalty, but also the compensation to the victim; that means that a part of our civil liability tends to become criminal in the modern law. Moreover, conditional sentence is granted not only in cases adjudged by the Courts, but also whenever the Prosecuting Attorney and the police authorities issue a *forelaeg*, that is, a criminal warrant which can be used with the express consent of the delinquent, because only fines can be imposed. The necessary requirements are: a. That the person or fine penalty be commensurate with the offense; and b. That peculiar circumstances concur in the defendant, like age (less than 18 years old), good conduct (not having been previously punished for certain offenses), little importance of the offense, conditions under which the offense was committed (grief, provocation, incidental drunkenness), full and sincere confession, satisfaction given to the victim or readiness to do so, etc. But none of these circumstances is so important that no conditional sentence can be pronounced without them. The term of suspension is of three years, during which time the execution of the sentence is carried out in case of recidivism or failure to compensate; although even recidivism does not altogether determine the fulfilment of the sentence, a fact which constitutes an altogether new feature of the system.

Conditional sentence is still the object of lively discussion everywhere. Beginning with the communications presented by Prins and Lammasch to the Brussels meeting of the International Union of Criminal Law, the theme has been taken up by penitentiary congresses, academies, scientific societies, and technical reviews, forming thus a bulky literature.

The Union has made of it its " pet child " as Liszt confesses; and from the time it recommended the Belgian law to the legislators of other countries, it has continually followed its progress, collecting in its " Bulletins " all the advances it has made. Conditional sentence, even in the present transitory form, violates so many classical principles and dogmas that it is not to be wondered at if it has gained also resolute opponents.

Among its partisans are: Liszt, Prins, Van Hamel, Lammasch, Leveillé, Dreyfus, Puibaraud, Lejeune, Beltrani Scalia, Puglia, Setti, Notaristefani, Tallack, Howard Vincent, Wines, Rosenfeld, Aschrott, Seuffert, Bachem, Simonson, Fuld, Heinemann, Mayer, Fayer, Stoos, Sitter, Harold, Hagerup, Uppstrom, Wulfert, Taganzeff, Sloutchowsky, Piontkowsky, etc.

Among its adversaries are: Kirchenheim, Wachs, Appelius, Rolin, Binding, Vierhaus, Meyer, Finger, Ofner, Pfenninger, Domela Nievenhuis, Levy, Thalberg, Petit, Manduca, etc.

An intermediary group which accepts the system with certain restrictions is composed of men like Garofalo, Ferri, Foinitzky, Gautier, Goos, Schmolder, Ditzen, Bar, Schulze, Brzobohaty, Pessina, Chiarone, etc.[1]

In ancient penal systems prison penalties were seldom inflicted. They were mainly limited to what we call to-day *preventive detention*. Prisoners awaited in their cells the judgment and the repression which were of quite a different form. They consisted either of bloody and collective eliminations by which the legislators, " like the ancient heroes of Greece tried to rid their States of monsters " (Guizot), or of mutilations and other corporal punishments, or of hard labor in the King's mines or galleys, or of lighter public services and various forms of work, etc. But from the time of Beccaria's reform and the Revolution, penology began to be centralized on these penalties which to-day have become typical and unique through a series of causes summed up thus by Garofalo: " The idea that the deprivation of freedom is an affliction equally felt by all; the idea that civilization cannot tolerate corporal punishments; and the necessity of equality and symmetry in all things, have ended by giving the preference to this class of punishments which are susceptible of almost infinite divisions and subdivisions." [2]

But, short sentences have proven everywhere powerless to repress small offenses; and what is worse, they have greatly and decidedly fomented recidivism. Not being able to

---

[1] This classification is taken from the first edition of this work, and was made at a time when the polemic was at its height. Since now it has been decided in its favor, it would be impossible to enumerate all its adherents.

[2] *Bulletin de l'Union Internationale de Droit Pénal*, May, 1889.

correct — for, what correction can be obtained in their short terms? — or to intimidate, for modern prisons offer material conditions of life superior to those enjoyed by the lower classes of society from which delinquency is mainly recruited, they offer no hope except to the few who from the point of view of absolute justice believe that the debt is paid and society satisfied from the moment the sentence is served. On the contrary, the punishment itself produces recidivism in the man who enters a prison for the first time. His honorable and industrious existence having been marred and destroyed by a small offense or misdemeanor (the number of which are being constantly increased by the exaggerated activity of the police), turned out from the workshop, and mistrusted by everybody, he will be led back to prison through the paths of idleness and drunkenness, like the unmarried mother who returns to prostitution.

What shall we substitute, then, for the short sentence?

First of all, money penalty is out of the question when we consider the economical condition of the delinquent class. Other substitutes arranged in logical order and suggested by the association of ideas are as follows: At first one thought of detention, substituting the home for the prison (domiciliary arrest). Then, recourse was had to other forms that are now in disuse, although some of them are to be found in modern Codes, like *judicial warnings* and *security*, or certain kinds of *hard labor* without imprisonment. They even recurred to a *reconciliation* with the victim and to the *reparation* of damages as penalty; and, going to the other extreme, it was asked whether it was not time to make the modern prison more severe by going back to the *hard prison* of the old régime.[1] At this time the conditional sentence

---

[1] Cf. the papers read before the Amberes meetings of the Union by Ofner and Felisch; *Bulletin*, V, 1895.

and pardon as another manifestation of the same idea reached Europe.

Immediately, a group of the most progressive reformers of criminal law and of penitentiary science saw in it " the most simple and efficacious means of checking the excessive development of the short sentence " (Liszt). Scalia finds it " such an ingenious disposition and so adequate for many purposes, that it is impossible to conceive how any Code can do without it." [1]

Besides, it is not an innovation without precedents. It represents both security and reprehension. It is that " correction by the judge's mouth " spoken of by Domat — and which the great magistrates of olden times, like D'Aguesseau, Servan, and Lamoignon claimed to employ — as well as a *material reprehension*, because of the constant psychic coercion which it produces in the delinquent. If this coercion produces results, can there be anything better than to redeem the delinquent without handing him and his family over to poverty and shame? If it produces no results, he will not remain unpunished, for penalties accumulate. Young delinquents, occasional criminals, and authors of small offenses find their best treatment in the conditional sentence, which affords exercise in self-control, and is far superior to the inertia and contagion of the prison. It even strengthens prison penalties which by their constant application have lost all their value.

The foes of the conditional sentence, although recognizing the inconveniences of short sentences, propose to reform and not to abolish them, claiming that the former is irreconcilable with the principle of retributive justice. " The conditional sentence," says Appelius, " cannot be accepted unless we place

[1] Beltrani Scalia; quoted by Setti in *La condanna condizionale, Rivista di discipline carcerarie*, XX, 350.

criminal law on a different basis." Others have referred to the
sanctity of the sentence, its greater or less incompatibility
with the prerogative of pardon and with certain principles of
procedure, etc.

The conditional sentence, according to Appelius, answers
to a new conception of punishment. The American *probation
officer* is really a *tutor dativus* (the guardian of the Roman Law).
But, what shall we say of the European system in which there
is neither guardian nor physician, and the delinquent is left
to himself? At first, both the pardon and the suspension of
penalty seem incompatible with the demands of a solicitous
and beneficent treatment; but, on further study, one notices
that both form part of that same system understood in all its
subtlety. Who does not know that at times the best remedy
is a kind of *laissez faire* allowed to the healing virtue of the
organism, a discrete *abstention* from interference that might
prove a hindrance? Inactivity and waiting for developments
is a rational process which ought to be applied in this case as
in other things. The conditional sentence and the pardon
mean, therefore, the recognition of certain *tempora tacendi*
as Vives would say. They are not measures of *grace* and
mercy, but of a higher and enlightened *justice*. Undoubtedly,
their application requires greater initiative, superior conscience, and more profound knowledge on the part of the
judge; but, as Prins remarks, the function of the latter becomes, thus, nobler and higher.

Let us glance, in conclusion, at the strange contrast offered
by the existence of these systems fused with the group of
traditional systems of punishment. The former are, according
to Ferri, an eclectic graft on the old stock of criminal law and
procedure, whose result is best expressed by the Italian
proverb: " the first fault is pardoned and the second whipped."
In fact, when we consider that the " sword of Damocles,"

the "persistent hanging threat" is the metaphor that best explains the power of the two new creations, then we will understand the reason why Leveillé considers and calls them the *prologue of penology*. But the future destines them to form a *part of penology itself*, when the conception of the latter is so changed as to admit that the first fault is pardoned and the second whipped, as long as the fallen will is redeemed.

If it should be asked which of the two systems is preferable, the probation or the conditional sentence system, we would say that although the latter may suffice in some cases when the automatic correction of the delinquent can be expected, it ought to be accompanied by the former especially in the case of minors; for it is the only ethical manifestation of tutelary punishment in modern law.

Section 39. (*b*) *Recidivism — Deportation — Indeterminate Sentence — Reformatories — Capital Punishment.*

In contrast with mitigation for delinquents without criminal record we have aggravation for recidivists.

Deportation. — This first solution is of old origin. Primitive communities practised the easy and unhindered method of *elimination* both in the *relative* and in the *absolute* form mentioned by Garofalo. The expulsion from the soil and the withdrawal of the protection of the law was one of the first ideas recorded by writers. The malefactor was taken to the seashore with bound hands, placed in an unmasted and, perhaps, leaking boat, and abandoned to the caprice of the waves.[1] Subjectively, as Makarewicz remarks, this man exists no longer for the community; he is *civilly* dead as he would have to be called, and in reality he is not far from

---

[1] Makarewicz (*Evolution de la peine*) attributes this custom to the old Germans and to the inhabitants of the Island of Tobi. It must have been practised with slight variations in old maritime towns.

natural death either. Yet, the community is not satisfied; it returns inland, nails down the doors of the malefactor's house, razes it to the ground, fills up his wells, devastates his fields and scatters salt over them so as to render them unproductive. These are the energetic features of primitive elimination. The same idea that caused more or less violent exile and banishment produced, also, the *deportation* of delinquents to places far from the community that expelled them. But, as the known parts of the earth were covered with men, these punishments fell into disuse until the discovery of new worlds and territories brought them back in the struggle against crime.

Russia, England, and France are the three nations that in modern times have practised deportation on a large scale. England has ended her cycle of penitentiary colonization; legendary Australia offers an ideal example which other countries would fain follow. In Germany, the cry of *away with jails* has already been raised; [1] and in Italy, Eritrea has been pointed out as a penal colony.

The example of Australia seems to have had sad results in France, where by the law of May 27, 1885, there was organized the system of deportation, imitated later by Portugal (law of April 21, 1891), and probably to be followed by Argentina (Draft Code of 1906). The French penologists (headed by Leveillé, Vidal, Garçon, etc.), with some exceptions, as in the case of Larnaude, look with favor upon deportation and penal colonization, and have advocated their cause, basing their faith on a precedent. Under the influence of an example the principle of deportation has spread to the

[1] *Fort mit den Züchthäusern*, Breslau, 1894, is the title of a pamphlet by Bruch, who is the author of other works of the same nature (*Neu Deutschland und seine Pioniere*, Breslau, 1896; and the paper read before the Congress of the Union at Lisbon). Together with Freund, he is a staunch advocate of deportation and penal colonization in Germany.

extent that at the Penitentiary Congress of Paris it was declared fitting " for serving out long sentences due to serious crimes, and for the repression of habitual criminals and obstinate recidivists." Under the same influence, the International Union declared in Lisbon that deportation could play a part in the modern penal system. Almost at the same time, a communication was sent by Feillet, Governor of New Caledonia, to the General Prisons Association[1] showing the failure of the system from a penal as well as colonizing standpoint. These authorized revelations created a great sensation. The government itself is planning to abandon the attempt according to the report of another writer who visited Caledonia not long ago.[2] If we add to this the change of policy of Russia which has limited deportation to the island of Sakhalin, we will easily understand why the general state of mind is one of mistrustful prevention before a disaster.

Nor are there wanting men who, like Fani,[3] believe that deportation is the secret of penitentiary science and the neutral field on which classicists and positivists clasp hands, forgetting, as Viazzi affirms, that if in its favor are found men like Ellero, Canonico, and Garofalo, the opposite side is championed by Brusa, Pessina, Beltrani Scalia, Nocito, Lombroso, Laschi, Drill, and others.

Without examining the arguments of either side, it can be affirmed that the *penalties of elimination* as such, like deportation with abandonment, which Garofalo advocates theoretically — " if there could be imagined the existence in Oceania of an island by which no ship could sail," or " if the Robinsons did not end by meeting always human beings " — would

[1] *La colonisation pénale en Nouvelle Calédonie;* in the *Revue Pénitentiaire,* XXII, pp. 646–656.

[2] D. Drill, in his communication to the Congress of the Union at Lisbon.

[3] *La deportazione,* Rome, 1896.

still remain intolerable *inferior systems*. From these they have passed to *colonizations* that might clean large centers of their vicious elements, and to *labors of the soil* by which, according to an oft-repeated phrase, the convict must prepare the abode for the honest and free man. But, on the other hand, the first answer the English colonies gave to the attempts of the mother country to send them her criminals would still be right: What would you do — they answered — if we should send you our rattle-snakes? That must be the end of the one-sided and selfish point of view. As for the labors of the soil, the idea is opposed by a conviction which is gaining the conscience of true, honest, and free men, that it is they who are duty-bound to prepare the soil and the new life for delinquents. The terms have been reversed and the consciousness of this duty forbids making of them *servants by law* of a favored social class, as they were once of royal mines and galleys.

We are scarcely rid of these systems of elimination. But, should we condemn and eliminate them? The idea of exclusion from one environment or of deportation to another seems, in these days when its influence is so emphasized, too important to abandon. The *change of climate* can become a remedy as in medicine. At times the mere *transfer* can suffice. Is not the simple fact of making distance intervene, a piece of foresight used at every instant both in the penal sphere as well as in private life, as we can see by the results empiricism shows us? But, in other cases, perhaps the more numerous and surely the more important, of what avail would deportation be if the delinquent were not removed to a well selected and well prepared environment as is done in the choice of climate and watering places for the sick? If, as Plato says,[1] there were for the moral welfare countries placed under the

[1] *Laws:* Book V.

influence of a beneficent spirit with springs of psychological virtues . . . that would offer the remedy.

This has given birth to the so-called *agricultural penal colonies*, which, beginning with the famous one of Mettray (Indre et Loire), are finding their way in all civilized countries. They are intended for *rest, nutrition*, and *moral recuperation*. They seem to realize the punitive equivalent of the treatment given the insane in the Belgian town of Gheel, so much longed for by some thinkers (Kropotkin), since, as in the colony of Val d'Yèvre (Cher), one enjoys freedom and the cultivation of the soil — " man acting upon the soil and *vice versa* " — as well as the home treatment.

From all that has been said we can draw one conclusion. While penalties inflicted through segregation have had no other object than the segregation itself, their results have been similar to those produced by prison penalties whose only object was the prison itself. Things being so, one might as well fill the prisons with delinquents as dump them upon the colonies. The discussion between the advocates of the one and of the other is of no serious weight. Both forms are equally undesirable. The same cannot be said for the form that has produced an Elmira Reformatory or a Colony of Mettray. The important point is to discriminate and to individualize as much as possible by applying to each class of delinquents the most suitable form for them and by distinguishing under what circumstances and treatment it is to be applied. Only then, as a physician prescribing for his patient what is best for him, will the judge believe that he is doing a true work of *distributive justice*.

Indeterminate sentence.—As a contrast, the conditional or suspended sentence suggests the idea of a penalty extending over an indefinite period of time. Thus, it must have been this association of ideas that gave birth to the indeterminate sentence.

Ferri states that a system of accumulated or progressive sentences, by means of which the penalty increased almost in geometrical proportion at each relapse, had been proposed by Viel and Walton Pearson back in 1871, having already been sanctioned in the penal code of India, while a Japanese law condemned a man who relapsed for the fourth time to life imprisonment.[1]

Less developed than the conditional sentence, the indeterminate sentence, in its form of indefinite detention, is found in many American States (Massachusetts, New York, Ohio, Minnesota, etc.), and in the Norwegian Penal Code of 1902, which, according to section 65, grants that dangerous delinquents can be detained even after having served the ordinary sentence, as a measure of safety, for a period not exceeding three times the length of the sentence or fifteen years. Plans for analogous measures for the treatment of recidivists are found in England (Draft of indeterminate segregation for habitual criminals, approved by the House of Commons, June 22, 1904), in Switzerland (Draft of the Federal Code, 1893), and in Russia (Draft of the Penal Code of 1903).

Nevertheless, we can easily understand how the principle of indeterminate sentence, or rather, the principle of sentence without previous determination is applicable to the general problem of fixed penalty. Thus stated, it is related to the corrective doctrine. It is difficult to understand how a writer like Garofalo may criticize it; because while, on one hand, he declares that the object of punishment is the correction of the delinquent, on the other, he establishes a fixed term for each crime, that is, a certain number of days, months, or years in a State institution.[2] Garofalo's Spanish translator, Dorado Montero, has felt it his duty to rectify this statement,

[1] *Sociologia criminale* (4th edition, Turin, 1900), p. 892.
[2] *Criminalogia*, p. 162.

citing against it the name of a Spanish correctionalist,[1] who in several of his works has fought fixed penalty, even before the time when Kraepelin [2] and Willert [3] asked for the *abolition of fixed penalty*. The last mentioned, a judge by profession, has said that " to establish a fixed term for each crime would be the same as if a physician prescribed a treatment for a patient determining on which day he was to leave the hospital whether cured or not."

Gautier, in his " The *pro* and the *con* of Indeterminate Sentences," [4] has admirably summed up the arguments in favor and against, stating the opinions of Kraepelin, Willert, Liszt, etc., for the *pro;* and those of Wach, Mittelstadt, Sternau, Zucher, Lammasch, etc., for the *con*.

The arguments in favor have already been stated. If the object of punishment lies in the future and appears uncertain, how can the sentence be fixed at a certain number of days? On the side of the opposition, there are some who advocate the opposite penal significance, that is, that of retributive justice; others who protest in the name of the victory of the Revolution that abolished judicial discretion; and still others, who, while accepting for the sake of argument the original principle of indeterminate sentence, ask for the proof of the correction that ends the sentence.

[1] He refers to F. Giner. This is what he says in his *Principios de Derecho Penal* (Madrid, 1873, p. 170): " Among the many historical negations of the right understanding of punishment must be mentioned . . the serious error of determining *a priori* and in an absolute way the duration of the penalty announced in the sentence, *as if it could be anything but the one thing necessary to accomplish the end in view*, and which, at the time the term is served, is still extremely uncertain."

[2] *Die Abschaffung des Strafmasses*, Leipzig, 1880.

[3] *Das Postulat des Abschaffungs des Strafmasses mit der dagegen erhobenen Einwendung.*

[4] *Pour et contre les peines indeterminées*, in the *Schweizerische Zeitschrift für Strafrechts*, IV. — Cf. also Levy, *Des sentences indeterminées,* Paris. 1897.

Among the first, Tarde, who is the most noted and who considers punishment as the *wages of crime*, says that punishment like wages ought not to be indeterminate. In fact, from this point of view, the indeterminate sentence has no reason to exist. In the " exchange of values," of which Carrara speaks, punishment must have the same value as the crime; and if it were possible to verify this mathematical operation, the principle would be just. But, apart from the confirmed decrepitude of the theory of retribution, to desire to measure the crime by the punishment is the same as to ask, according to Moddermann's old remark, how many kilograms of iron are necessary to make a suit of clothes? In reality, it is more absurd than that; for, after all, the condition of the market would solve the strange problem, while in our case it is a question of measuring something for which there is no measure, something which is beyond the traffic of men. As Max Nordau would say, this is " the greatest conventional lie of modern Byzantium."

The second group numbers men like Berenger, Leveillé and Foinitzky, who claim that we ought not to endanger by a debatable reform one of the most precious victories of the Revolution. Sternau, for instance, says that "with the indeterminate sentence the citizens would lose the *palladium* of their safety, the warrant against a judicial decision which fixes the time and the length that a culprit must be deprived of his freedom."

It is well known that, as Boitard affirms,[1] the criminal law posterior to the Revolution was almost entirely different from that anterior to 1789, and that one of its novelties consists in having suppressed the vast and fearful arbitrariness of the old penology. " Punishments are despotic in this kingdom " said the French practitioners; and they could

[1] Cf. Dorado Montero's *Problemas*, I, 19.

have said the same thing of other countries. Therefore, in consequence of the abuses suggested by the ill-sounding word *arbitrariness* in law, the Revolution accomplished two things: it protected the citizen against the abuses of the judge; and checked the latter by a very explicit law, which defined everything, measured everything, and was to be applied by the judge mechanically.

Now, as these guaranties have been asserting themselves so as to become an integral part of that law which does not need to be expressed in the statutes, the double work of the Revolution is on the point of dissolution. People think that so much security, " as long as it is wrongly used to protect the individual, constitutes the very weakness of criminal law " (Garofalo). Judicial discretion is regaining what it had lost, and rids itself of the unfortunate note as the magistrate gains in *science* and *conscience*.

The latest approved Codes and the Drafts which are being drawn everywhere bear witness to what has been said. It suffices to give a glance at the Dutch Code, which is pointed out as a model, to see that judicial discretion is such that the magistrate can pass from the maximum penalty of life imprisonment to the minimum one of a single day.

Perhaps of more importance is the other feature of the movement suggested by Garofalo's statement quoted above. When one considers that, as Liszt remarks, " no matter how paradoxical it may seem, criminal law is the Magna Charta of the criminal," for, as a result of those guaranties, it " protects neither legal order nor society, but only the individual who is rebellious to its dictates "; then the indeterminate sentence, almost to the point of becoming *perpetual*, is reserved for the habitual criminal, the incorrigible recidivist.

This is one side on which the indeterminate sentence tries to find its way into the penal system of to-day. The idea is vaguely outlined in the Union's by-laws and made clear by Van Hamel, one of the founders. This writer (in a paper read before the Paris Congress of the Union) would like to recommend the *absolutely indeterminate sentence* for incorrigible criminals, that is, for those whose confirmed criminal instincts threaten society with permanent danger; and for its application, he would recommend the process of applying the measure after the ordinary sentence, and in the cases pointed out by the law, by means of deliberations and periodical orders with trials of provisional freedom and the possibility of ultimate liberty, to be carried out by the judicial authorities with a procedure resembling the ordinary one. Gautier also, after having analyzed one by one the advantages and disadvantages of the indeterminate sentence, "fascinated by its theoretical side and repelled by the obstacles offered by its application," ends by recommending it only for incorrigible criminals. Griffiths, General Inspector of the English Prisons, classifies the criminals of all countries in two large groups: those who should *never enter* a prison and those who should *never leave* it (a paper read before the Congress of Criminal Anthropology at Geneva on "The Practical Treatment of Recidivists"). After all, this is but another expression of the war against recidivism. Are not the police asking everywhere for an anthropometric and medical analysis that would afford a sure and indelible mark of the personality through which the recidivist can be detected? Then follow the new methods against this plague. The progressive aggravation of penalties for the recidivist is an accomplished fact; a step further and we reach life sentence. But men stop at this point. Van Hamel himself only dares to suggest the possibility of a detention "until a very advanced age."

On the other hand, Prins reserves the indeterminate sen-

tence for *minors worthy of protection*. Gautier would add
delinquents who are in such pathological conditions that
the cure is revealed by positive marks, as in the case of drunkards. Griffiths advocates a " system suited to the Saxon
taste " as Rivière remarks; a system, according to which,
the duration of the penalty, instead of being fixed *a priori* by
the judge, should be fixed *a posteriori* by a special commission
according to individual circumstances. Liszt asks for a
general treatment in which the penalty should fluctuate
between a maximum and a minimum: its completion depending on the decision of a mixed commission (judicial administrative). Others propose new systems dealing only with
the details.

It is certain, however, that in the midst of so much discussion the principle of indeterminate sentence appears here
and there, now within the maximum (recidivists: incorrigibles), now within the minimum limit of the fixed law
handed down by the Revolution. Leveillé took no notice,
or did not wish to take notice, of this double invasion, which
will finally unite, when at the session of the Union in Paris
he said: " The indeterminate sentence is as simple as a false
idea."

According to Foinitzky, the future belongs to it; and this
is not a prophecy, but the result of prolonged observations.

The argument of practical application is also set forth
against the indeterminate sentence. How can it be proved
that we have reached the end of its period? What will assure
us that the penal function has been fulfilled?

These questions have already been answered by asking:
how does the physician know that his patient has regained
health? How does the teacher know that his task has been
accomplished? They will never know if we look upon life
as a period of constant education where everything must be

learned, from articulate speech to death. But we may look upon the work of the indeterminate sentence as well as upon that of the physician and of the teacher as the minimum needed for the object in view. The correction of the delinquent is not a process of sanctification. It has more modest claims. It aims at endowing him with moral strength enough to prevent him from relapse. "A delinquent can be considered as reformed when such a change has taken place in him that on returning to a life of freedom he will not offend again"; his reform is "the reasonable probability that he will not break the law again" (Smith).

These probabilities, as in any other phase of life, are manifested by exterior signs, daily manifestations, and repeated tests and experiments. To this modern law adds another institution which we shall now discuss.

Reformatories. — In the evolution of prison penalties, we distinguish two main features. In the first place, since the prison is a place of punishment, everything tends to deprive the prisoner of certain comforts of life considered secondary or superfluous, and to diminish the most important ones, like air, light, food, and rest; penitentiary prohibition includes all. In the second place, deprivation of freedom is understood to be the simple means of isolating the delinquent from bad influences and of making him the recipient of good ones which the penitentiary treatment places at his disposal.

Beginning with John Howard, the history of penitentiary treatment in the prisons is well known. The system of *life in common* among prisoners is immediately followed by systems of *classification* (sex, age, crime, character); and, as a contrast, by that of *absolute isolation*. Later it is changed to *relative isolation*. The *Auburn system* separates the convicts only at night, allotting to each a separate cell; while, in the daytime, according to Rolder,[1] real isolation is substituted by a fictitious, artificial, and superficial one, consisting in compulsory silence. Finally, there appears the *cellular system* as the result of selection from these first schemes dealing with prison penalties. The system of *individualization* succeeds that of *classification*. It isolates each convict from the rest, forming thus a class by himself; it borrows the *cell* from the Pennsylvania and the Auburn types; isolates the delinquent in it, as in an antiseptic treatment; and places him under the healthful influence of an environment composed of supervisors, physician, superintendent, teacher, etc.

For some time, the cellular system corrected by *progressive Irish and English methods*, has been accepted as the last word of penitentiary science. It is only at present that opposition, which is sure to accompany every theory and system, assumes form and asserts itself through the hostile position taken by the positivistic school. Enrico Ferri has more than any other voiced this opposition by qualifying the cellular system as one of the " greatest aberrations of the 19th century." It was at his suggestion that Italy, by the law of June 26, 1904, abandoned the already adopted cellular system and sent her convicts to clear the fields and drain the regions infected by malaria. As Rivière remarks,[2] it is strange that a school so imbued with the influence of social environment should be hostile to individual isolation and advocate the methods of classification. When Ferri says that although environment acts powerfully upon the individual, he is a man and therefore a social being whom we cannot isolate without leading him to insanity or suicide, he does not really criticize the cellular

[1] *Reforma del sistema español mediante el régimen celular;* in the *Doctrinas fundamentales reinantes sobre el delito y la pena;* translated by F. Giner, Madrid, 1876.

[2] *Le Congrès d'Anthropologie criminelle de Génève;* in Larnaude's *Revue de Droit public,* 1897, p. 378.

system, but the extreme types fashioned after that of
Auburn.[1]

In general, it is not only the cellular system defectively
applied, save a few exceptions, but also all prison penalties
that are facing a crisis. After a century of penitentiary
reform, never has the prison been attacked as in our days.
It is at this point that Kropotkin's name is coupled with
that of statesmen of all countries. The reader can find a
large collection of significant phrases in the last chapter of
Colajanni's " Criminal Sociology," devoted to repression as
a powerful factor of crime. The delinquent himself has
expressed his opinion of prisons in all the documents which
modern literature collects under the title of *penitentiary
po'impsest.* Far from the Dantesque visions which the
jurists imagine through a psychological automorphism, " he
who has seen a prison," said some time ago Lauvergne, one
of the first to make a direct examination of prisons, " can
boast of having witnessed a picture of happy life."

> " Qua sol trovi i fratelli e qua gli amici,
> Danari, ben mangiare e allegra pace;
> Fuori sei sempre in mezzo ai tuoi nemici,
> Se non puoi lavorar muori di fame." [2]

The penitentiary is only an accident of the profession not

---

[1] The cellular system has rightly been opposed from this point of view.
Read, as an example of severe sentimental criticism, E. de Goncourt's
Fille Elise; a novel of great interest for criminologists, since it is the story
of a prostitute who committed murder in a fit of psychic epilepsy. She
was condemned to death, but the penalty was changed to life imprisonment in an institution on the Auburn plan. The struggle against the rule
of silence forms the main episode of the story. Elise finally succumbs.
When visited by an illustrious philanthropist, the sub-prefect asks her
to speak, but she does not answer, she has become dumb. " Sub-pre-
fects," says the novel in conclusion, " lack the power of bringing the dead
back to life."

[2] " Here alone you will find brothers, friends, money, good fare, and
cheerful peace; outside you will always be in the midst of your enemies,
and if you find no work you will starve." Quoted by Lombroso and reproduced by Garofalo in his " *Criminalogia*," p. 223.

to be greatly feared; it is a higher school in which to continue its practice, and even a resting place from the agitated life of the career.

Hence the discredit cast upon the prison. Hence why, from Kropotkin to Griffiths, we continually hear that "a prison can never be *bettered*, it is necessary to do away with it."

In fact, the penitentiary is losing ground every day. The substitutes offered for short sentences diminish its usefulness. Domiciliary arrests, reprehension, securities, work outside of the jail, are daily becoming popular and cutting off the retreat of the penitentiary in the latest criminal codes and drafts. On the other hand, deportation tends to rob the prison of long terms and severe penalties. So general, persistent, and uninterrupted is the movement that for a time these efforts seem like two workmen who, attacking an obstacle from opposite directions, hear their blows getting nearer and finally meet at the same point.

The famous and moving episode of Pinel, when, together with the asylum warden Pussin, who had already practised similar ideas, he unfastened the chains of the insane,[1] has been cited everywhere by many thinkers of distinct tendencies. By many, from the radical Kropotkin to Solovieff, the episode has been cited, at times in the imperative form of an ideal desire; at other times, by those who abominate it, as a fearful intimation of what the future has in store. On examining this variety of opinions, one cannot help asking in a concrete form: Will prison penalty be abolished as was abolished imprisonment for debt, and as will shortly be abolished the subsidiary prison for civil responsibilities?

[1] The first was a madman, the soldier Chevinge, who burst into tears when he saw himself treated for the first time in a humane and kind way. From that time on, he remained in Pinel's service, whom he never abandoned, according to the historians who record this memorable episode.

The word *abolition* so often used in these pages — and for no other reason than for its frequent use around us — must not be taken in the sense of *destruction*, as one might be tempted to take it. Someone has said that the snake gets rid of its skin because it has already another defensive epidermis ready. So with men; behind every abolition there is another law that perpetuates in more delicate and happy forms a common idea whose continuity is not being destroyed by the novelty.

Looking around at what happens in the world for an answer to our question, we notice that while one thing disappears another takes its place. Simple *deprivation of freedom* reappears, and if this means prison, then the prison persists. But when we connect this word with the mass of ideas suggested by *prison penalty*, we can hardly make the same statement.

In the first place, these new institutions for delinquents are not called by any of those names whose most developed form corresponds to the penitentiary (*casa de fuerza*). They are called *reformatories*, *bridewells*, etc., and therefore their inmates are not called *convicts*, but *inmates*, *wards*, etc. Even the exterior of these institutions offers a contrast to the imposing fortresses of the old régime; for, being light constructions for recreation surrounded by gardens, their walls are of brick and not of granite, and their windows have more glass than iron bars. What shall we say of their interior if such is the exterior? They contain all the means with which to reorganize human life. A choice and intelligent staff: psychologists, pedagogues, physicians, etc., carefully apply them, studying their effects and results.

Excellent institutions of this type are found scattered in civilized countries. Some of them, the most numerous, are for children and young delinquents; others for men; and a smaller number for women. England and the United States, the promised land of penitentiary reform, possess the largest number and the most noted. They differ somewhat according to the civilizations of the two countries. The English institutions have a simple, almost severe aspect; while the American [1] are sometimes sumptuous and a little extravagant.

The Elmira Reformatory can be called the archetype of them all.[2] It was founded by an act of the New York legislature of 1876, chapter 207. It can be said to be the living expression of all that has been accomplished in regard to crime and punishment for many years, " the most advanced institution in the world," " the first that has shown in a practical way what men must do in order to act rationally and humanly, and at the same time the just and utilitarian treatment of delinquents." But, it did not drop out of the sky, and cannot be considered perfect. The first remark is suggested by writings which represent it as without ancestors, forgetting an entire generation of not less remarkable types associated with names like Suringar, Ducpetiaux, Obermaier, Guillaume, Maconochie, Crofton, Lucas, and so many others who have little by little gathered all the stones of the great edifice. The second seems an idle remark, for nothing is perfect in this world. But, when in the midst of so many kind attentions and cares which comfort the soul and fill

[1] After the establishment of the Elmira Reformatory, which is really the greatest penal institution of our times, this extravagance has become more apparent in similar institutions, which, taking it as a model, have sought to excel it. But the ridiculous is as distant from the sublime as the Tarpean rock is from the Capitol. It is not to be wondered at how far certain imitations have gone. In Aschrott's excellent work (*Aus dem Straf und Gefängniswesen Nord Amerikas*, Hamburg, 1889), the reader can find data on this degeneration and extravagance. At the soirée given by the inmates' *club*, at which Aschrott himself was present, full of astonishment, the inmates were all in evening dress with a fashionable flower in the buttonhole.

[2] Dorado, *El Reformatorio de Elmira*, Madrid, 1898.

it with hopes, we recall the presence of corporal punishments,
the whip, and the red-hot iron,[1] one ends by believing that
there is something monstrous even in connection with the
Reformatory. The cells which can be deprived of natural
light represent the last vestige of the traditional *dungeon*.

Perhaps, even this Reformatory possesses no scanty measure
of mechanism and rigor, as seen in its clear-cut and uncompromising classifications and gradations. Something
might even be said on the life in common of the inmates.
But, after all, it is the only institution where it has been
possible for " a delinquent by instinct, whose criminality has
found a favorable environment in which to develop, absolutely
ignorant, without employment or means to honorably earn
a livelihood, and with a weak and vicious physical organism,
to be so benefited as to come out strong in health, with an

---

[1] Towards the end of 1892, the New York press denounced the practice
of corporal punishment in the Elmira institution, affecting popular
opinion so much that the Governor of the State was obliged to appoint
a commission of investigation composed of a judge, a lawyer, and a physician. The Board of Managers in the meantime suspended Mr. Brockway,
the Director of the Reformatory, from office. At the time, it seemed that
the institution had kept the matter of corporal punishment secret, even in
its annual reports to the Legislature. The Commission, undoubtedly, was
expected to find out whether the measure had been abused, and to decide
whether, granted the positive legislation, this means of discipline was
legal or not. It was found that two corporal punishmen's were being
practised at Elmira: the whip and the red-hot iron, in order to force
rebellious inmates to leave their cells; but that it was done only as a
threat, and that they were never applied to the body. As for abuses
and cruelties, the Commission discovered only one serious case. The
opinion was that corporal punishment was being wisely applied by the
General Superintendent in person. Undoubtedly, the judge and the
lawyer believed that it was not strictly according to the laws of 1847
and 1869. The Board of Managers also believed that ch. CCCLXXXII
of the law of 1869 limited corporal punishment to federal prisons. The
result of this incident was to justly reënstate Mr. Brockway in office;
but corporal punishment was abolished, beginning from the 26th of
September, 1893. The proceedings of this investigation were published
in the *Nineteenth Year Book*, 1899.

education suitable to his condition, and with a trade or manual skill which he can put to use in an honorable environment." [1]

How this is being accomplished, the reader will find in Dorado's book. Here we can only give a resumé of Mr. Brockway's account of the means employed in the Reformatory for the correction of the inmates, " keeping in mind that they are given in the order of their efficacy, that is, in the order of the greater or less promptitude with which the inmates respond to their action, as it is shown by the progress obtained in the most susceptible of them ": 1. The desire for freedom, used for the amelioration of the individual by means of the indeterminate sentence and the monetary marking system. 2. The stimulus derived from the division into grades by means of the increase of comforts and privileges as they pass from the lowest to the highest, and the different wages which they earn in the various grades. 3. The benefits derived from a perfect system of education including all the inmates, from the most ignorant to those having received an academic training, and which is imparted by means of progressive methods. 4. The beneficent influence of military organization and drill, carried on persistently, which give in substance the same military education as the best conducted military academy. 5. The technical and industrial education given to all the inmates, which affords them the best practical preparation for life as free men with a profession or a lawful occupation, and whose chief aim is to enable them to earn their living by their own efforts as workmen in legitimate occupations.[2] 6. Physical training scientifically taught in

[1] Words of Dr. A. Flint, President of the New York State Medical Association, quoted by Dorado.

[2] This ought to be the nature of the work assigned to delinquents: a means for honest life — the best way to obtain it, — and not a punishment as it has been customary. Compare the " huge wheels the prisoners had to move with their feet, developing power enough to operate a thou-

a well-fitted gymnasium by a competent instructor under the
supervision of the physician of the institution. 7. Manual
training for those afflicted by some peculiar perversity due
to the lack of development or disorder of the mental faculties.
8. A progressive use of adequate elements of nutrition, so
as to build up the tissues, and to produce or favor good health,
to strengthen and tone up the nervous system, and to promote
habits and aptitudes for the exercise of a regular and continuous work.[1] 9. In addition to all these measures, they bring

sand mills," as reported by Bentham, who found this occupation —
which has lasted in England till a short time ago — excellent, " being
nothing else but a *different way of climbing a hill* "(*!*). According to this,
death penalty is only a different way of beginning another life.

[1] These three items deal with the *education* or *medical treatment* of
the delinquent imparted through three main agencies: a. Physical
education, so powerful — especially with the Saxon race — as to revive
the Olympic games in our days; b. The teachings of modern psycho-
physics, which show in the character of each individual the rôle played
by his peculiar anatomy and physiology; c. The teachings of criminal
anthropology, which point out in every delinquent what is abnormal and
pathological, whether it be much or little, horrible or imperceptible at
first sight. Thus arose the idea of a physical treatment for delinquents,
since the physical in them, as in every person, is a factor of their conduct.
In Elmira, for instance, they adopted since 1895 a series of bodily exercises to strengthen and balance the psychic functions by means of certain
manual activities, chosen and expressly prescribed for determinate groups
or individuals; for, physiology teaches that for every part of the body
submitted to the exercise of the will there exists a cerebral center that
regulates its movements (cf. Ferrero's *Le ultime esperienze del Riformatorio
di Elmira*, in the *Archivio di Psichiatria*, XVII, 631; and *Twentieth
Century Book*, New York State Reformatory, 1896). Certain medicines
and drugs (like bromure and copper for epileptics, phosphorus for the
weak-minded, mercury and gold for syphilitics), certain surgical opera-
tions(the boring of the skull for traumatic epilepsy, etc.), and normal
and hypnotic suggestions for some cases, have been proposed and are
already being tried (cf. Lombroso's paper read before the Geneva Congress on the " cure of the occasional and born delinquents, according to
sex, age, type, etc.''; Vaudelet's *De L'éducation physique rationelle chez
les jeunes detenus*, Paris, 1896; the works of Beriilon on suggestion, etc.).
All this suggests remarks which would be too lengthy for a foot-note.
It suffices to point out what we have, which in itself is enough to suggest
the same ideas in everybody.

into play moral and religious influences so as to increase
and strengthen the ethical power of the inmates.[1]

In short, the system is based on the application of intelligent
corrective methods, extended over a sufficiently wide period
— although fixed,[2] — with conditional freedom as a test.

The Board of Managers governing the Reformatory acts,
also, as a Parole Court, and grants conditional freedom on
parole four times a year. The General Superintendent, or
Director, acting as a reporter in these procedures, gives an
account of the deserving candidates. They appear before
the Board and undergo a kind of examination showing that
they are fit for social life. In general, the candidates presented
by the Director are nearly always released on parole; but,
the inmates whose names are not included in the list, can,
always under the general provisions of conditional freedom,
appear before the Board and solicit the release in person.

After a man has been released on parole, he will not enjoy
his privilege immediately. Two requisites must still be met.
First, the Superintendent and the Board find him a steady
and suitable occupation; and, secondly, he must earn in the
Reformatory shops the necessary means of transportation
to the place assigned him, and must live at his own expense
as soon as he receives the first payment for his work as a
free man.

When these two conditions have been fulfilled, the Superintendent states that he has found employment for his charge.
The Reformatory report, on the other hand, mentions the
activity the paroled has displayed in the shops in order to

---

[1] *Year Book* of 1895, p. 25.

[2] During the first years of its existence, the sentence was indeterminate only when it represented the minimum term. But, afterwards,
by the Fassett law of 1889, the system was suppressed. After that, both
maximum and minimum terms were fixed in the sentence. In either case,
the duration of the treatment wavers according to the conditions of the
delinquent.

enter upon a life of freedom. Then the paroled receives a certificate of provisional freedom. This credential or passport is not like the shameful yellow paper of the discharged convict, which has caused so much oratory, the paper that sent Jean Valjean back to a life of crime. The Reformatory certificate is couched in words full of respect and trust for the man who is supposed to be reformed. The Board imposes certain conditions which he must fulfill in order to obtain ultimate freedom. At all events, it offers him the protection which it is able to grant for the last time. The most important condition is that he must make a monthly report of his life, which, examined and indorsed by the agents who are to be found in every State of the Union, is sent to the institution. These agents, like the Probation Officers, although without the public character of the latter, protect and watch over the paroled.

At the end of eighteen months, or less when the maximum of the sentence does not cover that period, the provisional freedom becomes absolute if the paroled fulfills the conditions and the reports of the agent are favorable. Otherwise, the Board of Managers appoints a commission of investigation or sends a Transfer Officer, who is equipped with a regular prison warrant, and, on verification of the bad behavior of the paroled, brings him back to the Reformatory. The paroled who loses his employment or occupation returns also to the Reformatory, but not as a prisoner.

As can be seen, the whole system is a happy combination of the principle of conditional freedom with that of supervision.

Doubtless, it is difficult to recognize by exterior marks the purely internal and invisible change that can take place in the mind of the delinquent. The most painstaking psychologist can be deceived. But, does not the same thing happen

in the treatment of the child by the father, of the pupil by
his teacher, and of the patient by the physician? Do any
of these renounce or give up the task?

The man to be reformed does not come down from the
clouds as an enigma to be solved. We know his antecedents,
we have direct observation, and the observation and experiences obtained from many others with whom he must necessarily have many traits in common. Elmira, for instance,
carefully keeps trustworthy notes of the past and antecedents
of every inmate and his family, draws up *biographical statistics*, and possesses *human documents* of the same nature.

Another indication is found in the inmate's behavior in
the establishment. Here we must mention an observation
made by all. In the penal systems with fixed terms, the
prisoner awaits the termination of his sentence in a complete
mental inertia which renders him less and less capable to
guide his own destiny. Convinced that the last day of his
term will come without his doing anything, his interest lies
in simply adapting himself to the mechanical treatment of the
establishment in order to avoid disciplinary punishments
and to gain the good will of the chiefs and employés. His
conduct, far from being bad, is really exemplary from this
point of view. All agree, strange as it may seem, that the
worst delinquents make excellent *prisoners*. This kind of
behavior, then, cannot accomplish the desired end. The
behavior to be desired must be the result of the activity of
the faculties and conditions peculiar to each man which will
help him to earn his freedom, and enable him to hasten it
or lose it indefinitely. To give him his freedom means to
suppress in him personal effort upon which his redemption
depends.

During the experiment, the moral worth of the individual
cannot help revealing itself to the eyes of the Director of the

prison; even if he happens to have been recently appointed to the *care of souls*, from him must be expected the virtue and the inspiration accompanying the office of his priesthood or of his magistracy. The limitations that surround the trial of social questions will often hinder the testing of the *specific character* of the delinquent (murderer, swindler, lewd . . .), who must be examined through his general aptitude in a place lacking the means and the incentives that might betray him. In case of relapse, the man who was thought reformed must be returned to prison, the same as a discharged patient who not seldom must be resubmitted to the former treatment, as the absolved sinner who confesses the same sin to his spiritual adviser, or as the pupil who recites the same lessons to his teacher. It is an incident that accompanies every educational work without exception. But, while the system of conditional freedom tries to overcome this as far as it is possible by advocating a *gymnastics of the will* that may strengthen and reform it, not otherwise than muscular exercise in producing strong men and intellectual exercise in producing logical men, the system of captivity fixed by the law crushes the little corrective energy that remains, and at the hour appointed returns the delinquent to society without worrying over the certain relapse.

Death penalty. — Whether there are incorrigible delinquents or not, the question of death penalty still exists, mustering arguments from the philosophy of every epoch. The question resembles in some of its features that phenomenon which scientists call *mimitism.*

After having clothed itself with the philosophical doctrine of every epoch and borrowed the arguments accepted by all, to-day, at the height of a Darwinistic age, it calls upon the law of selection for further argument. In vain one looks in the work of the great naturalist for a passage upon which to base the selective function of the death penalty. Häckel is the one that affirms it,[1] and upon his words its advocates wish to base the simple argument. Lombroso favors it at times;[2] Garofalo does so always. According to the latter, social authority by allowing itself to be seduced by the advocates of abolition will act contrary to the progress of science.

In reality, it is to Ferri that we owe the turning point of this current in favor of the death penalty in modern Italian criminology.

First of all, Ferri remarks that the selective point of view (Darwinistic, although not in Darwin's mind) must be complemented both in the natural and in the social life by the point of view of adaptation to environment (Lamarckism); so that the influence of the social environment upon the pathogenesis of crime must have as much value when dealing with the social sanction against crime as when dealing with the rehabilitation of the criminal in social life.

On the other hand — going back to the point of view of

---

[1] " Death penalty has an immediate good result, because it is a process of artificial selection." (Häckel's *Naturliche Schopfungsgeschichte*, quoted by Makarewicz in his *Evolution de la peine*, who considers death penalty " as an infallible remedy to purify the atmosphere.")

[2] The second French edition of " Male Offender " contains, as an expression of support which pleased Lombroso most, a letter from Taine ending thus: " Your book shows us lewd orang-outangs with human faces, who, being as they are, cannot act otherwise. If they kill, rob, or commit rape, it is due to their nature and their past. One reason more of getting rid of them as soon as they show that they are and will always be orang-outangs. From this point of view, no objection ought to be raised against the death penalty as long as society is benefited by it." But, who will prove that they are and will always be orang-outangs? Lombroso has nobly declared afterwards, in a letter to the French deputy Reinach, that having been an advocate of the death penalty at the beginning, long reflection led him to finally oppose it (Cf. *Scuola Positiva*, 1906).

selection, — if penal justice is to be an exclusive function of artificial selection, then it ought to have the logical and practical courage of inflicting the death penalty on a large scale, and make true hecatombs surpassing the proportions in which it was applied in the Middle Ages.

De Flury, who does not lack this courage, demands, among other repressive measures, the " mitigation of the means and the multiplying of executions." [1] Garofalo shows the same courage when he tries to prove that the execution of born criminals would not arouse the sympathy of any one; because, sympathy proceeds from resemblance, and, psychologically speaking, nobody can feel sympathy for them; and because, when the deed, apparently evil, is committed with altruistic ends, it offends no one.

Yet, the abolition tendency is spreading with more or less intensity and fluctuation everywhere, including Spain itself.

Section 40. (3) PREVENTION OF DELINQUENCY.

Thus far we have dealt with the treatment of delinquency aiming at preventing relapse. But, would it not be possible to anticipate crime and apply a similar preventive agency when less grave symptoms revealed the diagnosis of the evil and the prognosis of the necessity of a corrective treatment?

Hence there arises the idea of prevention before criminality, starting with situations and states bordering upon it, and spreading thus through successive circles over the entire social environment as a part of what English writers call *Eugenics*, or the arrangement of influences which improve the quality of the race.

Starting with the idea of successive circles, we reach the one immediately surrounding the focus of criminality, the smallest

[1] *L'âme du criminel*, Paris, 1898.

and most intense, and consequently containing the preventive activity directed upon the combined dangerous and equivocal classes that constitute the borderland of the criminal world.

The most important of these classes is represented by vagrancy, which becomes even the generic symbol for the rest.

There is nothing more variable and heterogeneous than the legal conception by which the defensive mind of legislators, rising against all logic, binds together, under pretext of a crime *per se* or an aggravation of some accompanying offense, all kinds of suspects, including sometimes even the sick.[1] And, indeed, even after reducing vagrancy to its natural trait — namely, inability for regular and continuous work, and, consequently, social segregation with a posterior parasitical readaptation, — we find in it differently constituted individualities, as:

a. The *ethnical* vagrancy of transplanted peoples who lead a nomadic life and move among communities enjoying an old and stable civilization, like the rivers which for a certain time cut through the surface of the sea without mingling with it. Such are the gypsies — already diminishing in numbers — and the other nomadic peoples of the Balkans, where the mountains separate and defend Europe from Asiatic immigration;

b. The *atavistic* vagrancy through ancestral influences which determine incompatibility with civilized life;

c. The *physiological* vagrancy of children when it is due to a simple inner impulse, which represents in the individual ontogeny the nomadic phase of the racial philogeny;

---

[1] " The general fear caused by the pestilence " — wrote Florian and Cavaglieri (*I Vagabondi*, Turin, 1897–1900) — " induced the legislator to treat persons infected with the plague as vagrants " (I James, 1, ch. 31).

d. The *pathologic* vagrancy dependent in its causation and progress upon various psychopathic states;

e. The *economical* vagrancy due to social conditions (lack of occupation, the breaking up of the family, criminal record, etc.), which, in the long run, fixes itself upon the personality and becomes hardened.

From the abandoned child to the human wreck which **Gorki** calls "ex-man," [1] the vagrant class, to which Florian and Cavaglieri have devoted the most painstaking work perhaps ever published, offers without doubt some dangerous characters — from the simple thief to the Sadistic murderer — although it numbers also varieties truly inoffensive.[2] From this point of view, Konn [3] divides them into the antisocial and the extrasocial class: the latter composed of primitive types, hermits, preferring the country; and the former including degenerate types of the city, like panders, *apaches*, etc., who live in bands for the sake of the gay life, for fear of solitude, and also for love of depraved pleasures.

Many of them lead this life from childhood. Therefore, our attention is called to that part of the problem which deals

[1] Cf. our study: *Los vagabundos según Maxim Gorki*, in the volume: *Alrededor del delito y de la pena*, Madrid, 1904.

[2] Such as Onésime Loyé, a former University professor, who answered his judge in Alexandrine verses:

"What is your name?"
"*Onésime Loyé, c'est ainsi qu'on me nomme.*"
"Your age?"
"*Voilà bien cinquante ans que je suis honnête homme.*"
"Where do you live?"
"*La terre est mon seul lit; mon rideau le ciel bleu.*"
"What is your profession?"
"*Aimer, chanter, prier, croire, espérer en Dieu.*"
"Why were you found begging?"
"*J'avais faim, magistrat; aucune loi du monde.*"
"*Ne saurait m'arrêter, quand mon estomac gronde.*" (From a French communication to the *Corriere della sera*, November, 1905.)

[3] *Gazeta Sizitawa Warzawska*, 1906.

with the abandoned child, and which is of such importance for penology; for, as Morrison remarks,[1] the passage from occasional to habitual delinquency rarely takes place in the adult age.

The efforts displayed for the reduction of vagrancy are many and always interesting. The interest grows when we study child vagrancy. This is due chiefly to sentiment; for, neither valetudinarian neglect nor adult pauperism engraving upon the walls their pictures of misery move us as does unhappy childhood. But this sentimental impulse is accompanied also by thoughtful reasons. Every protected child — as someone has said — represents a rescued generation. Moreover, the rescue can be accomplished with the minimum effort, and with the maximum result compared with the effort required for the regeneration of adults. Therefore, without neglecting the latter, the efforts are especially focused upon the young.

In Juderías' " The Protection of Childhood Abroad," [2] the reader will find the most complete exposition of the laws and institutions adopted in the civilized world. We will only add that the traits which best characterize the movement are the principle of guardianship and the placing of minors among homelike surroundings, where moral influence will improve their psychical organism. This represents a fruitful renewal of the old cellular system based upon better biological foundations. For, instead of isolating the subject between the four walls of a cell, he is placed in a living cell, namely, an honest family into which he can be more easily absorbed.

Continuing our simile, if we pass to a second circle of wider prophylaxis, we shall find that the struggle against alcoholism

---

[1] *Juvenile Offenders*, London, 1896. Joly, Raux, Ferriani, Cuello Calon, Guarnieri Ventimiglia, etc., are of the same opinion.

[2] *La protección á la infancia en el extranjero*, Madrid, 1908.

on the part of modern communities is as intense as the power of alcoholism itself. Thus, the writings on this subject — alcohol, alcoholism, and antialcoholism — take up in Abderhalden's bibliography more than 500 pages, with 15 or 20 titles in each.[1] We will add a few works published later. On the relation of alcoholism and criminality we have Hoppe's " Alcohol and Criminality in all its Relations," [2] and Pistolese's " Alcoholism and Delinquency." [3] On the campaign against alcoholism, there is J. Bertillon's " Alcoholism and the means of fighting it according to experience," [4] and Miomande's " The Struggle against Alcohol." [5] Baudry de Saunier's " His Majesty, Alcohol " [6] treats of both topics.

This campaign is of great interest to criminology, since a large number of crimes are due to alcohol and the tavern, now directly and indirectly as illustrated by the so-called " alcoholic murder " (caused by acute intoxication without apparent motive and followed by amnesia [Sullivan]), now in an indirect, distant, and very remote way, as in the crimes committed by the descendants of drunkards. Criminology is interested also in the means adopted to fight the evil, from the system — somewhat naïve and trusting too much in the omnipotence of the law — of *absolute prohibition of the sale* of all alcoholic drinks, reserving it only to druggists as it was at the beginning, to the *high tariff* on alcohol, which, although diminishing the output, increases the strength, and the most profitable systems, as that of *limiting the number of licenses* and that of *leasing the monopoly of alcohol* to corporations of

[1] *Bibliographie der gesamten wissenschaftlichen Literatur über den Alkohol und der Alkoholismus*, Berlin and Vienna, 1904.

[2] *Alkohol und Kriminalität in allen Beziehungen*, Wiesbaden, 1906.

[3] *Alcoolismo e delinquenza*, Turin, 1907.

[4] *L'alcool et les moyens de le combattre jugés par l'experience*, Paris, 1905.

[5] *La lutte contre l'alcool*, Paris, 1906.

[6] *Sa Majesté l'Alcool*, Paris, 1906.

public utility.[1] To this must be added the spread of *temperance societies* and of *drunkards' asylums*. Finally, there is what Ferri calls the *social remedy*, the uplifting of the common life (reduction of the hours of labor, raising of wages, more attractive home life, hygienic amusements, etc.), which will attenuate and eliminate alcoholism from the lower classes of society, as it did the drunkenness of the well-to-do classes so widespread in the Middle Ages, and which has almost disappeared on account of the great change wrought in their social conditions.[2]

Finally, reaching the last circle — after culture, reformation, and fully applied justice, — it is interesting to mention measures like the establishment of public baths and the rebuilding of forests for the modification of impulsive and sanguinary tendencies; for the trees help in bringing systematic rains which they retain, thus changing a dry, exciting environment into a damp, sedative one.

Section 41. (4) REPARATION OF THE INJURY CAUSED BY THE CRIME.

Ought the criminal system to take more thought of the indemnification of the victims of crime? This question has for several years been the order of the day of all Congresses of penal science; for, as Prins says,[3] " modern criminal law has altogether neglected the offended party and the entire notion of the reparation of the injury in order to give prominence to the Public Prosecution exercising justice in the name of all."

[1] The Gotenburg system, the most efficacious of all; cf. Laquer's *Gotenburger System und Alkoholismus*, 1907; Rubenson's *Das Gotenburger System*, etc., Leipzig, 1907.

[2] *La justice pénale, son évolution, ses défauts, son avenir* (Brussels, 1898), paragraph VII.

[3] A paper read before the Congress of the International Union of Criminal Law at Christiania.

Bentham and Spencer have been prominent in our century in calling attention to this memorable criminal question. Spencer's theory set forth in his " Essay on the Morality of Prisons " is very interesting. Proceeding with his characteristic method of illustrations, he tells us how criminal reformers, like Maconochie, Crofton, Mettray, Obermaier, Montesinos, etc., have best known how to rid themselves of the old conception of the jail, keeping its doors wide open and giving more freedom to the prisoners. Therefore, he proposes a new treatment which seems to bear some analogy to the two types of society which he considers fundamental, namely, soldiers and merchants. This system is, in fact, a new manifestation of the contract; it is the *security* or the *bail* for the judgment of penalties. According to Spencer, the duration of the penalty must depend on the time the culprit takes to make reparation for the injury caused by the crime, granted a creditable person takes him under his protection and promises to return him to the authorities as soon as he sees him go wrong. Thus, Spencer believes to find a kind of *automatic regulator;* for, the author of the most loathsome crime would never find a person to go security for him, and his custody would be perpetual. Recidivists would also find it difficult; while the authors of light or excusable offenses, the injury once repaired, would be exempt from punishment on account of the facility with which they would find security and also on account of their good behavior.

Among contemporaries, Garofalo advocates in his " Criminology," in his " Indemnification of the Victims of Crime," [1] and in various papers read before Congresses, a system which demands the *strict obligation of repairing injury* as the only repressive measure for certain light offenses committed by delinquents from whom, on account of their behavior and con-

[1] *Riparazione alle vittime dei delitti*, Turin, 1887.

dition, no relapse is to be feared. For these a double fine would suffice, one for the benefit of the State as a reparation for the disturbance caused and a reimbursement of costs, the other for the benefit of the injured party. As the trunk returns to the trunk and the root to the root according to a maxim of our common law, so the two branches of the system of penalties whose bifurcation is pointed out by Makarewicz — the fine and the civil compensation — come together in this theory.

But, how can these reparations be obtained?

"As for *solvent* defendants," says Garofalo, "extreme severity should be adopted. The injured party ought to have a judgment lien on the defendant's real estate and a special creditor's lien on his other property; and this not from the time the final sentence is pronounced, but from the time suit began. This would give the defendant no time to dispose of his property. In case the injured party renounces the indemnification, the defendant ought to be compelled to deposit the corresponding fine in a *fine fund* destined to advance sums to indigent persons who have suffered in consequence of crime. As for *insolvent* defendants, they ought to be compelled, for the benefit of the State and of the injured party, or, in case of renunciation, for the benefit of the *fine fund*, to hand over the share of their income beyond what is *absolutely* indispensable for the strictest necessities of life, namely, board and lodging. In the case of factory employés, the employers should be compelled to retain the wages of the defendant save what is absolutely necessary for his support. Finally, those who prove unmanageable, those who find it impossible to save, the vagrants, the idle, and those without a home, should be compelled to join a gang of laborers working for the State. They would receive nominal wages not inferior to those received by free workmen; the State would give them what it deemed sufficient for their maintenance, and the rest would be gradually deposited in the *fine fund* with which to indemnify the injured party."

Here we have, then, a complete plan of legislation defending the interests of the victim of crime. Out of consideration for these interests and also because of its being another means to avoid short sentences, the International Union decided that "in the case of slight offenses against property, there is no necessity of pronouncing sentence if the non-recidivist has previously indemnified the victim" (Christiania Session of 1891); it recommended also in similar cases reconciliation with the injured party. Perhaps, only in some cases, the consideration for the rights of the victim is so great, that by conceding to him also a kind of *vindictive satisfaction*, as Bentham would call it, some writers (Garofalo himself, for instance, in the case of the conditional sentence which he does not admit without a previous indemnification to the victim) subordinate the penal treatment properly speaking to the reparation of the injury.

5. CRIMINAL LAW AND PENITENTIARY SCIENCE IN SPAIN AND IN SPANISH AMERICA.

A. Spain.

Section 42. (a) *Ideas*.

"The characteristic peculiarity of Spanish penal science at the beginning of the 20th century," writes Dorado Montero,[1] "seems worthy of attention. The alliance of metaphysicians and positivists on this question has never been better realized than in Spain. We might say that correctionalism furnishes the mold, the meaning of the penal function; and that positivism contributes the data with which to fill this

[1] *Balance penal de España en el siglo XX;* in the volume *De Criminalogía y Penología*, Madrid, 1906.

mold and which serve as a basis and a proof for that meaning.
Somebody in Ribot's 'Revue Philosophique' [1] has spoken
of a Spanish School. Never before could such a statement
have been made. . . ."

We already know that the origin of this phenomenon is
due to Röder's direct influence in our country. His correc-
tionalistic ideal drew later from Giner, Calderón, and Montero, the progressive exposition binding together anthropology and criminal sociology: a union which is not frequently
met elsewhere. Undoubtedly, it is to this that Richard refers
when he speaks of a "Spanish School"; but, even if not
so characteristic, the retrogressive deviations from that cor-
rectionalistic ideal are more frequent although minimized
in the case of magistrates (González del Alba) and of penitentiary experts (Armengol, Lastres, Cadalso, and especially
Concepción Arenal). [2]

Concepción Arenal, a sister of the order of St. Theresa of
Jesus, lived in different times, and distinguished herself by
the intensity of her work. [3] She addressed herself to the
delinquent as well as to judges and private citizens, and
aimed at the purification of the perverted penal function.
It would be impossible to call her a correctionalist as has been
done at times. "From no thought of correction," she wrote,
"they have ended by using nothing but correction; the

[1] Alluding to G Richard, the distinguished critic of criminal sociological publications in Durkheim's *L'année sociologique*, and always well
disposed toward Spanish productions.

[2] Silvela, *El Derecho penal estudiado en principios y en la legislación
vigente en España*, second edition, Madrid, 1902. — Aramburu's *La
Nueva Ciencia penal*, previously cited; the notes in the translation of
Pessina's *Elementos de Derecho penal;* and Valdés, Rueda, etc.
Aramburu's work drew forth an answer by Ferri, included in his
Polemica in difesa della scuola criminale positiva (Bologna, 1886, including
writings by Lombroso, Ferri, Garofalo, and Fioretti).

[3] *Cartas á los delincuentes, Manual del visitador del preso, Estudios
penitenciarios, etc.*

prisoner is given lessons that may enable him to suffer the least possible. The ideal seems to lie in correcting without causing pain." Her main position in relation to the problem seems to be one of neutralization of the correctional idea by means of the conception of expiation through grief, which, "when it is not made to play the part of the executioner becomes a great teacher." Thus, more than penal science, it is mysticism that we find in Concepción Arenal.

Section 43. (b) Laws.

The integral reform of the present penal Code started almost simultaneously with the date of its promulgation. In 1873, Minister Salmerón appointed a Commission which during its existence succeeded in producing the first book of a Code inspired by the corrective principle and including the inevitable abolition of capital punishment. Then follow the unsuccessful drafts drawn by Alvarez Bugallal (1880-81), Alonso Martínez (1882), Silvela (1884), Villaverde (1891), and Montilla (1902); the last was not even presented to Congress on account of its reformatory tendencies. The Code of 1870 — already in operation since 1848 — still stands on its feet, aged and paralytic, while a few special laws try to modernize it by placing it on a better defensive.

The principle of conditional sentence has finally become a law (March 17, 1908), although organized in a timid and not very original way. Another law, enacted the 31st of December, 1908, on the preventive detention of juvenile delinquents, could not be more unhappy in its precepts.

No draft exists against recidivism; but it is amusing to note an inferior substitute for the indeterminate sentence in the police practice of the so-called "fortnights." [1]

[1] The "fortnights" treatment is applied to habitual offenders for blasphemy. An article of the Provincial law (art. 22) authorizes the

As for conditional freedom, a first concession can be seen in the state of resistance established by the royal decree of May 6, 1907.

Finally, the death penalty is bound to disappear. A law of April 9, 1900 (Pulido law), prohibited the publicity of executions, alleging the immorality of the spectacle as one of the reasons. A later draft, dated November 2, 1906 (Morote draft), aims at its definite abolition.

Section 44. (c) *Institutions.*

The reform in the application of penalties, so backward in our country, is making lately some interesting progress.

Apart from the progress recorded only by the " Official Gazette," that is, the reforms which were not carried out (like the important royal decree of May 18, 1903, on the tutelage and correction of prisoners), we will mention the founding, through a royal decree of March 12, 1903, of a " School of Criminology " for the training of the penitentiary personnel, which is conducted under the direction of an appointed professor (Salillas, Simarro, Cossio, Aramburu, Olóriz, Anton).

Private initiative gave birth to the protective league. That for juvenile prisoners in Madrid has been recently

Governors to impose upon those who blaspheme in public, as an offense against public morals and decency, a fine not exceeding 500 *pesetas*. The said article has served as a basis for this law. As soon as an habitual offender is known to the police, he is immediately considered a dangerous subject and can be arrested as often as they please so as to prevent his relapsing. This is done through a juridical fiction by presuming that he has violated the above article. The maximum fine is then imposed, which, through a presumed insolvency, is changed to imprisonment not exceeding a fortnight; this can be repeated indefinitely, thus taking the place of the indeterminate sentence. In as far as showing the creation of juridical customs, it is curious as well as instructive to notice how, in the presence of the necessity of defense not provided by ordinary laws, it has been possible to devise a complementary system, which, rudimentary and defective as it may be, presents traits of marked originality.

founded and is trying the regenerative system of placing the young in families.

Section 45. (B) Spanish America.

Among the various Hispano-American countries, Argentina excels in penal and penitentiary reform.

Worthy of notice is the Argentina draft of penal Code of 1906, elaborated by a Commission composed of five lawyers and a physician (Beazley, Rivarola, Saavedra, Moyano, Gacitúa, Pinero, Ramos Mejía). It is true that on account perhaps of the barbarity of some sections of the country this draft includes the death penalty, yet it contains many features which are in harmony with the modern tendencies of criminology (a consideration of the motives of the crime and of the antecedents of the delinquent, the individualization of punishment, wide scope for judicial discernment, conditional freedom, suppression of the cellular treatment included in life sentences, of statutory limitations, of amnesty, etc.).

Besides these drafts there was established in 1907 an "Institute of Criminology" under the direction of Ingegnieros and connected with the National Penitentiary now in charge of A. Ballvé.[1]

The Institute enjoys a wider scope and greater intervention in the administration of criminal justice than our "School of Criminology."

According to the by-laws, the institution will have charge of all the studies becoming an Institute of Criminology. The Director will plan the corresponding tasks, the books, registers, pamphlets, bulletins, etc., which he may deem necessary, and will decide according to his scientific judgment upon the

[1] Cf. Ballvé's *La Penitenciaría nacional de Buenos Aires*, Buenos Aires, 1907; and E. Gómez' *Estudios penitenciarios*, Buenos Aires, 1906.

methods of investigation which criminological science has adopted or is on the point of adopting.

Without interfering with the other tasks of the Institute, a " medico-psychological bulletin " will be quickly issued for every convict serving his term in the above-mentioned establishment or in any other; a bulletin to be filed with the general memorandum of each prisoner and to be kept constantly up to date (criminological clinic).

The Institute is also charged with the examination and permanent study of all prisoners who show symptoms of mental alienation and of prisoners supposed to be epileptics alcoholists, or victims of some other physio-psychological disturbance. For these cases, the Institute will make medical reports dealing with the subjects studied and with the result of the examination, which will be submitted to the judges in charge of the cases or to be used in connection with further trials in the case of persons against whom final sentence has been pronounced (Criminal Psychiatry).

The Institute can also exercise direct intervention by undertaking the appropriate investigation and examination of all cases of actual or attempted suicide which are committed in the establishment.

Chapter III.

SCIENTIFIC INVESTIGATION OF CRIME.

I. Origins.

Section 46.

By scientific investigation of crime we mean the application of scientific data to criminal investigations which will guide in establishing the identity of a suspect, in determining the rôle a person or an object has played in a criminal matter, and in detecting the methods employed by the various classes of criminals.[1]

Studied from its origins, we can say that this function has passed through three phases: (a) an *equivocal* phase, when its personnel — including the chief of police, as in the case of Vidocq — was recruited from the midst of the delinquents themselves, believing that they were better acquainted with the character and skill of criminals; (b) an *empirical* phase, when the personnel not recruited from criminals struggle against them in an empirical way with the aid of mere natural faculties, common or exceptional as they may be, as in the case of Auguste Dupin, Corentin, Lecoq, and Sherlock Holmes, all fantastic characters created by Edgar Poe, Balzac, Gaboriau, and Conan Doyle;[2] (c) a *scientific* phase, in which

[1] This is the definition given by Niceforo at the 6th Congress of Criminal Anthropology held in Turin, 1906. The last clause of the definition is taken from Reiss' *Les méthodes scientifiques dans les enquêtes judiciares*, in the *Archives d'Anthropologie criminelle*, 1906.

[2] On the last mentioned, cf. Bercher's *L'œuvre de Conan Doyle et la Police scientifique au XX siècle*, Paris, 1906.

these natural faculties are coupled with methods of investigation based on observation and experiment.

When were criminal investigations formulated into a science?

It may be said that the science has a threefold origin. First, we have the work of the empiricists themselves (Vidocq in France and Ave Lallemant in Germany). Then come the practical criminalists who, at the beginning of the 19th century, founded the so-called "judicial psychology" in Germany (Metzger, Platner, Mittermaier). In direct line with this movement comes our contemporary Gross, who preserves its traditions and methods as seen in his " Manual of Judicial Investigations as a System of Criminality," and " Criminal Psychology," [1] constituting with all the heterogeneous material of information useful to the judge, the police, and the gendarme, what he calls *Criminalistica*, which is not without very old precedents.[2]   Finally, legal medicine and chemistry have offered and still offer an important agency. The entire subject of the revelation of hidden traces and the study of obvious ones based on organic principles proceeds from them.

All these tendencies come together with the establishment of Criminal Anthropology. Receiving their impulse from the latter, they are being systematized in accordance with modern Criminology. At the Paris Congress of Criminal Anthropology (1889), Alongi, Ottolenghi, and Romiti spoke of the possibility of the police making use of modern studies on the natural history of the delinquent.

[1] *Handbuch für Untersuchungsrichter als System der Kriminalistik*, Graz, 1894. Translated by J. Adam in 1906. — *Kriminalpsychologie*, Graz, 1898; translated in the Modern Criminal Science Series of the American Institute (Boston, Little, Brown, & Co., 1911).

[2] Manzini, for instance (in his *Trattato di Diritto penale Italiano*, vol. I. ch. I, paragraph 8, note, Turin, 1908), mentions Cospi's *Il giudice criminalis'a* (Florence, 1643), which contains even a chapter on Judicial Astrology.

The possibility has become a fact. Gross' books, Alongi's "Manual of Scientific Investigation of Crime," [1] and especially the recent treatise by Niceforo on "The Police and the Scientific Investigation of Crime " [2] bear witness to the fact.

II. APPLICATIONS.

Section 47. (1) THE IDENTIFICATION OF CRIMINALS.

The problem of individual identification, especially in reference to the delinquent's personality, is the most important of all.

When analyzed in all its magnitude, it divides itself into two questions: (a) the determination of the author of the crime; and (b) the determination of his penal antecedents.

The first question is connected with the general problem of the investigation of the traces of the crime. The second resolves itself into a determination of recidivism. But we cannot separate them altogether, since every method used for the determination of personality — and in this lies one of its advantages — serves indiscriminately for both purposes.

From the point of view of both questions, the problem is so important as to justify the efforts its wonderful solution has called forth. First, then, it is necessary to discover the criminal, who, perhaps, as experience shows, has had himself arrested for a light offense in order to ward off the inquiry into a serious crime. Secondly, it is necessary to discover whether he is a recidivist or not.

In olden times, the second part of the problem was solved by the simple and radical method of branding the criminal with the pontifical keys, the French fleur-de-lis, or the L of our abridged laws.

[1] *Manuale di Polizia scientifica*, Milan, 1897.
[2] *La Police et l'Enquête judiciaire scientifiques*, Paris, 1907.

The penalty of public shame in the pillory and at the whipping-post can be also considered as pointing out the criminal to the town with the same preventive aim.[1]

But the last method had a very limited sphere of action; and the system of branding, although universal and indelible, was abolished with the humanitarian reform wrought into penology after the appearance of Beccaria's work. It was then that people felt the need of some bloodless method for the identification of criminals.

An account of the various methods devised can be found in Ramos' " Identification," [2] and in Ortíz' " Criminological Identification." [3]   In general, these methods can be reduced to two groups: those of measurements and those of description.

In the competition that ensued, the first group, after having enjoyed a certain amount of popularity, yielded place to the second. The reason for this is that while methods of measurements are subject to the personal errors of the expert, those of description — especially when applied through a natural process — are not in such a danger, and are, therefore, more trustworthy.

Section 48. (A) Anthropometry.

Alphonse Bertillon bases his system mainly upon the anthropometry of the subject.[4]

Every person who falls into the hands of the law is submitted to a series of tests whose object is to ascertain his

---

[1] Cf. our book, La Picota (crímines y castigos en el pais castellano en los tiempos medios), Madrid, 1907.

[2] Da identificaçao, Rio de Janeiro, 1896.

[3] La identificación criminológica, in the Derecho y Sociología, Habana, 1906.

[4] Instructions signalétiques pour l'identification anthropométrique, second edition, Melun, 1893.

peculiarities both as to measurements and as to color, and also his distinctive marks.

Peculiarities of measurement include:

a. Height,
b. Arm,
c. Trunk,
d. Length of the head,
e. Width of the head,
f. Bizygomatical diameter,
g. Length of the right ear,
h. Length of the left foot,
i. Length of the left middle finger,
j. Length of the left ear,
k. Length of the left forearm.

The description gives the color of:

a. Eyes,
b. Beard and hair,
c. Skin.

The special marks are:

a. Scars,
b. Moles,
c. Tattooings.

The result of the three tests is put down on a card and filed with a photograph full front and in profile of the subject. The Paris bureaus of judicial identity go through these tests in five minutes, thanks to a system of abbreviations and to the skill of the employés. They need no tachyanthropometers as the one proposed by Anfosso in his " Central Court Catalogue." [1] This writer proposes also a descriptive system of identification based on cranial profile (craniogram) and on the opening between the forefinger and the middle finger (digital triangle).

[1] *Il Casellario giudiziario centrale,* Turin, 1896.

The card having been filled, an investigation is made to see whether the bureau of identification has a similar card describing the criminal record of the delinquent.

But, how can this be done, when, as in Bertillon's office, there are hundreds of thousands of cards?

This difficulty has been overcome thanks to a system of grouping the cards according to homogeneous measurements, which reduces the number of those needed for comparison to a few dozens.

Section 49. (B) Dactyloscopy.

All this is very ingenious.   It is impossible to find two men exactly alike in measurements, in color and in peculiar characteristics.   But, the securing of these characteristics will inevitably be accompanied with some error sufficient to cause confusion.   On the other hand, the Bertillon system, especially as related to the examination of peculiar marks, leads to an investigation in which personal dignity suffers.   On this account the problem was not considered as solved and a better solution was sought.

The better and perfect solution has been found in the descriptive method of dactyloscopy, that is, the investigation of the papillary lines of the finger tips, whose structure is permanent and lasting from the seventh month of womb life till the decomposition of the textures after death, and is absolutely distinct in every individual.

Perhaps prehistoric observers were already acquainted with this peculiarity, according to a note by Ivert [1] in reference to some of Poirier's remarks; but the merit is due to **Purkinje** of having made in 1823 the first anatomical description of the

[1] *L'identification pour les empreintes digitales palmaires*, Lyons, 1904.

digital lines without conceiving the practical applications to which it could be put.[1]

At the beginning (Herschell, Thompson), these applications were limited to a kind of autographical, authentical signature for receipts and civil documents by pressing upon the paper in the manner of a seal one or more fingers soaked in ink.

Galton,[2] Potecher, and others applied the discovery in distinct ways to the identification of criminals. Finally, the Argentine Vucetich has simplified the system so successfully that his method has spread everywhere.[3]

Vucetich distinguishes only the following four main types:

a. Arch (A, or 1).

b. Internal loop (I, or 2).

c. External loop (E, or 3).

d. Vertical (V, or 4).

An impression of the five fingers of each hand is made upon the card; then, in view of the dactylogram obtained, one can establish the dactylographic formula of the subject, representing the type to which each finger corresponds by preëstablished figures. The thumb is excluded and is designated always by the letter of the type to which it belongs. Take, for instance:

V 3242 — I 3343

---

[1] Roscher: *Der Altmeister der Dactyloscopie,* in the *Archiv für Kriminalanthropologie und Kriminalistik,* XXII, 1907. Purkinje distinguished as many as eight shapes of papillary lines in the finger tips: (1) *flexuræ transversæ;* (2) *stria centralis longitudinalis;* (3) *stria obliqua;* (4) *sinus obliqus;* (5) *amygdalus;* (6) *spirula;* (7) *circulus;* (8) *vortex duplicatus.* In our days, Kollmann has investigated the cause for the distribution of the lines, and concludes that they correspond to the space between the papillæ, while the crests separated by them contain the tactillpapillæ and the orifices of the sudoriferous glands.

[2] *Finger Print Directories,* London, 1895.

[3] *Dactiloscopia comparada,* La Plata, 1904.

This formula represents a subject with the following papillary structures:

Right Hand

Thumb = Vertical (V).

Forefinger = External loop (3).

Middle finger = Internal loop (2).

Ring-finger = Vertical (4).

Little finger = Internal loop (2).

Left Hand

Thumb = Internal loop (I).

Forefinger = External loop (3).

Middle finger = External loop (3).

Ring-finger = Vertical (4).

Little finger = External loop (3).

The combined ten alphabetical or numerical designations yield a large number of formulæ which allow and facilitate the classification of the cards.

But how can we compare two different prints of the same type and obtain the identification?

Stockis sums up the various methods in his " Investigation and Identification of Finger Prints." [1]

According to him, Windt enumerates the papillary lines from the delta to the bifurcations, the ends of the lines, and the points or lines fastened among the others.

Galton and Henry, tracing a line, join the center of the print with the delta and count the lines thus crossed, the points touching one another, etc.

Sarachaga bases his comparison of the distinct types of the vertical on the number of lines, the elevation of the loop, the inclination (horizontal, oblique, vertical), and the direction (rectilinear or curvilinear) of the axis of the drawing, the opening of the central angle of the print, and, finally, on the apparent scars.

Roscher and Gasti emphasize the number of the lines and the configuration of the crests composing the delta.

Vucetich compares, above all, the directive lines and

[1] *La recherche et l'identification des empreintes digitales ;* in the *Rivista di Polizia giudiziaria scientifica,* edited by Niceforo, 1907.

the characteristic points (bifurcations, pitchforks, islands, etc.).

Daae also investigates the characteristic points.

Giribaldi distinguishes the varieties of verticals, the scars that can possibly cross the print, and the details of the lines.

Pottecher bases his observation mainly on the enumeration of the lines.

Niceforo recommends the investigation of the directive lines, the number of the furrows, the characteristic points (starting point of the lines, bifurcations, rings, points), and the casual or anomalous peculiarities (scars, pustules, syndactyliæ, etc.).

Finally, Reiss calls attention to the photographic method of the superposition of the two enlarged pictures, the first on paper and the second on a transparent film, or by passing simultaneously in the projecting lantern two photographic plates of the two prints natural size, one on glass and the other on stiff film. In either case the identification is obtained from the matching of the lines.

It is impossible to discuss the advantages and the inconveniences of all these methods. Their multiplicity offers a serious obstacle for international investigations. Yet, the advantages offered by Vucetich's system are such as to win him popularity in both hemispheres. A place seems to be reserved for his system in the international dactyloscopic catalogue which some are planning.[1]

Section 50. (C) The Word Portrait.

The problem of identification seems, then, entirely solved by means of dactyloscopic methods. Nevertheless, in some cases — as, for instance, in the case of the arrest of known

[1] Locard's *Les services actuels d'Identification et la Fiche internationale*, Lyon, 1906.

criminals in the streets or on the highway, — the method of the word portrait becomes very useful. It is also due to Bertillon, and can be traced to Leonardo da Vinci, the most versatile genius the world has ever known.[1] The system is fully discussed in Reiss' " The Word Portrait." [2]

It simply consists in a description by conventional abbreviations of the peculiar traits of the face, which by means of a system of annotations records with severe exactness the shape, the contour, and the dimensions of the features.

We cannot give here the very extensive nomenclature of the morphology of the various parts of the face; we can only give a classification of their dimensions:

Very short $= s$
Short $= s$
Slightly short $= (s)$
Slightly long $= (l)$
Long $= l$
Very long $= l$ [3]

Influenced by one of Ottet's studies on the classification of anthropometric cards based on the decimal system, Reiss, in "Telegraphic Code of the Word Portrait," [4] thought of changing the vocabulary of the word portrait into a simple numerical system which is very logical and useful. He makes ten decimals correspond to ten characteristics of the portrait; thus, the forehead $= 0,1$; the nose $= 0,2$; the ear $= 0,3$; the

[1] Cf. *Il portrait parlé dato da Leonardo da Vinci;* in the *Scuola Positiva,* October, 1909.

[2] *Le Portrait parlé,* Paris, 1905.

[3] As can be seen the first letter of each trait is taken; therefore, in Spanish, French, and Italian, the letters used are: *p*, p (p), (g), g, *g.* — (Note of the Tr.).

[4] *Un Code télégraphique du portrait parlé;* in the *Archives d'Anthropologie Criminelle,* 1907.

mouth = 0,4; etc. Each characteristic of the forehead is
marked by the addition of a figure to 0,1. For instance:

0,121 forehead in profile very receding,
0,122   "   "   "   receding,
0,123   "   "   "   slightly receding,
0,124   "   "   "   intermediate,
0,125   "   "   "   slightly vertical,
0,126   "   "   "   vertical,
0,127   "   "   "   projecting.

By means of this numerical system, the use of the word
portrait could become international. Two police offices
could, without needing to know the language of each other's
country, send and read the full description of an individual.
Moreover, it has the advantage of translating by means of a
few figures a long description which would cause great telegraphic expense. Lately, Icard has simplified and perfected
the system.[1]

Section 51. (D) The Biographical Ledger and the Album of the Investigation of Criminals.

For the discovery of notorious delinquents (exiles, fugitives
from justice, rebels), Alphonse Bertillon has by combining
the anthropometric card with the word portrait invented the
so-called *Album D K V*, in order to condense the main trait
(*Deq.* stands for the lobule of the ear with sloping outlines;
Car. for the concave or rectilinear antitragus in profile; *Vex.*
for the lower convex fold) which serves in itself for the identification of the suspect.

Ottolenghi has likewise devised a *biographical ledger* with
a complete physical and organic description of criminals.[2]

[1] *Archives d'Anthropologie Criminelle*, 1909.
[2] *La nuova cartella biografica dei pregiudicati adottata nell' Ammini-
strazione di Pubblica Sicurezza ;* in the *Scuola Positiva*, 1905.

The following is table V of the ledger, the most interesting of all:

Psychical characteristics and biographical information.

(for dangerous subjects)

(The officer will underline the quality of the characteristic, or fill out the space as he makes his observations and verifications).

I. Psychical Characteristics.

Intelligence and its manifestations: deficient, ordinary, high; — cunning, sincerity; — excited, depressed, unbalanced, raving.

Manual occupations: skilful, ordinary, clumsy.

Reading: whether he reads or not; the books he prefers . . . ; what periodicals. . . .

Writing: handwriting: childish, ordinary, careful; — conventional letters, peculiar signs, secret writing; — aptitude for writing: little, ordinary, developed.

Culture: deficient, ordinary, fair, high; — languages he knows . . .; — publications. . . .

Speech: talkative, laconic, silent; — careful, vulgar, obscene; — whether he knows slang or not.

Carriage: ordinary, vain, dejected, timid.

Facial expression: intelligent, indifferent, stupid; — good, indifferent, ferocious; — attentive, indifferent, distracted; — gay, indifferent, sad, changeable; — calm, indifferent, restless, frightened; — open, indifferent, suspicious, false; — insolent, indifferent, timid.

Temperament: calm, restless, emotional, not emotional; — uniform, changeable, apathetic, excitable, violent; — balanced, unbalanced, maniacal.

Character: weak, easily influenced, strong, obstinate; — constant, inconstant; — mild, brusque; — merry, indifferent, sad; — selfish, altruistic; — expansive, reserved; — timid,

proud, insolent; — sociable, misanthropic; — sincere, hypo-
critical, simulative; — scrupulous, honest, dishonest.

Behavior in the family: with parents; with wife; **does** he
live with her or not; — does he treat her well or not; — **does**
he support or exploit her; — *does he live with another woman or
not;* — with the children: does he look after them or not,
does he abandon them; does he treat them well or not; does
he support or exploit them.

Industry: works assiduously, little; does not work; un-
employed, changes occupation; does he take part in strikes
actively or passively; the opinion his employers have of
him. . . .

Attitude in business: enterprising, adventurous, without
initiative; honest, not very scrupulous, rascal.

Sexuality: accentuated, ordinary, abnormal. . . .

Religiosity: believer, unbeliever; **does he practice his**
religious exercises or not; pious.

Dissipation, prodigality: yes or no.

Inclination to vagrancy: yes or no.

Vices: drunkard, gambler, fond of women, **debauchee.**

Litigation: is he inclined to contest in law or not.

Impulsiveness, brutality: yes or no.

Attitude towards authorities: obsequious, arrogant, scornful,
rebellious, mistrustful.

Relation with suspects (malefactors, prostitutes, etc.): yes
or no.

Predominant criminal aptitude. . . .

Dangerousness. . . .

Signs of regeneration. . . .

II. Biography.

Family: parents, brothers and sisters, wife, children (condition of life, economic condition, morality, mental state of each).

Childhood and youth: behavior in the family.

Behavior at school and in charitable institutions.

Behavior in the house of correction.

Aptitude shown for study, work, vagrancy, pauperism, delinquency.

Studies, titles, vicissitudes in work and in business and family matters.

Military life: behavior, rank, offenses.

Civil life: mode of life, employments, reputation.

Men acquaintances.

Women acquaintances.

Change of domicile.

Vicissitudes abroad: occupation, journeys, acquaintances, expulsion.

Vicissitudes in jail and during the period of vigilance: insubordination, rebellion, simulation, attempt to commit suicide, etc.

Important events in which he took part.

Physical infirmities.

Mental infirmities: epileptic fits, hysterical fits, paranoias, excitement, depression, suicidal attempts.

The human document is registered as a whole.

Section 52. (2) THE REVELATION OF THE TRACES OF CRIME.

Empirical investigation rested on the general dualism of crimes that left traces and those that did not. "Scientific investigation," says Niceforo,[1] "must always start with the supposition that all murderers and thieves leave some traces at the scene of the crime. These traces are often visible,

[1] *Guía para el estudio y la enseñanza de la Criminología,* third part, Madrid, 1904.

although at times they are not. Therefore, every effort must
be directed to discover on the carpet, on the glass, on the
floor, on the victim's neck, on the shining metal of the
bell, on the steel of the strong-box, the traces which the
criminal *undoubtedly* leaves behind. In these investigations
the microscope comes to the aid of chemistry and
photography."

In our days, the main effort in the investigation of traces is
directed to the discovery of dactylograms which the delinquent
almost inevitably leaves behind. The value of this examination is seen in the case of the murderer Schoeffer, who was
arrested and convicted because of a blood-stained dactylogram
left on a window pane and which was identified by the tenacious Bertillon. Robbers have been identified by means of
dactylograms in relief left on the fallen wax of a candle;
another malefactor was detected through the revelation of a
print left on paper by his fingers moistened in ferrocyanide
of potassium . . . and which became visible by the application of acidified perchloride of iron. Thus, among the directions Reiss gives the Swiss police and to be found in all police
posts, there is one that reads: " . . . the officer will not
touch any object with a smooth surface found at the scene
of the crime, especially broken glass and its fragments. Window panes exposed to the rain will be covered with wax-
cloth. . . ."

The prints once visible, direct photography or the mold in
case of prints in relief will be found sufficient.

At other times, more elementary devices can bring them to
light. The print can be superposed on black material and a
strong light thrown against it; or, if the print is on glass, the
tarnish of the breath will suffice.

There are cases when we must have recourse to more delicate
methods. For instance, in the case of prints on glass, Stockis'

" Investigations and Identification of Finger Prints "[1] enumerates the following:

a. The application of an 8 per cent. solution of nitrate of silver, exposure to the light, and revelation by means of a photographic revealer.

b. The application of a coating of ink.

c. Coloring by means of osmic acid.

d. The use of iodine vapors.

e. The use of hydrofluoric acid, which attacks the glass between the papillary lines.

f. Coloring by means of eosin, etc.

g. The application of an alcoholic solution of Sudan red III, etc.

In all these experiments the usefulness of the photograph is evident.

As Niceforo says,[2] " every print which does not of itself present to the eye differences of tone on account of the imperfection of the optical organ can be brought to light on the photographic plate. A blood-stained handkerchief washed several times appears perfectly white to the eye; but, if a photograph of it is taken, black stains will be detected. The almost invisible traces of a pencil on a page placed under the paper on which the writing was made will also appear on the photographic plate. A burned letter, properly prepared and laid out by the aid of varnish, prints its writing on the photographic plate."

This is not all; every invisible print leaving a light impression on the photographic plate can be strengthened by chemical means, that is, by employing the so-called orthochromatic plates, or microphotographic preparations.

---

[1] *Les recherches et l'identification des empreintes digitales.*
[2] *Guía para el estudio y la enseñanza de la Criminología.*

Bertillon's " Judicial Photography," [1] Reiss' book of the same
title, Paul's " Manual of Criminal Photography," [2] etc.,
which, on account of their technicality, cannot be reviewed
here, have discussed this subject. It suffices to know that
the human eye can acquire surprising power by the aid of
these wonderful improvements.

Section 53. (3) INSPECTION OF THE PLACE, OF THE EFFECTS, AND OF THE VICTIM OF THE CRIME.

At this point a new application can be made of judicial
photography.

Criminal investigation, if it is to bear results, requires that
the place of crime be indefinitely kept as it was found at the
time of the discovery. This necessity cannot be completely
met by a written description, the drawing of a plan, or even
by ordinary photography.

Alphonse Bertillon has thought of a better device, namely,
metrical photography, by means of which and without the
need of trigonometrical calculations, we can obtain likenesses
whose various elements of height and distance are susceptible
of an easy and immediate measurement on the positive itself
placed between two lateral scales.

" This method," says Niceforo,[3] " can be of great service.
A witness declares to have seen the scene from a definite
point. The metrical photograph or its reproduction on a
geometrical plan will show whether it is materially possible
for him to have seen it. Can the height of a window allow
an entrance without any aid? Is the size of an aperture
sufficiently large to let a man through? etc."

Partial photographs and the enlarging of sections and

[1] *La Photographie judiciaire*, Paris, 1890.
[2] *Handbuch der Kriminalistischen Photographie*, Berlin, 1900.
[3] *La Police et l'Enquête judiciaire scientifique*, chapter I, Paris, 1907.

details of the place of crime or of the *corpus delicti* are equally useful.

In the photography for the identification of corpses, methods (the corpse toilette) are used which tend to render the face almost as if alive (friction of the skin with talc, washing with a solution of chloride of lime, injection of glycerine in the eye-ball or washing of the eyes with aluminum sulphate, rouge on the lips, etc.).

Niceforo's " The Police and the scientific Investigation of Crime " [1] contains some fine reproductions of photographic negatives obtained from the Police Bureaus of Paris, Berlin, Dresden, and Lausanne.

Section 54. (4) THE VALUE OF TESTIMONIAL EVIDENCE.

Criminal justice is based on testimonial evidence as well as on the revelations obtained from the traces of the crime. How much weight should be put on testimonial evidence?

Apart from wilful false testimony, our contemporaries realize how much this kind of evidence is to be mistrusted.

In 1904, Liszt arranged a mock murderous attempt in his class in criminal law before 60 students who were not aware of the fact. After an address given by Tarde, Liszt asked if any one in the audience wished to speak before the lecturer summed up his conclusions. One of the students spoke in favor of Tarde's argument from the point of view of Christian morality. Another qualified the argument as shameful. Insults and threats were exchanged until one of them pulling out a revolver attempted to shoot the other. Then Liszt asked the students to testify. Scarcely ten out of sixty gave a faithful account of what had happened, while the others made more or less grave errors, especially in reference to details.

[1] *La Police et l'Enquête judiciaire scientifique,* chapter I, Paris, 1907.

Gross also related in his "Criminal Psychology" that being present at an execution during which the hangman wore gloves, he asked afterwards four persons present of what color the gloves were. One said that they were white, another that they were black, a third that they were gray, and the fourth maintained that he wore no gloves.

Claparède's experiments are also worth remembering. Once, during a lesson, he distributed among his pupils a list of questions concerning certain peculiarities of the University building. The questions were: "Is there an inner window in the University cloister opposite the window of the janitor's lodge?" "How many columns are there in the vestibule of the University?" "How many busts?" etc.

Out of 54 answers, none was altogether exact. The existence of the window before which the students passed every day was denied by 44 witnesses.

Another day, a masked man entered the hall gesticulating and uttering incoherent words. The professor asked him to leave, and on his refusal he had him put out by force. The scene took place the day after the Geneva celebration of the so-called "Scalade." The students thought that on that account some one had made a wager, and therefore they did not suspect that the scene had been arranged beforehand. After the expulsion of the intruder, Claparède continued his lecture as if nothing had happened. Only a week later he alluded to the event and asked the students to answer the following questions: "Did the man wear a hat?" "What kind of hat?" "What was the color of his hair?" "Did he wear gloves?" etc., etc.

After giving the answers, the witnesses were asked to recognize the mask from among nine others.

Not only were they unable to recognize it, but every one gave a different description of the masked man.

Nothing is more difficult than truth.

As Lombroso says,[1] " we only need to consider how our senses perceive a thing and how we come to represent it to ourselves, to become convinced that we rarely perceive all the details that accompany it."

The anomalies found in the constitution and operation of the senses, as numerous as they are complex, their so-called illusions, the mechanism of attention, the suggestions and auto-suggestions, the process of memory (amnesic, paramnesic, and hypermnesic), modify the value of testimonial evidence and often annul it altogether. A whole review, founded by Stern[2] in 1902, analyzes this class of problems which would require long psychological diversions to explain.

In conclusion, we only need to point out that the question of testimonial evidence is in some respects solved differently than it was done by old practitioners. For instance, the rule " *testis unus testis nullus* " loses its value if it is believed that a single witness can give a faithful testimony. Also, the witness who doubts, wavers, and testifies with partial or progressive amnesias, is nearly always more trustworthy than the one who affirms or denies flatly and unconcernedly, elaborating his deposition with details and minutiæ.

In any càse, the testimony of children and feeble-minded needs a very careful examination.

(5) MODERN INVESTIGATION OF CRIME IN SPAIN AND IN SPANISH AMERICA.

Section 55.   (A) Spain.

In Spain, modern investigation of crime has not gone beyond the methods of identification.

---

[1] *La psicologia dei testimoni nei processi penali;* in the *Scuola Positiva,* 1905.

[2] *Beiträge zur Psychologie der Aussage.*

The first allusion to Bertillon's anthropometric system, lamenting that it could not be immediately adopted, is found in the declaration of motives contained in the Royal decree of June 24, 1890, which sets forth that, in the future, papers sent in by the judicial authorities to the Central Registration Bureau should contain data for identification. These data were limited to height, weight, size of hands and feet, color of the iris, color of the beard and hair, color of the face, and scars.

No scientific criterion had determined the selection of the characteristics to be noted, which, as in the case of weight, suffer constant oscillations.

Six years later, a Royal decree of September 10, 1896, established the service of anthropometric identification according to the Bertillon system. The Bureau of the Madrid Cellular Prison was to act as a Central Bureau under the Department of Justice. The late Dr. Simancas organized the Bureau and was its first Director.

The service of identification was organized on February 18, 1901, by uniting the Central Bureau of Anthropometry with the Bureau of Registration for convicts and rebels, which had been established in 1878. Dr. Olóriz was charged with the direction of the service.

Under this new administration, the service has developed to such an extent as to adopt dactyloscopy.

Olóriz has devised a dactyloscopic system, which can be summed up as follows:

1. The main types were reduced to only two: *circle* and *angle;*

2. Their disposition in the five fingers of each hand capable of 32 combinations were classified by a logical key, as in the words of a dictionary, consisting of the numbers 1 to 32;

3. The individual dactylographic formula was expressed

by a fraction whose numerator represented the combination of the fingers of the right hand and the denominator those of the fingers of the left;

4. But, since two of the dactylographic formulæ — namely: " angles in the ten fingers " and " circles in the ten fingers " — are so frequent, especially the first, as to include ten per cent. of the cases, he introduced at this point anthropometry for the measurements of the two diameters of the head; not for the sake of subdividing, but in order to arrange the dactylograms obtained in a continuous series, thus facilitating the task of identification.

Later, Olóriz abandoned his system and accepted with a slight modification that of Vucetich.

Section 56. (B) Spanish America.

As we have seen, the great South American contribution is the simplification and perfecting of dactyloscopy crowned by Vucetich's method.

The 3rd Scientific Latin-American Congress (Río Janeiro, 1905) approved Vucetich's conclusions with no other opposition than a defense of the Bertillon system by Dr. Giribaldi, of Uruguay. The Congress declared that:

"The system to be adopted was the South-American dactyloscopy as advocated by Lacassagne, Locard, and Yvert of the Lyons University, because:

" a. It is simple, rapid, and safe, and makes it possible to find the individual dactyloscope in the file with promptitude and certainty. The subdivision by families corresponding to the four main types: Arch $= A = 1$, Internal loop $= 1 = 2$, External loop $= E = 3$, and Vertical $= V = 4$, allows an infinite extension of the analytic division, and has the advantage of being less expensive, affording more facility of diffusion and more respect for the prerogatives of human personality;

" b. With the dactyloscopic system, certainty does not depend absolutely on the operator; any impression, no matter how often repeated, gives always the same result. No two fingers have the identical papillary design; the impression of a single finger is sufficient for the mathematical identification of any person;

" c. The digital design never changes from the last months of womb life to the decomposition of the body. Dactyloscopy alone permits an exact identification of minors and corpses. The possible accidents that may occur in the course of a man's life only emphasize the individuality of the impression. The *restitutio ad integrum* of the papillary designs in case of exterior burns or other slight injuries is a fact demonstrated by science;

" d. The bloody digito-palmar and plantar impressions, like the revealed invisible ones, can determine and facilitate the discovery of the criminal;

" e. It would be very advantageous to replace all the old systems by the application of the simple digital impression which can be used to advantage in deeds connected with civil, commercial, and military life, reserving morphological filiation, peculiar marks, and visible scars for the capture of criminals in public thoroughfares. The importance of photography in the matter of identification is relative; it is necessary to restrict its application to persons convicted of crimes against property and of serious offenses against the person;

" f. Anthropometry in itself *does not identify;* in order to reach a *probable identification*, it needs morphological filiation, photography, peculiar marks, scars, and tattooings, obliging the delinquent to strip down to his waist. But, in the dactyloscopic individualization, personal identity is determined in a way that all the police in the world can read, whatever be the classification adopted. Thus, the dactyloscopic system becomes a *true universal language*."

In the same year, the South-American Inter-police Congress declared itself in favor of Vucetich's method, thus beginning the internationalization of the system.

III. THE CRIMINAL'S REPLY.

Section 57.

This intelligent attack is met by an equally intelligent defense on the part of the criminal world.

The novel reflects the struggle. Sherlock Holmes, that clever *detective*, finds a worthy rival in Hornung's Raffles or in Leblanc's Arsene Lupin. Meade and Eustace's "The Brotherhood of the Seven Kings," and Goron's "The Flower of the Penitentiary" recount the wonderful deeds of scientific criminals — Madame de Koluchy, the Baron de Sainte Magloire, etc. — who kill with different methods. They subject the unsuspecting victims to the action of the X rays of a fragment of radium; they get rid of compromising articles, like a goblet zealously watched and which by playing music containing the specific note of vibration the resonance will break it into pieces; criminals in short who realize their evil instincts by methods that would arouse the enthusiasm of the Society fancied by Thomas de Quincey which considered murder a Fine Art.[1]

---

[1] It is only a humorous outburst, and in no way — as some maliciously suppose — a result of disappointed desires. No; the mind that created " Levana " and passages possessing such profound beauties of style has a deep hatred for crime. In the history of literature, there cannot be found a more touching description of crime than the one of Williams' murders. One feels the real presence of the criminal behind him, as in Poe's description of the man in the crowd we see him walking before us. The powerful description, altogether epic and fired with indignation against the assassin, forms a strange and striking contrast with the cold ironies of the Memoirs of the Club of homicidal experts. We take pleasure in writing these lines in defense of the illustrious writer, who lived Gorki's beautiful story, " Once, in autumn . . . ," fifty years before the latter wrote it. De Quincey also was debtor for bread, warmth, and love

This is only fiction; but, the reality is not far distant, as can be seen in Lombroso's "Old and Modern Crimes." [1]

Thus, as Ottolenghi [2] pointed out, if the Bertillon system led professional criminals to abandon tattooing, dactyloscopy makes them commit crime with gloves on in order to avoid the betraying dactylogram. Reiss [3] says that until now he only knows of one case of theft committed with gloves on, and that he hopes — since "a cat does not hunt with gloves on" — the fashion will not spread. He recalls Vidocq's anecdote, who, in order to put an end to the rumor that his agents stole from time to time, made them wear gloves when on duty.

Will the skill of the thief be ever overcome?

CONCLUSION

Section 58.

All that has been said in these pages concerning modern theories of criminality is only the shadow of a reality, impossible to express like all realities — an abstract remark, which, in spite of its reality, has not been made in order to absolve the author from the defects and errors with which he has expressed it. Although the book could end here, it seems fit to cast a glance over the whole for the purpose of forming an idea of the present situation and of the probable future toward which we are bound.

— not once, but many times — to an innocent prostitute, poor Ann, whom he also sought afterwards in vain — unless it be in the poisonous dreams of the opium, — and for whom he wrote words, which, would to God, had been efficacious.

[1] *Delitti vecchi e delitti nuovi*, Turin, 1902.

[2] *Applicazioni pratiche degli studi su 265 processi criminali;* in the *Archivio di Psichiatria*, vol. XVIII.

[3] *Osservazioni sulle impronte digitali e sulla dattiloscopia;* in the *Rivista di Polizia giudiziaria scientifica*, May, 1907.

I. THE MOVEMENT.
Section 59.

To the number of, properly speaking, *criminological* theories treated here — that is to say, theories which arise from and end in the pure conception of crime and punishment — we must add the various tendencies which modern communities are developing, intending them not for a universal rebirth which is in store only for our century, although all have hoped for it, but simply for the constant renovation of their structure and life in the calm continuity of History. After all, criminal law is a part of History, and, therefore, the whole *social question* and the various social tendencies, — in part or entirely — socialism, anarchy, feminism, internationalism, etc., are related to it entirely or incidentally. Nevertheless, we must isolate, as much as possible, what we may call the *legal question* from all the rest, although a blending of the former with the latter must have been noticed here and there in these pages, even if we have only pointed it out in a few concrete instances.

* * *

The question of the delinquent stands out preëminently and offers a clue for the others.

Criminal Anthropology, appearing twenty years ago in various places and almost at the same time — the works of Lombroso, Benedikt, and Maudsley appeared simultaneously in Italy, Austria, and England — like a ripe fruit which is bound to fall at a certain moment, offers numerous theories on the nature of the criminal. Those who in the name of criticism are intoxicated with these theories, take advantage of their variety in order to overwork the science, forgetting that, when examined from their positive side, they show many contradictions — not very serious after all. However, these theories and contradictions present in a unanimous and compact way the problem of the *male offender*, although when examined and explained their bonds loosen, disclosing signs of disintegration.

It can be safely stated that the movement started with Lombroso, whose name, like that of his predecessors, Röder and Beccaria, will form a landmark in History. His work, like that of the last two, does not consist in a mere collection of pages, but rather in a fruitful trend of thought which it has stimulated in the whole civilized world; thought which after 35 years of activity shows no signs of decline.

His book has been thought by some almost as a revelation, by others as the most baneful the Code has ever known, and by others, more kindly inclined, as an attempt to solve certain questions already known and discussed by a small professional circle, affirming the existence of a man fatally destined to crime by nature, absolutely incorrigible and ostensibly revealed in a monstrous type, with its list of unheard-of theories, like atavism, epilepsy, infantilism, etc. Yet, the work has stirred minds in a manner most brusque, arousing indignation in some, admiration in others, and in all an interest in the pursuit of the problem. In spite of errors and hasty conclusions, the book contains pages of real value, which will survive and be recorded in the future *digest* of science. Its greatest merit, however, will consist in having influenced thousands of men to unite in the study of a subject of supreme importance.

Whether delinquency is inherited or acquired; whatever may be the factors that determine it; whether it manifests itself in an organic or professional type, the fact remains that the consciousness of the problem's existence has become so general that, if some one should say that such a man is the same as other men, he must surely have a more complicated conception of human nature than that represented by simple free-will.

One of the greatest factors in the revision of modern criminal law is found in the studies on the nature of the delinquent, gathered and encouraged by Criminal Anthropology.

Although not the only factor, it is the most evident and the one brought to the attention of all.

A second movement, destined to revise our conception of penology, is found in the old penitentiary science. In order to gain an idea of this process it is necessary to go back to Beccaria.

The Milanese writer, after having reduced the evil of punishment to a minimum sufficient to make it lawful, — according to his formula, — only questioned the lawfulness of the death penalty, without suspecting — as it was seen later — that to question the utmost application of a principle is to question the principle itself. The sentiments of his epoch were satisfied with his humanitarian reforms; but a later epoch found them insufficient for its sentiments, which were more delicate and numerous on account of an inexhaustible natural selection. The minimum of a previous epoch was not considered such in a later one. The decadence of punishment reaches such a stage that, at an imperceptible moment in history, the terms of the penal problem are changed; the *quantitative* reform of punishment becomes an *essential* or *qualitative* one.

At this stage, the old question that concerned only the death penalty pervades all penalties, and the abolitionist of the former joins hands with the abolitionist of penal servitude as a whole. From Beccaria to Röder and from the latter to Vargha, Dorado, Poletti, and Solovieff, covering a period of a century, this process has gone on and still continues, being completed, from its positive side, by the elaboration of that penal substitute which is destined to better fulfill its function in civilized countries, namely, the system of tutelage which is being organized in penitentiary science.

* * *

Rarely do both factors overlap and mingle in modern theories and writers. Most of the latter adopt the one or the other, according to their source, and develop one-sided and incomplete systems. Criminal Anthropology, for instance, separated from the ethical reform movement on the significance of punishment, makes some writers fall back upon the significance of a crude or indifferent defense; while this second movement, without the teachings of the former, degenerates into a barren sentimentalism.

The present movement contains factors which— to a certain extent — do not participate in any of these two main influences; others which accept in various degrees only one; and still others which combine the two in various ways.

II.   THE PRESENT STATUS.
Section 60.

It has been said that this is a *transitional* and *critical* period. The transition and the crisis are so serious and evident that it is only because of their extreme *quantitative* features that the above statement can be accepted; for, all periods are transitory and critical, since human thought never stops in order to leap immediately into another state.

Signs of this extreme critical condition are everywhere visible.

Higher institutions, born of a profoundly educative and moral understanding of punishment, thrive within the same system which preserves the death penalty and which permits a regression to refined corporal punishments, like the electric and gradual torture planned in England, and the restoration of the whipping-post in Delaware.

The same feature characterizes all other questions of modern science. To speak of them now would be to rewrite the whole book, which, for better or for worse, must have left, perhaps, the impression of constant contrasts and anxieties. With the poet, we would describe modern science as being half beautiful, half ugly, and monstrous in the ensemble.

III. The Solution of the Future.
Section 61.

How will the crises be solved?

Without trying to prophesy or to conjecture, it can be affirmed on the mere observation of facts and their significance that humanity is directed toward penal tutelage, not by the straight and easy path of progress as it is generally conceived, but with a complication of movements in all its steps, very difficult to describe.

Once entered upon this course, as we have often pointed out, what can change its direction unless it be an aberration or an episodical incident not connected with its previous march?

It is often stated that humanity must be cured of a sentimental aberration. But, first of all, sentiment enters necessarily in everything; for, nothing can be done with it alone or without any of it. There is needed both *head* and *heart*, the *whole soul* of which they form a part. Moreover, if by sentimentalism is meant a morbid degeneration of certain virtues, it must be said that it is exactly these virtues in their healthy condition that penal tutelage is acquiring by a positive knowledge of the delinquent.

This tutelage, on account of its love, will not cause any

tears to be shed; yet, it will not play the part of the weak father who becomes an accomplice in the corruption of his children. Taking the place of the results hoped for in vain from punishment, it will realize them in a better way on account of its better nature.

On the other hand, we believe we have demonstrated that tutelage is not an incidental episode, but that it is closely connected with previous phases, although difficult to perceive, at a given moment, the change that has taken place. Penal tutelage is the uninterrupted continuation of punishment, having the same biological basis, namely, the reaction against crime. But modern communities cannot react as the old. The greater delicacy of their sentiments attenuates the response to the provocation and makes it pursue different courses; for, " as the lion," says Poletti, " gives all his movements a character of savage ferocity, so man gradually marks all his actions with the stamp of humanity."

* * *

Having attained this new conception, criminal law acquires the harmonious simplicity of truly superior institutions.

The intricate problem of responsibility, which disturbs scholars, disappears. Since the main object of the problem is to distinguish the *responsible* from the *irresponsible* in order to punish the one and acquit the other, the day when punishment disappears, shall we not be able to say that no one is responsible or that all are?

Both solutions, although expressed in different words, are identical at bottom. The notion of responsibility, which is eliminated in the first, returns and assumes infinite proportions in the second by including the heretofore irresponsible, the insane and weak-minded, the minors and the imprudent, the impulsive in the defense of their person, and the many *dangerous* subjects whose acquittal as well as their return to upright society constitutes the greatest immorality of modern systems. With a less formal and more ethical conception of crime it would be extended to new and numerous actions and omissions.

When the claims of *responsibility* make way for the claim of the *necessity of public tutelage,* there will be an end to the disputes between the advocates of *free-will* and those of *determinism;* for, whether crime is due to the most ungovernable freedom of choice, or to the more fatal pressure of invincible agencies, such necessity remains and is not changed by the intervention of foreign elements.

On the other hand, when from *corrective punishment* we pass to *penal tutelage,* is not another cause for contradictions also removed? If the *corrective* school has been obliged to modify its position, if not in regard to *born criminals* at least in regard to *incorrigible criminals, penal tutelage,* on the contrary, like medical science, keeps its *incurables,* or to use its own phrase, its *perpetual wards.*

In conclusion, what will the future do with the delinquent, judging by present indications?

Perhaps nothing. It may be that *abstention* will form a part of the penal system. The *verdicts of not guilty* rendered by juries, *legal pardons,* and *conditional sentences* predict that. If penal tutelage should prove *injurious* or *useless,* there is no necessity for its maintenance. At times, crime produces in certain natures the same effect as punishment, and serves as its own most powerful antidote through the agency of the conscience afflicted by that *natural punishment,* the first manifestation of all punishments, which Plato describes as the instantaneous and irremediable assimilation with the morally fallen through noble remorse for the deed, the empirical and automatic corrections, and the combined inhibitions of the moral nature of man.

Passing from *abstention* to *intervention*, it is safe to say that all forms that *cause human dignity to suffer* or submit it to shame and insult will be abolished. These having been eliminated, penal tutelage, through *indefinite, indeterminate,* or, at any event, *conditional* sentence, will take charge of delinquents and give to each what he needs by means of the consequent *individualization*. This kind of modern dosimetry which offers the same remedy for every crime and for every delinquent, varying only in quantity, will be replaced by methods difficult to foretell, because on this ground we find ourselves in the most elementary and incomplete empiricism. To declare, for instance, that the *cellular system,* or the *system of classification,* or any other, is the *only* penitentiary system, and discuss therefore their advantages and disadvantages, as some do in our days, is to defend an untenable position. If, for instance, in speaking against isolation, we use Dostoyewsky's terrible phrase that " it deprives the criminal of all strength and energy, enervates his soul by weakening and frightening it, and, finally, presents a desiccated half insane mummy as a model of repentance and correction," how can we help remembering that the worst torture suffered by the gifted writer himself during his period of imprisonment was that *forced companionship,* which does not allow a single moment of solitude? All this, then, must form the store of instruments to be used by the new tutelage, and their use and application must vary according to the individual and the given time, not otherwise than is done in a medical examination. Hence, modern criminal law seems to be always de-

pendent on the study of anthropological sciences, and the
first reform to carry out is the diffusion of their teachings
among all those who come in contact and have to deal with
delinquents.

* * *

These are indeed the *new horizons of criminal law*, no matter
how paradoxical a criminal law without penalties may appear
to some. What it has gained is so superior that it seems to
have reached the *non plus ultra;* since all its work consists
in extricating itself from the mire in which it shamefully
finds itself at present.

It is the duty of every one to proclaim these new horizons
and to serve them to the best of his ability.

POSTSCRIPT TO THE CHAPTER ON THE SCIENTIFIC INVESTIGATION OF CRIME.

Section 62.

How to procure the Confession of the Accused.

The ancients employed torture in order to procure the confession of crime from the accused. Can we procure it by kinder and more humanitarian methods?

Münsterberg [1] thinks to have succeeded, and defends the advantages and results of a method based on the principle of the association of ideas, as employed in psychological laboratories. The method consists in: (a) including in the series of topics one or more which recall the crime; and (b) in measuring the rapidity of the spoken associations by means of an electric device placed between the lips of the suspect. The instrument, by the least movement of speaking breaks an electric current passing through an electric clock, and causes its hand to move around a dial ten times in a second, like chronoscopes which measure the time of reaction.

The delay in answering the revealing associations would constitute a proof of guilt and a kind of implicit confession.

Suppose a case of murder. The suspect must orally and instantaneously express the association of ideas involved in the terms: moon, house, palm, *blood*, rose, ship, *struggle, weapon*, etc., etc. The murderer would give an immediate answer to the indifferent subjects; but he would feel obliged to stop and hesitate before answering the compromising ones.

McClure's Magazine, 1907.

It seems to us that this substitute for torture would lead to the same errors that accompanied the barbarous practice. It is well known, in fact, that at times torture was unable to draw a confession on account of that invulnerability possessed by the malefactors mentioned by Lombroso, or on account of their presence of mind; while, at other times, it caused innocent persons, overcome by pain, to declare themselves guilty. Thus, the born criminal, the cold-blooded assassin of Lauvergne may succeed in not compromising himself by answering to the revealing topics; while the innocent man, troubled by the weight of evidence, will often be disturbed and appear self-convicted.

The same can be said of the graphic method of the respiratory and circulatory movements.[1]

[1] For further references on this subject, cf. the bibliography collected by Professor Wigmore in his article on " Professor Münsterberg and the Psychology of Testimony " (Illinois Law Review, 1909, vol. III, p. 399), and Dr. Guy M. Whipple's paper in the American Psychological Bulletin for 1909. [Note of the T.]

INDEX